Richard Hurley has produced an informative and entertaining look at the impact of the Civil War on California and Californians' impact on the war. He intriguingly explores Golden State warriors' active roles throughout the Southwest and in the Eastern Theater, where their cavalry skills were desperately needed. Hurley's humor and frank insights enhance the enjoyment of reading this unique study.

—*Edward Bonekemper, author of six Civil War books, including* The Myth of the Lost Cause: Why the South Fought the Civil War and Why the North Won

California's Civil War impact was one of unquestionable significance, yet relatively few books have explored the state's many contributions to Union victory. Into this void steps Richard Hurley, his California and the Civil War *serving as a fresh reminder of a rich wartime history largely unknown to today's citizens. Hurley's lively and highly accessible narrative ranges far and wide, examining topics as diverse as the triumph of Union politics in the state, the indispensability of California gold in financing the war and the outsized contributions of Californians to aid societies that assisted soldiers and their families. The state's military contributions were also far from nominal. During 1861–65, California volunteers replaced army regulars throughout the Far West. Flocking to the colors in large numbers, they engaged numerous native tribes hostile to the expansionist United States, protected isolated settlements, ensured that the great western trails remained open, and kept a watchful eye out for pro-Confederate activities. Some Californians even traveled clear across the country to directly confront Rebel armies in Virginia. Addressing important military and homefront topics like these along with many others,* California and the Civil War *is a fine popular-style introduction to the state's fascinating and multi-faceted Civil War history.*

—*Andrew Wagenhoffer, editor,* Civil War Books and Authors

Although the Civil War's titanic battles all took place far to the east, California was roiled by the conflict too. In this book, Richard Hurley brings the stories and colorful characters of the Civil War–era Golden State to vivid life. Anyone who thinks the Civil War didn't affect the Pacific Coast will come away with a whole new perspective.

—*Christopher L. Kolakowski, author of* The Stones River and Tullahoma Campaigns: This Army Does Not Retreat *and* The Civil War at Perryville: Battling for the Bluegrass

Once I started reading California and the Civil War *by Richard Hurley, I couldn't stop. History is my passion and my profession, and this is the first book I've read that accurately interprets California prior to and during the Civil War, as well as its role in that great conflict. Richard's rich, moving narrative not only kept my attention, but my enthusiasm. I highly recommend this book to anyone who has the slightest interest in history or California or reading in general. Everyone who reads it will enjoy it.*

—*Ralph Gibson, museums administrator, Placer County Museums*

CALIFORNIA AND THE CIVIL WAR

RICHARD HURLEY

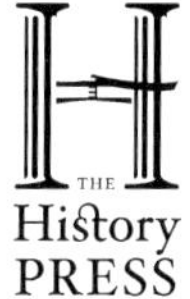

Published by The History Press
Charleston, SC
www.historypress.net

Front cover, top, left to right: White Bear (Sa-tan-ta). *Wikimedia Commons, original at National Archives and Records Administration*; Private Henry Fillebrown, first volunteer for the California Hundred. *Michael K. Sorenson Collection*; General James Carleton. *Courtesy Palace of the Governors Photo Archives (NMHM/DCA), 022938.*
Front cover, bottom: Starr King addressing a pro-Union rally on Market Street in San Francisco. *San Francisco History Center, San Francisco Public Library.*
Back cover, top: John Singleton Mosby and his officers. *Library of Congress*; *bottom*: Lincoln obsequies in San Francisco. *Library of Congress.*

First published 2017

Manufactured in the United States

ISBN 9781625858245

Library of Congress Control Number: 2017934945

CONTENTS

ACKNOWLEDGEMENTS

The visual side of this history is due entirely to the unerring eye of T.J. Meekins. Her skill at capturing history with a period drawing or photograph gave life to the multimedia show and museum exhibit that are the origin of this book. In many cases, all I had to do was build a word-trail from image to image.

Susan Spann generously helped me through the shoal waters of the legal side of writing. An author herself, she knows the perils we face—and our general helplessness in facing them. Thanks, Susan.

One of the chief pleasures of writing history is the opportunity to meet and compare notes with others who share a passionate interest in the past. Mike Sorensen and Keith and Larry Rogers are dedicated keepers of the memory of the California Hundred and Battalion. These scholars have been very kind in sharing their knowledge and allowing me access to the images that record the story of those remarkable soldiers.

The State of California is blessed with some very diligent employees who provided invaluable assistance in my hunt for data and images. Koren Benoit, capitol curator; Emily Blodget, California state documents librarian; Kris Quist, district museum curator; and Wil Jorae, museum curator II, have all been most gracious in helping me access state records and artifacts.

On the private side, Peter Benitz and the Benitz family provided the striking photograph of their clan assembled in Fort Ross in 1865. Mr. Rick Carlile volunteered his photo of Sylvanus Shaw, the archetype of a soldier. David Whittemore, commander of the Massachusetts MOLLUS (Military

Order of the Loyal Legion of the United States), very kindly offered the use of the photographic collection of that venerable organization. Joseph Pawlowski and John Hunicutt II both let me use their extraordinary photographs of the Southwest, which capture the essence of the forbidding landscapes that played such a commanding role in shaping California's past. Gary Spradlin (of the Monterey History and Art Association) helped mightily in the search for authentic imagery of Commodore Sloat's capture of that town. Jim Nugent, managing editor of the Dictionary of Unitarian and Universalist Biography, provided much-needed help in tracking down images and quotations relating to the great Thomas Starr King, the leading light of Unionism on the Pacific coast.

And as always, I tip my hat to my kind friends (Pat and Dick Calkins, Jeannie Harris and Charlie Johnson) who volunteered to critique this manuscript long before it was ready for prime time. And finally, a special callout to Ed Bonekemper, who made many valuable suggestions at the eleventh hour. My thanks to all.

AUTHOR'S NOTE

A crescent moon lit the night of June 30, 1864, as six heavily armed bandits sprang out of the brush and seized the stage from Virginia City as it neared the town of Placerville, in California's Mother Lode. Another coach drove up during the robbery, and it, too, was relieved of its treasure box. Estimates of the loot vary, but the haul was considerable—enough to warrant a dogged pursuit across several counties and a string of deadly gun battles, in which lawmen and bandits both died. One of the robbers was later hanged for his part in the affair.

Of itself, the incident hardly bears mentioning. Stagecoach robbery was a popular form of outdoor fundraising in California at the time, and large shipments of gold and silver from the mines were the favorite prey of men who sought to grow rich without the inconvenience of hard labor. What made the Bullion Bend Robbery (as it came to be known) special was the courtesy of the gang leader, who left behind a blank receipt for his victims to fill in. The receipt explained how the funds were being appropriated for "out-fitting recruits enlisted in California for the Confederate Army." It was signed "R. Henry Ingram, Captain, Commanding Company C.S.A."

Criminals rarely lack for imagination in justifying their acts. When the robbery first came to my attention, I assumed Captain Ingram was merely following the lead of countless villains before him in providing a fig leaf for his crimes. Further research revised my thinking. In the end, I had to admit that the punctilious stage robber was exactly who he said he was—a

Confederate officer (official or otherwise) who was raising money to take a band of partisans back east to fight.

The Bullion Bend story was my introduction to the realities of Civil War–era California. I soon learned that the state was not the Union bastion I had imagined—at least not at the start of the war. Demographically, California was a Border State, with an active, vociferous Southern majority in the lower half of the state. Transplanted Southerners and their allies ruled California through the first decade of statehood. In 1859, the state legislature passed a plan to split California, with the southern portion entering the Union as a slave state. In that same year, California's proslavery Supreme Court chief justice shot and killed the state's free-soil U.S. senator in a duel over the direction of the Democratic Party then dominating California. It was only this violent quarrel among the Democrats that allowed Abraham Lincoln, the Republican candidate, a chance at the state's electoral votes in 1860. Lincoln won California by about seven hundred votes—roughly half a percentage point. Less than one-third of the state's voters cast their ballots for him.

California's connection to the South, as manifested in the Bullion Bend Robbery, was the inspiration for *Queen of the Northern Mines*, a historical fiction set in Civil War–era California that I wrote with T.J. Meekins. To promote our book, we created a multimedia slide show entitled "California and the Civil War," which we presented at historical societies, libraries and museums across Northern California. This, in turn, led to an invitation to guest-curate an exhibit on the subject at the Folsom History Museum. Over time, we have expanded our research and our collection of stories until the present volume became inevitable.

In talking with our audiences, we discovered that almost no present-day Californians know the true story of the state's experience of the Civil War. Few are aware that California originally leaned South until an impassioned campaign by a brilliant orator, the Reverend Thomas Starr King, rallied complacent Unionists and spurred them to take control of their state government. Fewer still know that California's escape from the murderous bushwhacking and incendiarism of partisan warfare was due almost entirely to the sense of honor of a distinguished Southern officer, General Albert Sidney Johnston. Johnston commanded the U.S. Army Department of the Pacific at the start of the war and was perfectly positioned to arm and lead a Rebel force on the West Coast. Instead, he submitted his resignation—and served faithfully until a pro-Union general replaced him. Johnston then journeyed back east, where he died at the head of the Confederate army that almost destroyed Grant at the Battle of Shiloh.

Author's Note

California's experience of the war was—as any such experience must be—a collection of individual tales, shaped by the larger forces that affected the state as a whole. First among those forces was California's sheer remoteness, much greater in those days than most realize today. News of Lincoln's election came west by Pony Express—the fastest means available—and took ten days to reach the Pacific coast. Troops sent to or from California took months to reach their destination by crossing Panama or sailing around the tip of South America.

California's war was also shaped by its unique population of immigrants: an explosive mix of transplanted Northerners and Southerners, who brought their politics out with them, surrounded by large numbers of foreigners, who held no stake in the violent quarrel that was tearing the nation apart. The fact that California's population was composed largely of adventurous young men led to high recruitment rates—the highest, in fact, of any state in the Union, despite the state's divided loyalties.[1] California Volunteers took over the role of the entire prewar U.S. Army and campaigned all over the West.

California's curious history also played a role, albeit an ambiguous one. Admitted as a free state in 1850, California was, in fact, no stranger to slavery. Indians found off the reservation while not employed by whites were deemed liable to forced servitude under the Indian Law of 1850—an injustice that persisted well into the Civil War. On the other hand, the absence of a state-sanctioned system of black slavery also had an effect. Few Californians stood to gain or lose financially, no matter what fate befell the South's "peculiar institution." This must have affected the eagerness of Southerners to risk their lives and fortunes for an economic system they had left a thousand miles behind in their journey west.

Finally, there was the impact of gold itself. Americans from both North and South came to California—at great hazard and cost—to get rich, and the lure of boundless wealth remained powerful throughout the Civil War. One Southern partisan in California left a wonderfully candid record of a plot to seize the state government, relating how the conspirators' hunger for martial glory ebbed with each new report of rich strikes in the Comstock Lode in nearby Washoe Territory (present-day Nevada). Finally, the would-be guerrillas voted (in secret ballot) to defer their crusade for a Confederate California, pending personal inspection of the fabulous new discoveries.

Far from being detached from the great quarrel, Californians in the early 1860s were in it up to their necks. The fact that they didn't set about shooting one another in large numbers is, perhaps, the most surprising fact in all of California's history. There were distinct reasons for this mercy—reasons every bit as interesting as those that led to the wholesale bloodletting back east. California's experience of the Civil War is a great story, one I am pleased to share with readers who are curious about the state's improbable past.

Chapter 1

THE REMOTEST PLACE ON EARTH

Sailing westward around the tip of South America was a heroic undertaking in the early years of the nineteenth century. Only dire need or the prospect of great reward led skippers to drive their wooden ships into the howling ice storms and violent seas of the passage. Whalers and fur traders braved the Horn in those days, as did the Spanish and Mexican ships that sustained settlements along the Pacific shores. Until the advent of the steamship, passage from the Atlantic to the Pacific coast of North America remained a dangerous and costly business.

Access by land was even more challenging. Expeditions to California from Mexico crossed vast stretches of desert, where draft animals perished and mounted warriors from a variety of tribes attacked wagon trains almost at will. The central government of Mexico simply did not have the military resources to control what is now the American Southwest or even venture into it without the gravest precautions.

For citizens of the young United States, the Pacific coast was even more remote. More than 1,500 miles of mountain, prairie and desert separated the Mississippi Valley—the locus of American expansion in the 1830s and '40s—from the western shores of the continent. Any attempt to reach the Far West also had to pass through the domains of numerous native peoples, whose response to white intruders varied from welcoming to lethal.

Adventurous Yankee trappers, traders and sailors did reach Mexican California in the first decades of the nineteenth century. They brought back tales of a rich country of excellent climate, governed by a small

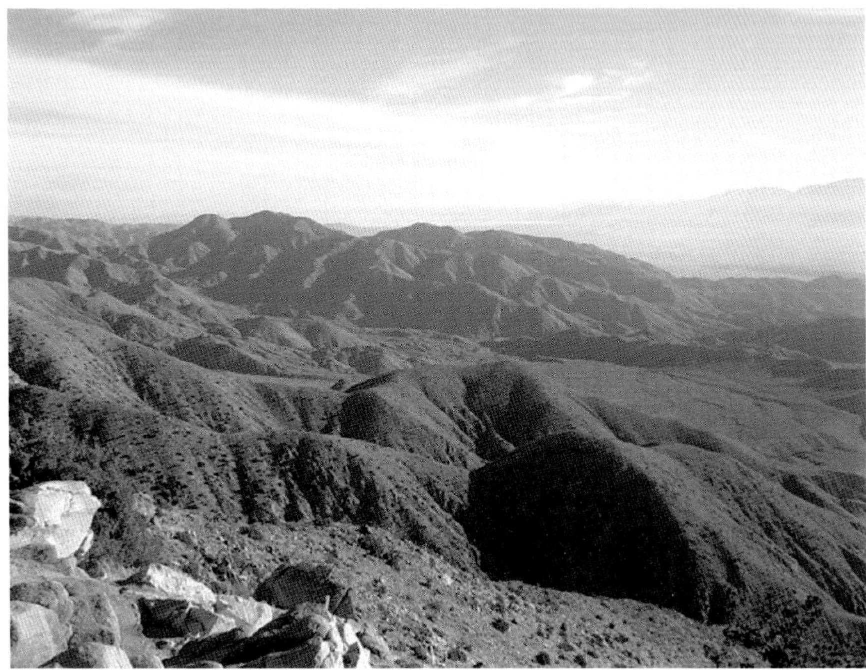

The land route between Alta California and Mexico was extremely difficult and dangerous. Expeditions were heavily guarded and infrequent. *Collection of Joe Pawlowski.*

population of Mexican ranchers and soldiers along its coast and inland valleys but still under the sway of its original inhabitants everywhere else. These early American explorers also carried back word of the fabulous Bay of San Francisco, the great natural harbor of western North America—a still-water haven where all the navies of the world could ride safely at anchor.

The strategic potential of San Francisco Bay was a magnet to any nation with ambitions in the Pacific. Great Britain and the United States sought to buy the harbor from a weak and divided Mexico, which desperately needed foreign currency. When Mexico refused all offers, the Polk administration, which assumed office in 1845 under the banner of "Manifest Destiny," proceeded to make other plans. Later that year, the administration welcomed the breakaway Mexican province of Texas into the Union—an act that Mexico had repeatedly threatened to oppose with force. Texas's admission was made all the more galling by the state's claim that its border was marked by the Rio Grande. Mexico held that the Nueces River constituted the dividing line.

National pride was engaged on both sides of the dispute, and Mexican forces duly sallied forth to attack the troops Polk sent into the contested area by way of live bait. Bitter recriminations ensued, and the two nations prepared for war.

It was clear from the beginning that America's aims extended far beyond Texas. Before news of the U.S. declaration of war reached California, Yankee settlers in the Sonoma Valley rose in the "Bear Flag" revolt, assisted by a party of sixty heavily armed "surveyors" under Captain John C. Frémont, who just happened to be in the neighborhood at the time. A few days later (and still before news of the U.S. declaration), Commodore John D. Sloat of the U.S. Pacific Squadron sent marines ashore to seize Monterey, the capital of Alta California.

Many native Californios had little use for the remote and ineffective government in Mexico City and were in favor of independence—or of

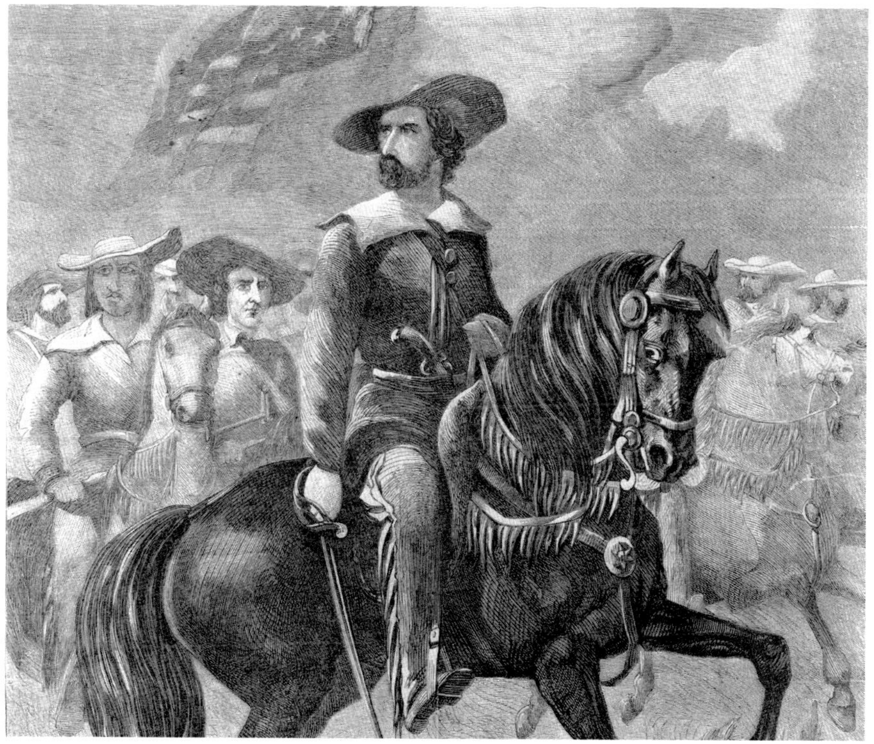

In 1843, Captain John C. Frémont was sent to explore the Far West. His mission was to survey a route to Oregon for American settlers, who would forestall British occupation of the territory. Frémont also visited California—and went home full of enthusiasm for what he saw there. *Library of Congress.*

gaining the protection of another power. In Sonoma, opposition to the Yankee rising had more to do with outrage at the high-handed behavior of the Bear Flaggers rather than opposition to American rule. Mexican resistance proved more determined farther south, where Andrés Pico and a troop of Californio lancers handed the American expeditionary force under Stephen Kearney a bloody check at the Battle of San Pasqual. In the end, Kearney's force combined with sailors and marines of the Pacific Squadron and with Yankee settlers to quell Californio resistance. In January 1847, Mexican forces in California capitulated. The American conquest was sealed by victories won later that year in Central Mexico by Generals Winfield Scott and Zachary Taylor, who broke Mexico's war-making power. In February 1848, the Treaty of Guadalupe Hidalgo formalized the "Mexican Cession"—the transfer from Mexico to the United States of a landmass the size of Western Europe, comprising the future states of California, Nevada and Utah, along with parts of New

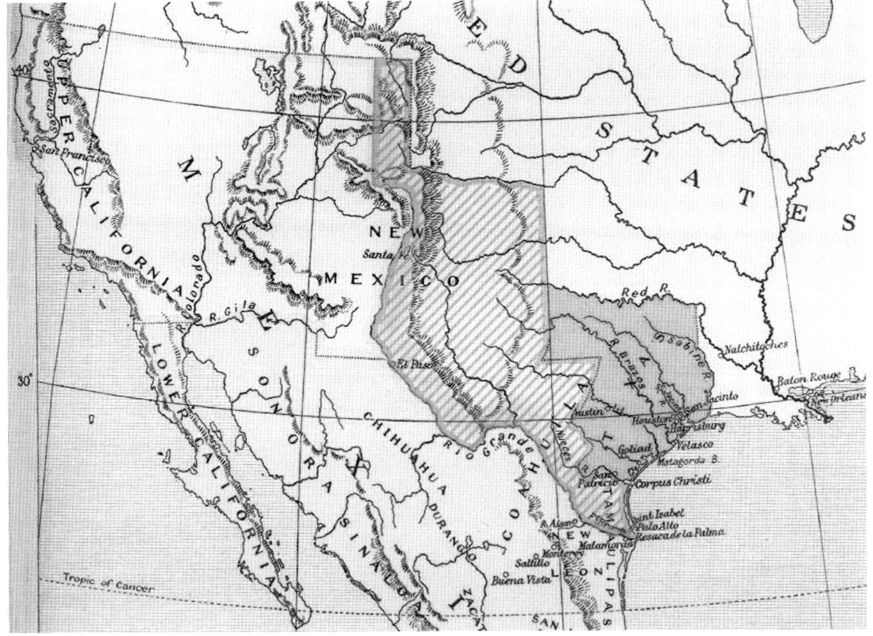

Mexico and the United States held different views about the size of Texas. The area in dispute (shown in diagonal hatching) was vast. Ironically, most of it was useless to white settlers, since great swathes of present-day Texas, New Mexico and Oklahoma were at that time under the control of the Comanche and their allies, who were not inclined to share. *Base image courtesy of the University of Texas Libraries, University of Texas at Austin.*

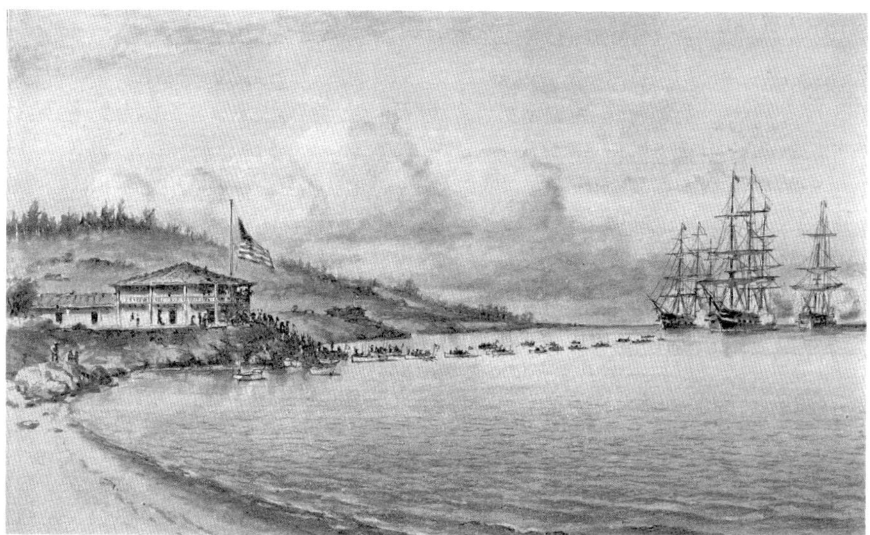

U.S. sailors and marines seized Monterey on July 7, 1846. Their commander, Commodore Sloat, was not the first American to take Monterey. In 1842, Commodore Thomas ap Catesby Jones of the Pacific Squadron had also raised the U.S. flag over the sleepy colonial town. Discovering that no war had been declared, the commodore apologized and sailed off. *From* The Life of Rear Admiral John Drake Sloat *by Edwin Sherman (1902).*

Mexico, Arizona, Colorado and Wyoming. Mexico received $15 million in compensation.

Nine days before the signing of this treaty, the defining event of California's history took place. On January 24, 1848, a carpenter named John Marshall discovered gold in the tail-race of Captain Sutter's sawmill at Coloma, in the foothills of the Sierra Nevada. Over the next two and a half years, a quarter million Argonauts—seekers of the Golden Fleece—poured in, transforming the remote colonial province into the bustling U.S. state of California.

Chapter 2

AMERICAN CALIFORNIA

For millennia, California's natural abundance supported a large population of native peoples. Pre-contact numbers are hard to estimate, but a commonly cited figure puts California's indigenous population at about 300,000 at the beginning of Spanish colonization in the late eighteenth century. Waves of European-derived illnesses sliced through the Indian population, both at the crowded missions (which provided ideal vectors for disease) and along trade routes that offered European-born pathogens free passage around the province. By the 1840s, the native population had been reduced to half its original size but still vastly outnumbered settlers of European descent, who numbered fewer than 10,000.

Both native and Mexican populations were overwhelmed by the onslaught of gold-seekers. California's Indian population collapsed, cut down by disease, starvation, murder, forced relocation and social disruption. Tribes who numbered in the thousands in the mid-1840s virtually disappeared in the first decade of American rule. Survivors were systematically driven from the gold fields and herded onto remote reservations, where disease and vicious "ethnic cleansing" continued unchecked. Indian political power, which had been considerable in Mexican California, disappeared in this era and did not play a role in California's experience of the Civil War. A few remote Indian tribes do enter the story, mainly as targets of military and paramilitary operations.[2]

California's Mexican population, by contrast, continued to play a role in the state's politics. Many Californios were substantial property owners—

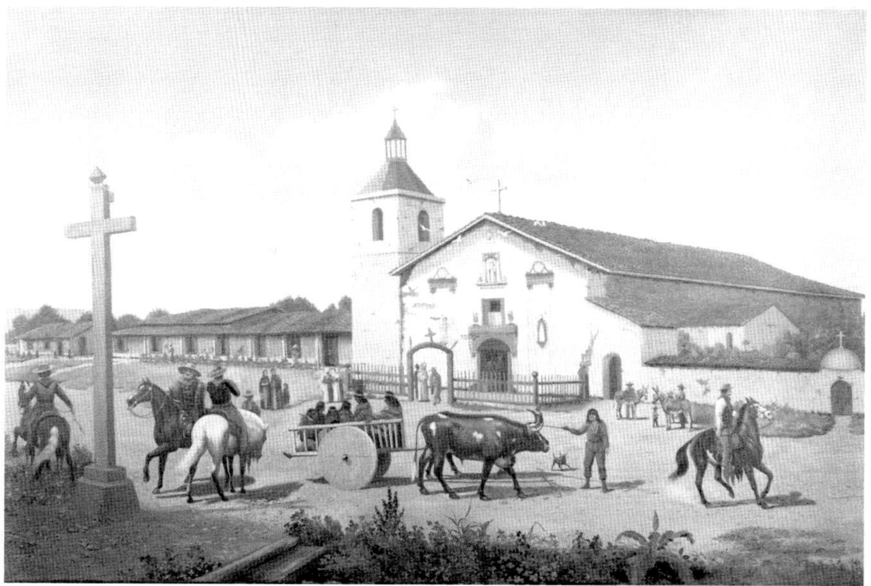

Mission Santa Clara, a crowded public place in California in the 1840s. *Image provided courtesy of Archives & Special Collections, Santa Clara University Library.*

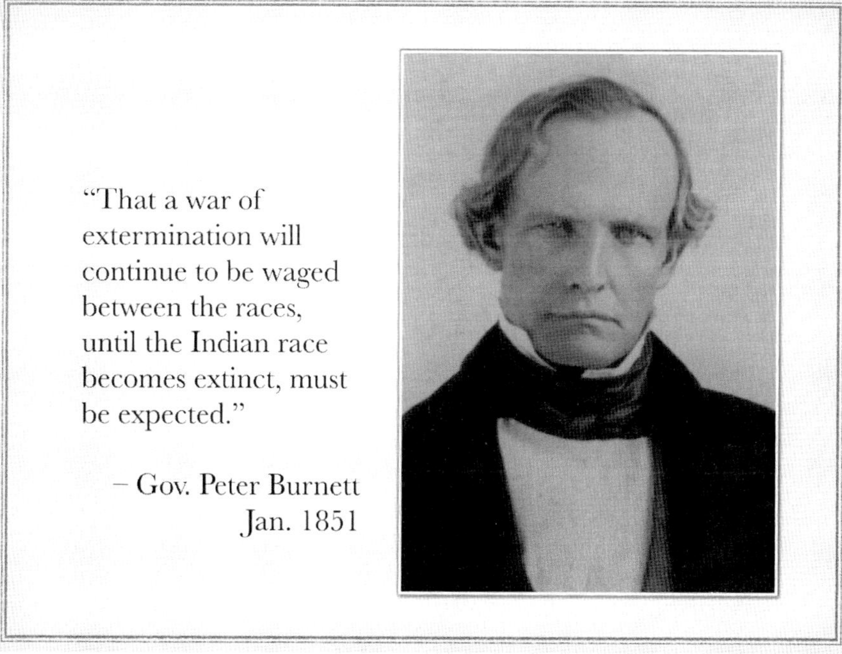

California's newly elected governor painted a dark picture of race relations in his first State of the State address. *Wikimedia Commons.*

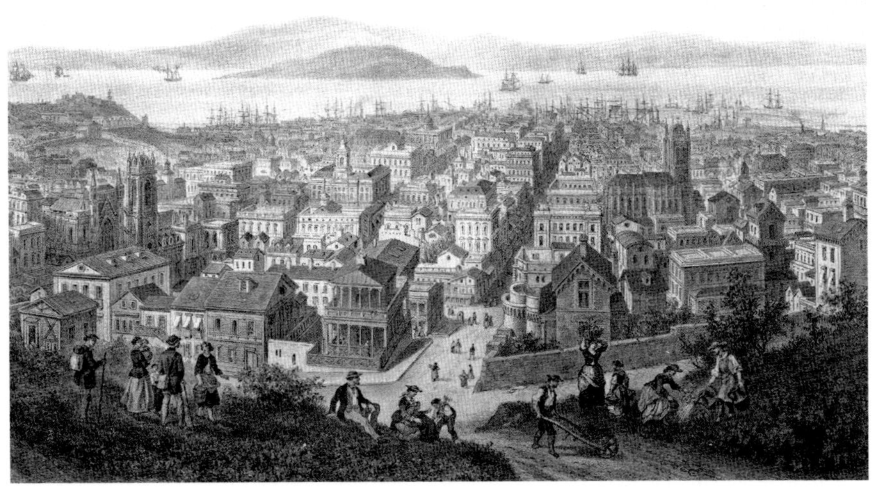

San Francisco, a crowded public place in California in 1860. *Library of Congress.*

California's gold rush coincided with a string of natural and man-made disasters around the world that displaced millions from their homelands. The Tai-ping Rebellion in China, the Irish Potato Famine and the brutal repression of Europe's revolutionaries of 1848 sent out tidal waves of suffering humanity. For refugees who could afford the sea voyage, migration to the gold fields offered a radiant promise of new life.

particularly in the southern half of the state—and their numbers were sufficient to retain a voice in the new society.

Ultimately, the lion's share of wealth and influence generated by gold mining fell to recent arrivals from the United States, the "Forty-niners," who poured into California by the tens of thousands following Marshall's discovery. These adventurers (almost all of them men) came from both North and South and brought their political beliefs, customs and social prejudices with them. They—and the tens of thousands of gold-seekers who arrived from Europe, China, Mexico, South America, Hawaii and Australia—formed the core of a new society that grew up almost overnight into the racial and cultural kaleidoscope that was American California. It was the interaction of these wildly differing peoples that determined the Golden State's response to the great crisis that overtook the United States in the tenth year of California statehood.

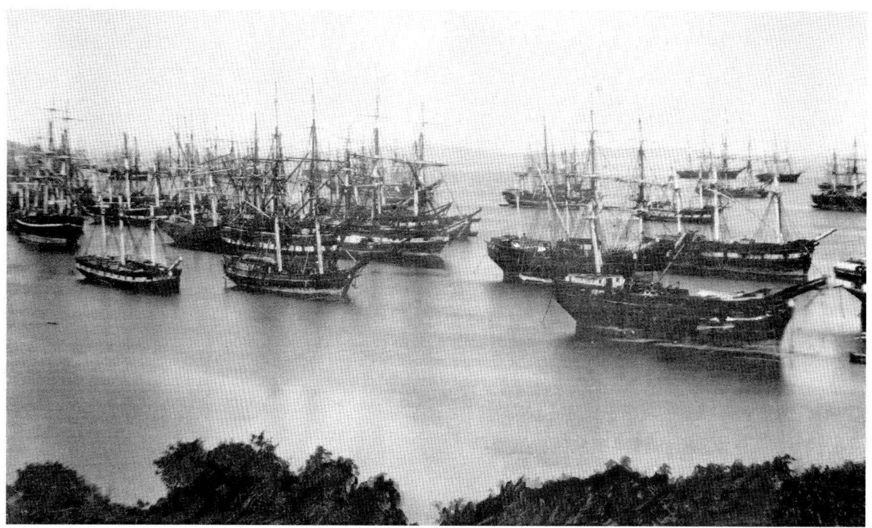

Abandoned ships in Yerba Buena cove, San Francisco, 1849–50. *Library of Congress.*

The surge of adventurers into California from around the globe was unprecedented in human history—and the patchwork U.S. military command that was supposed to govern it was desperately under-equipped for the job. Soldiers and sailors who should have kept order joined the exodus for the gold fields, leaving behind empty barracks and ships. Merchant seamen also deserted en masse. San Francisco's waterfront became a graveyard for hundreds of abandoned vessels, many of which lie there to this day under landfill.

INVENTING A GOVERNMENT

Mexican California's civil government had been based on the office of the *alcalde*—a kind of mayor and justice of the peace—and the system persisted in established areas, as stipulated by treaty. But the floods of miners pouring out over the valleys and up into the foothills caused new towns and cities to spring up overnight. Such communities were governed—to the extent they were governed at all—by ad hoc arrangements. Law enforcement and the administration of justice were pretty much do-it-yourself affairs, with the unsurprising result that early American California was a chaotic and violent place.

General Bennet Riley, California's last military governor, knew a thankless, impossible job when he saw one and acted swiftly to establish a civil government. Riley issued a decree in June 1849, calling for a convention to define California's borders and draw up a state constitution. In September, delegates elected to this convention assembled in Colton Hall at Monterey. In October, they issued a proposed state constitution, which California voters approved in November (voters in this instance being defined as white male U.S. citizens over twenty-one and Mexicans who opted to become American citizens). All that remained, as far as these Californians were concerned, was for the federal government to welcome them into the Union as the thirty-first state.

Back in Washington, discussions about the government of the territories acquired from Mexico was proceeding slowly and painfully, due to bitter disagreement over the extension of slavery. California's request to join the Union came out of the blue and struck Washington like a bombshell, widening the cracks that had already begun to show in the major political parties and hurling the nation to the edge of civil war. It was not that Congress and the administration were reluctant to bring in a new state. Far from it. The explosive part of California's request lay in its constitution, which forbade slavery.

WE SHALL KNOW WHAT TO DO

For decades, Southern politicians had watched in dismay as European immigration into the North increased free state representation in the House of Representatives. This ominous trend made the South cling ever more fiercely to the notion of a "balanced" Senate, which could serve as a bulwark against any threat to its "peculiar institution" of slavery. California's sudden appearance on the scene as a potential free state threatened to upend the delicate balance in the Senate, block Southern expansion to the Pacific and establish the precedent of Free Soil below the thirty-sixth parallel, the line established by earlier compromise to mark the boundary between free and slave territory in the West.

Southern politicians flung themselves into the battle against California's admission, and their impassioned oratory echoed through the House and Senate for month after grim, divisive month. Tempers soared and patience fled. One exasperated senator emphasized a point he was making

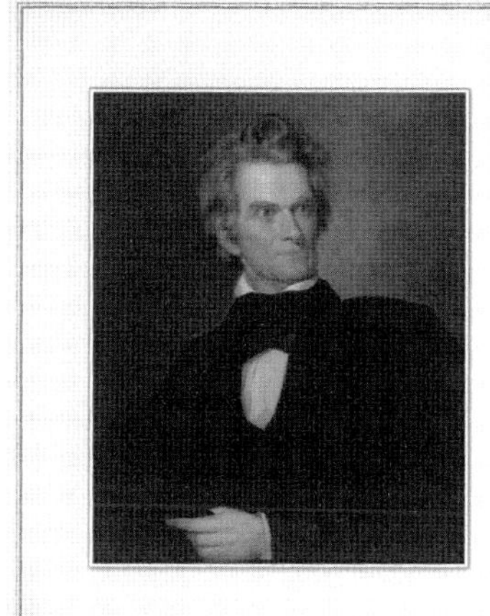

"…we shall know what to do when you reduce the question to submission or resistance."

—John C. Calhoun, opposing California's entry as a free state

John C. Calhoun of South Carolina was the senior statesman of the South in 1850. His farewell speech to the Senate was an impassioned plea against the admission of California. Calhoun was too ill to deliver the address himself, so he sat by while another senator read it. *National Portrait Gallery, Smithsonian Institution.*

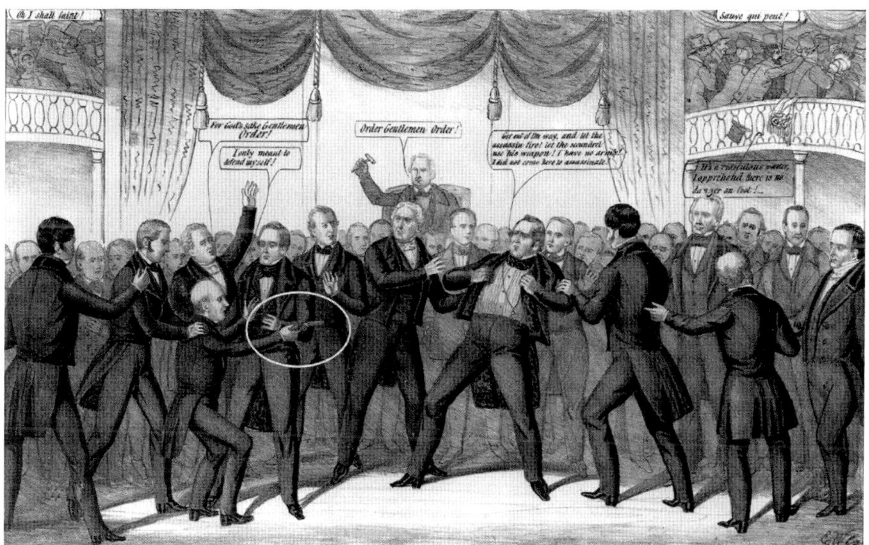

In this scene, Senator Foote threatens Senator Benton with a pistol. Washington was paralyzed by the great tug-of-war between North and South over the extension of slavery into the newly acquired territories. *Library of Congress.*

by leveling a loaded pistol at the heart of another, who did not share his opinion. "Secession conventions," meetings of political leaders of Southern nationalist persuasion, took place amidst white-hot talk of disunion. The breakup of the United States appeared to be at hand.

In the end, a trio of powerful senators (Webster, Clay and Douglas) hammered out an agreement that staved off disaster. A series of bills, known

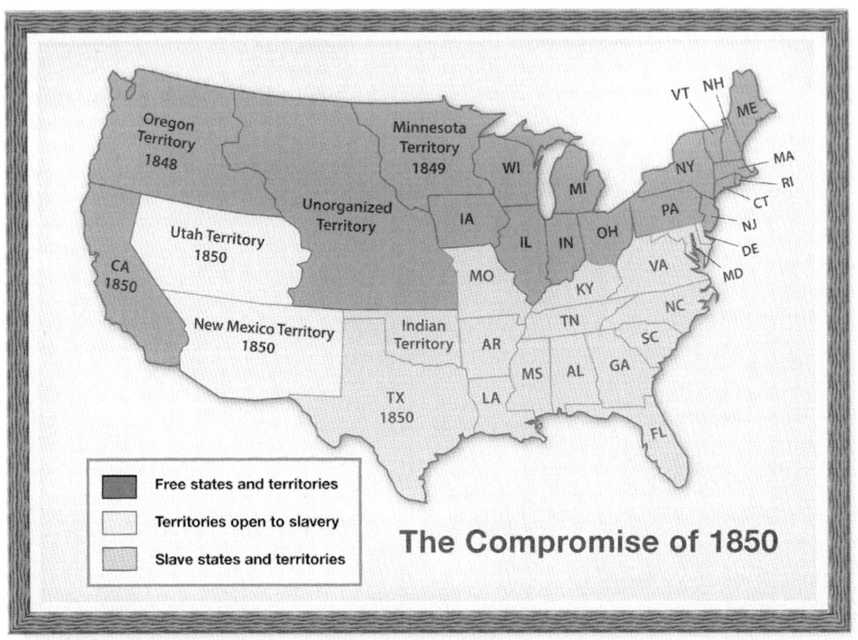

The Compromise of 1850 staved off war for a decade. *Map by the author.*

collectively as the Compromise of 1850, brought California into the Union as a free state, while other territories in the Southwest were expressly opened to slavery, if their settlers wished. A draconian Fugitive Slave Act was included in the package, allowing federal authorities to demand the assistance of state agencies in capturing runaways. Northern officials and private citizens who sheltered fugitives were subject to heavy fines.

The great irony about the quarrel that accompanied California's admission was that the proslavery leadership need not have worried at all. The new state's government fell promptly into the hands of Southern Democrats—and stayed there for most of the state's first decade.

NOT-SO-FREE CALIFORNIA

That "free" California aligned so swiftly with the South might seem odd at first glance, but the mystery disappears on close examination. California's adoption of a Free Soil constitution had nothing to do with political theory or concern for the rights of black people. (In fact, the Colton Hall Convention very nearly banned blacks from California altogether.) More to the point was the fact that gold mining is hard physical labor. No miner—from North *or* South—wanted to compete with slave-powered mining companies.

The handful of Southerners who brought out slaves to challenge the state's free status soon found themselves at odds with local "miners' councils," which provided the nearest thing to political and judicial authority to be found in the gold fields. The position of the councils was clear and consistent: no black slaves would be tolerated on a working claim.

As a practical matter, black slavery—even when redirected from mining—was hard to maintain in an area as chaotic and ill governed as gold rush California. The tightly woven social system that kept blacks enslaved in the South simply did not exist on the West Coast—a fact that slaves in California grasped quickly. Running away, they discovered, was a much less risky endeavor in a state where law enforcement was sketchy at best and where much of the population was indifferent or unsympathetic to black slavery.

Indian slavery was a different matter. Mexican California had a history of impressed Indian agricultural laborers, despite the fact that Mexico outlawed slavery after achieving independence from Spain. Sensing an opportunity, the legislature of "free" California passed, in its very first session, an Act for the Government and Protection of Indians.

This 1850 Indian law established a system of servitude for any Indian declared to be "vagrant" by a white justice of the peace. "Vagrant" Indians could then be parceled out to the friends, family and cronies of the court as domestic servants or field laborers. An Indian dragged before one of these courts could not testify but had to rely on a sympathetic white to speak in his or her defense. In practice, this often boiled down to a white farmer appearing in court and saying, "This is my Indian. I need him for harvest."

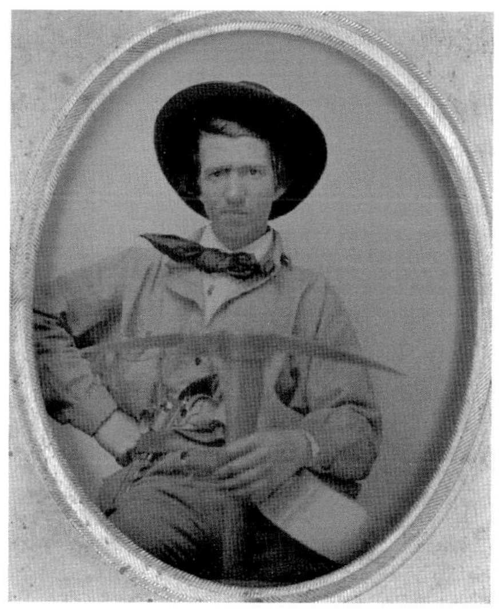

"One man, one claim" was the rule in early gold rush California. *Courtesy of the Bancroft Library, University of California, Berkeley.*

At the peak of the system, in the early 1860s, captive Indian boys could be held in service until they reached the age of thirty. Girls could

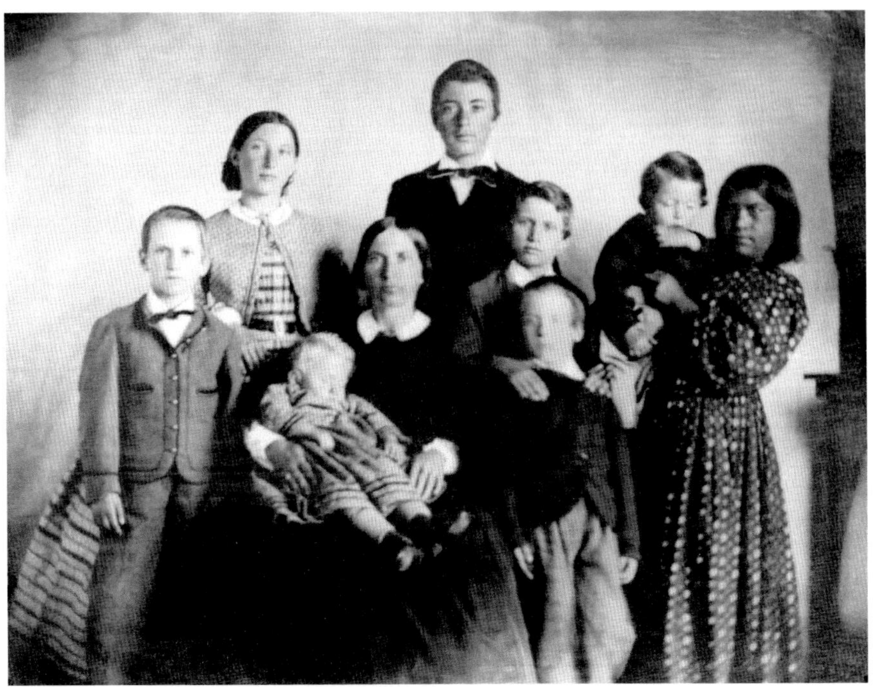

Benitz family at Fort Ross, circa 1865.

Working for or intermarrying with pioneer families was an essential survival strategy for many California Indians. The young woman at right is most likely Maria Meyer, the daughter of the business partner of William Benitz, the father of the household shown in the photo. *Courtesy of the Benitz family.*

be held until age twenty-five. Indian men and women who were captured as adults could be worked for a period of ten years. The market in young Indian "servants" was highly profitable—so much so that slavers took to raiding Indian villages, gunning down the adults and capturing the children, who fetched between $50 and $200 a head. Possession of an Indian "servant" was common in households throughout the state during the 1850s and '60s. Large numbers of Indians worked as agricultural laborers.

The reality of mid-nineteenth-century America was that full-blown white supremacism was the norm—a set of beliefs shared by white Northerners and Southerners. What varied was the way those beliefs played out in law. In California, black slavery never took root, whereas Indian domestic and agricultural "service" was widespread. This is what made it easy for California's electorate to rally around a charismatic Mississippi slave owner who dominated the state's Democratic Party for almost a decade.

Chapter 3

IN THE SOUTHERN ORBIT

Most people who traveled to California did so in pursuit of gold. William M. Gwin sailed into San Francisco Bay in June 1849 looking for political power—and found a bonanza.

Gwin was a seasoned pro. In his younger days, he had been secretary to Andrew Jackson. Later, he served a term as a Democratic congressman from Mississippi. He had given and received patronage jobs and knew intimately how the system worked. In the wide-open, make-it-up-as-you-go politics of the gold rush, Gwin's training and experience proved invaluable. Two months after his arrival in California, he won election to the Colton Hall Convention, where he played a leading role in drafting California's new constitution. Gwin then went on tour to promote the proposal, building up a formidable political machine in the process. When California's first legislature met, William Gwin was chosen alongside John C. Frémont as one of California's first U.S. senators. The two drew straws to see who would serve the longer term. Gwin won.

Gwin dominated California's politics for the first decade of statehood, demonstrating along the way an uncanny ability at balancing contradictory political forces while keeping his hands firmly on the reins of power. Gwin was a slave owner with a plantation back in Mississippi, but he astutely joined the rest of the delegates at Colton Hall in voting against slavery, thereby winning favor with the miners and making California's entry into the Union more palatable to Northern states.

Once in office, Gwin played the Southerner through and through. He supported efforts at establishing slavery in California and backed proslavery legislation at the national level. Gwin's political machine in California was run largely by and for Southerners, who were known as "the Chivalry." Gwin's mastery of the patronage system ensured that his supporters never lacked for employment. In Gwin's heyday, the San Francisco Customs House was dubbed "the Virginia poorhouse" because of the number of Southerners who relied on it for their daily bread.

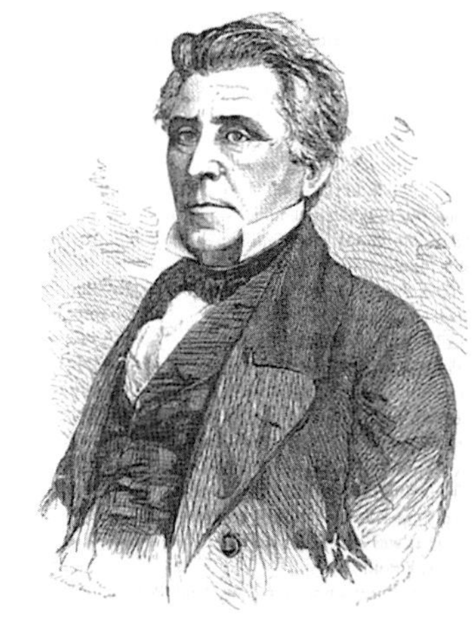

Senator William M. Gwin. *From* The Annals of San Francisco *by Frank Soulé (1855).*

In the Senate, Gwin made sure that federal funds flowed freely to the new state. In addition to a customs house and a branch of the U.S. Mint, Gwin secured money for lighthouses along the coast and a naval shipyard on Mare Island. Gwin's success in Washington came at a cost, however, since it kept him away from the pulse of California politics, where a rival Democratic clique was gaining power. This new faction was led by a Northerner named David Broderick, who had also come to California in search of political glory.

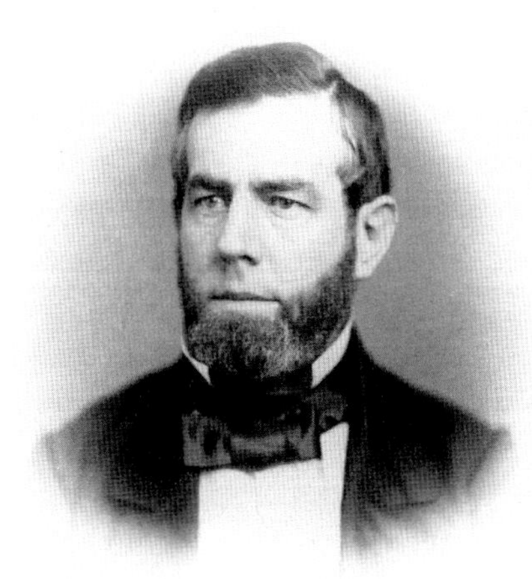

Senator David Broderick. *Library of Congress.*

Broderick served his political apprenticeship in Tammany Hall in New York City, a peerless preparatory school for the bare-knuckle style of machine politics practiced in early San Francisco. He was brave and cool in a crisis, characteristics he demonstrated early on as a firefighter—an occupation even more dangerous in an era lacking building codes and effective firefighting equipment. Broderick was a champion of the working man (his father was a stonemason) and opposed the institution of slavery. Broderick's power base, 1850s San Francisco, featured the most

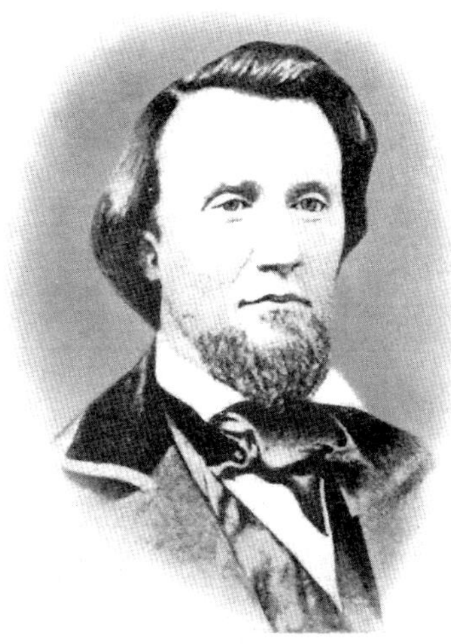

Political violence was not new to David Terry. During San Francisco's "Vigilance Committee" upheavals, Terry once expressed his judicial opinion by stabbing a vigilante in the neck. Terry escaped hanging when the man unexpectedly survived. *From* The Last of the California Rangers *by Jill Cossley-Batt (1928).*

violent and corrupt urban politics in the United States. Elections were determined largely by physical possession of the ballot boxes, and toughs were routinely employed to secure that possession. (This is where Broderick's background as a firefighter paid off. Disciplined companies of hearty young men were ideal sources of political muscle.)

Broderick was not known to be personally corrupt, but his machine exacted tribute from every politician it placed in office. His iron grip on San Francisco gave him the political and financial base to expand his domain. Broderick's climb to the top was long and hard and marked by brutal contests with rival politicians, but by 1857, he had amassed enough influence in Sacramento to be chosen as California's junior U.S. senator.

While the Democratic Party continued to dominate California in the late 1850s, infighting between its Northern and Southern wings became more and more bitter. The rivalry eventually spilled over into a series of duels, culminating in the famed encounter between Senator Broderick and David Terry, chief justice of the Supreme Court of California.

Terry was an ardent "Southern man," originally associated with the Whig Party. The collapse of the Whigs in the early '50s led Terry first to the Know-Nothings (a nativist party that flourished briefly) and then to the Chivalry, where he became a de facto ally of Gwin. Terry had been a friend of Broderick's, but when Terry lost his bid for reelection to the Supreme Court in 1859, he blamed his defeat on Northern Democrats in general and on Broderick in particular. The men traded public slurs until a duel became inevitable.

The circumstances surrounding the duel were suspicious. The pistols Terry provided were known to be hair-triggered; after the duel, Broderick partisans claimed the weapons were unequal, with one being thought to fire prematurely. In the encounter, Broderick's pistol went off as he lifted it, and the bullet plowed into the dirt. Terry's bullet struck home, wounding Broderick in the lung. Broderick died three days later.[3]

As the critical election of 1860 approached, the Democratic Party in California was in tatters. Many Californians believed that the Chivalry had murdered Senator Broderick in cold blood. California voters were fed up with the open strife in Democratic ranks and began to take a more serious look at the upstart Republican Party.

Two (or More) Californias

As political tensions approached the breaking point, a number of schemes were floated to reshape California for partisan advantage. Foremost of these was a plan put forward in 1859 by Andrés Pico and an unlikely alliance of old-time Californios and proslavery Southerners.

The Pico Act proposed to create a separate, slaveholding "Territory of Colorado" out of the six southernmost counties of California. This notion appealed to Californio landowners in the area, who felt numerically overwhelmed by the Americans in the north and believed their taxes were being diverted to the advantage of mining interests. Slaveholding Southerners favored the scheme because it would firmly establish slavery on the Pacific coast and because the new territory would later seek admission to the Union as a slave state, thereby redressing the "imbalance" in the U.S. Senate that Southerners found so alarming.

The power of the prewar Chivalry is demonstrated by the fact that the Pico Act was approved by the state legislature in Sacramento and sent on to Washington. The war broke out shortly afterward, however, rendering the issue of a new slave state on the Pacific moot.

The alliance between the Californios and the Chivalry proved short-lived. Mexican attitudes toward race were generally more relaxed than those of U.S. Southerners. (Andrés Pico himself had African and Indian blood.) When the United States finally broke apart, many Californios sided with the Union and ended up donning the blue uniform of the California Volunteers.[4]

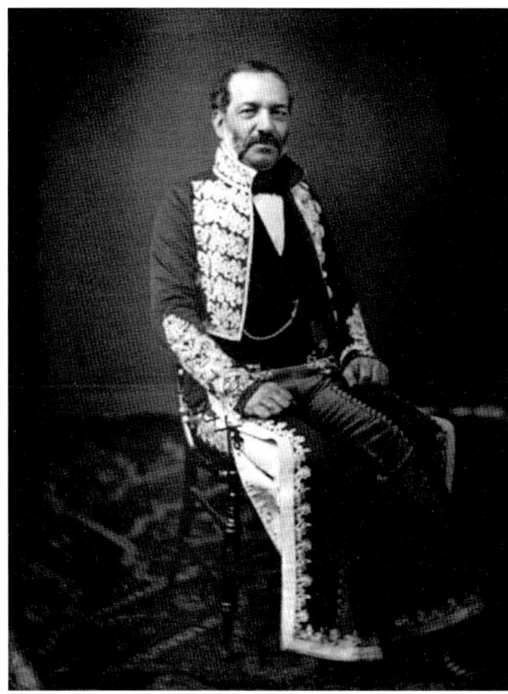

Andrés Pico and his brother, Pio, both served as governors of Mexican Alta California. They retained considerable political power under the new American government. *Seaver Center for Western History Research, Natural History Museum of Los Angeles County, California/Wikimedia Commons.*

The Republic of the Pacific

There was another prewar plan to reshape the political geography of the West Coast to Southern tastes, this one involving the creation of a new nation, the "Republic of the Pacific," to be composed of Oregon and California. This scheme was favored by powerful Chiv politicians who anticipated a breakup of the United States over slavery. John Weller and Milton Latham are examples of state officials who backed this idea at one time or another. Both were Ohio-born Democrats who had lived in the South before moving to California. Both served as U.S. senator and governor of California (though Latham served only five days as governor before taking up the martyred Broderick's seat in the U.S. Senate). Both men backed the "Lecompton Constitution" for Kansas, a proslavery document that became a litmus test for membership in the Southern wing of the Democratic Party. Weller expressed his abhorrence of abolitionism and espousal of Pacific Coast separatism in the clearest possible terms: "If the wild spirit of fanaticism which now pervades the land should destroy the [Union]—which God forbid—California will not go with the south or north, but here on the

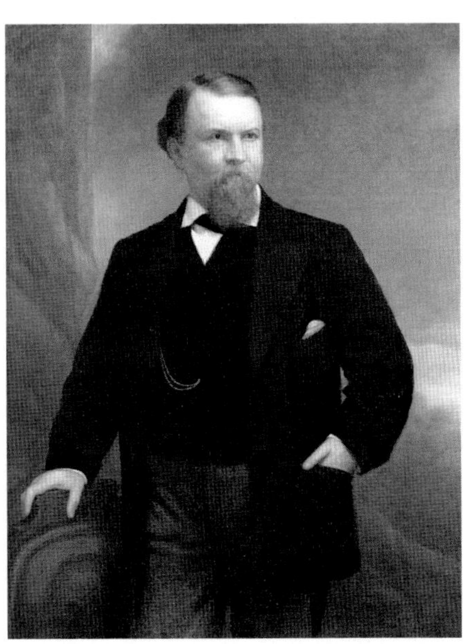

Milton Latham's gifts as a political chameleon baffled friend and foe alike. As a prewar U.S. senator from California, he railed against Northern overreach and threatened secession—but as sentiment in California swung toward the Union, Latham swung with it. In the end, he became the only leading Chiv politician to have a Union army training camp named after him. *Courtesy of the State of California/Department of General Services/Facilities Management Division/Capitol Historic Region.*

shores of the Pacific, found a mighty republic, which may in the end prove the greatest of all."[5]

That midwestern-born men holding high office in California should publicly espouse such views may seem odd today, but we know the outcome of the war and have grown used to the idea of a strong federal government. At the time, California's enormous distance from the eastern states made plans for an independent nation more plausible, as did a widespread feeling of grievance on the part of Californians at what they felt was neglect of their state by the national government. Many Californians saw the proposed Republic of the Pacific as a sensible way of saying "a plague on both your houses" to a North and South that were manifestly unable to manage the nation's affairs. As Asbury Harpending, a Confederate partisan in California, put it in his memoirs, "In 1860, the ties that bound the Pacific to the Government at Washington were nowhere very strong."[6]

Chapter 4

THE NATIONAL CRISIS

California, with its Border State demographics, reflected the politics of the Union at large in the 1850s—a Union that was hurtling full-throttle toward a trainwreck. Relations between Northerners and Southerners in Congress turned ever more bitter because of the tug-of-war over slavery in the territories acquired from Mexico. Although the Compromise of 1850 succeeded in bringing California into the Union as a free state, Southerners were left deeply dissatisfied, since by their lights, the settlement did not leave enough room for the expansion of slavery.

The Kansas-Nebraska Act of 1854 was an attempt to defuse tensions by deferring decisions about slavery to the settlers of the new territories. The scheme looked plausible enough from the floor of Congress but failed spectacularly in its first field test. In the new territory of Kansas, pro- and antislavery partisans promptly set up rival governments and attacked each other with shocking ferocity.

Pouring fuel onto the fire, the Supreme Court handed down in 1857 its infamous Dred Scott decision, an attempt to settle the debate over slavery once and for all—on Southern terms.

Dred Scott was a slave who lived for a number of years in a free state. He returned with his master to a slave state, where his master died. Abolitionist lawyers sued for Scott's freedom, and the case ended up before the U.S. Supreme Court. Chief Justice Roger Taney's decision maintained that blacks were not citizens of the United States and never could be.[7] Southerners could move into any territory or state they liked and bring their human

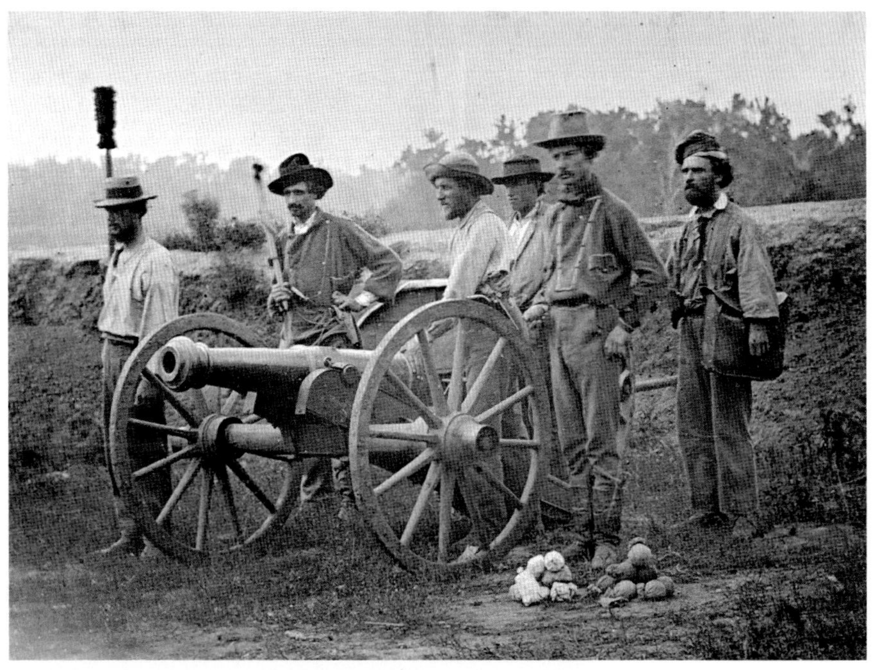

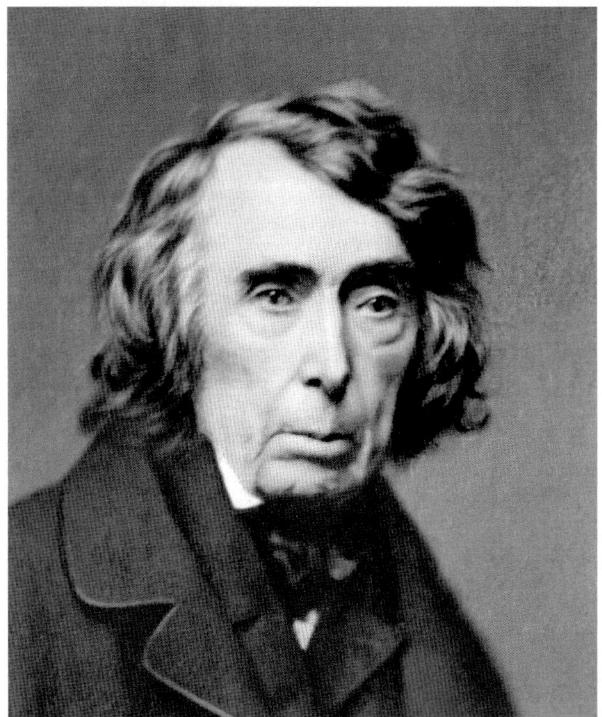

Above: Free-Soil debating team in prewar Kansas. *Kansas State Historical Society.*

Left: Chief Justice Taney held that "[blacks have] no rights which the white man was bound to respect.…The negro might justly and lawfully be reduced to slavery for his benefit. He [can be] bought and sold and treated as an ordinary article of merchandise and traffic, whenever profit could be made by it." *Library of Congress.*

property with them, happy in the knowledge that the federal government would protect their "rights." Unsurprisingly, Taney's ruling provoked outrage across the North.

The final blow to the old Union was struck by John Brown, a blood-soaked veteran of the fighting in Kansas. In 1859, Brown launched a raid on Harpers Ferry, Virginia, in hope of starting a slave rebellion. Brown's effort was quickly contained by local militia and then put down by U.S. Marines under the command of Colonel Robert E. Lee. Two of Brown's sons died in the fighting. Brown was badly wounded and died on the gallows shortly afterward.

Brown's act was widely repudiated in the North, but most Southerners brushed aside these disavowals. In their eyes, the North's true agenda had been exposed at last.

THE TIPPING POINT

The political fabric of the United States tore apart in the months preceding the presidential election of 1860. The Democratic Party, unable to select a candidate by the rules then in place (which required a two-thirds majority), split into Southern and Northern factions, each with its own candidate. In the upper South, a new party arose, the Constitutional Union Party, which sought to preserve the Union but with firm protections for slavery. When the pre-election dust settled, voters were left with four candidates for president.

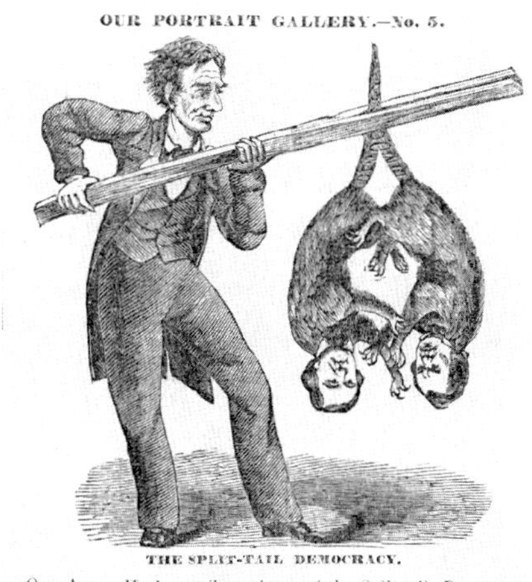

Lincoln gets the better of "Split-tail Democracy." *From* The Rail Splitter, *July 21, 1860.*

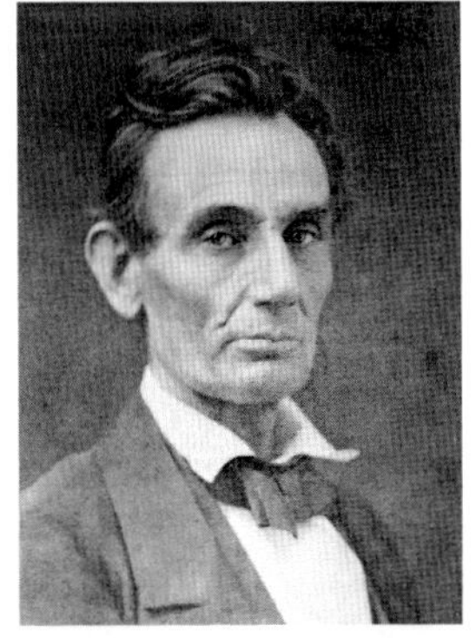

THE REPUBLICAN PARTY was dedicated to the exclusion of slavery from the western territories. This was not necessarily because of concern for the fate of black people. Most Republicans shared the white supremacist assumptions of the day. But they disliked slavery as an institution and feared economic competition from it. They did not want to see it expand into the new territories.

The Republican candidate, Abraham Lincoln, was seen as a moderate in the North but was written off as a wild-eyed fanatic throughout much of the South, where his name did not appear on the ballot.

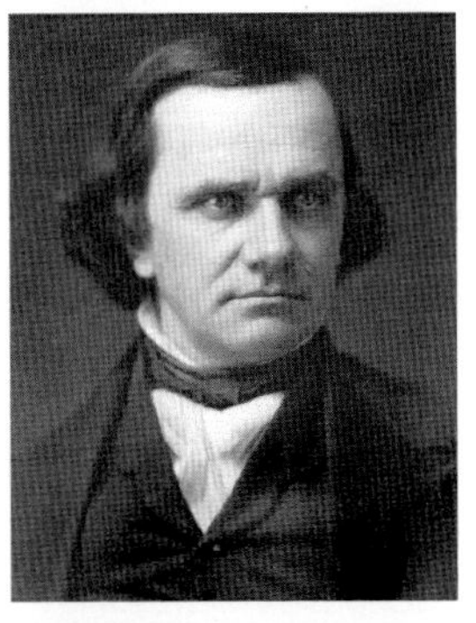

NORTHERN DEMOCRATS tended to be "soft" on slavery, if only to keep the Democratic Party united and in control of Washington. Their candidate, Stephen Douglas, promoted the concept of "popular sovereignty," allowing settlers of the new western territories to decide for themselves about slavery. Douglas believed his position would be seen as a workable compromise by Southern members of his party. He was mistaken.

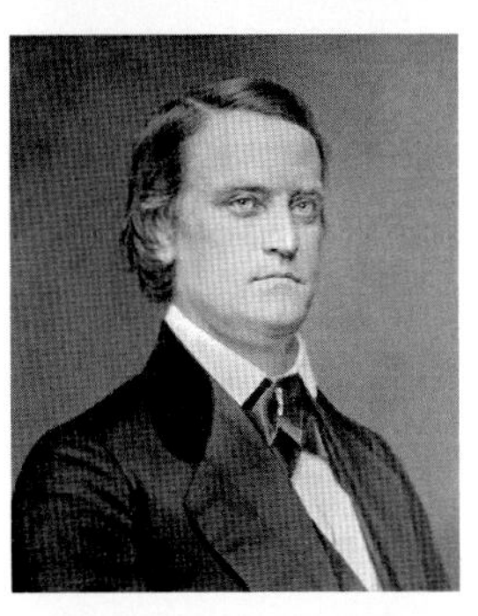

SOUTHERN DEMOCRATS were energetically proslavery, pro–states' rights and favored strict enforcement of the national Fugitive Slave laws. Their candidate, John Breckinridge, eventually became a general in the Confederate army.

California's ruling Democratic clique (Gwin's "Chivalry") was aligned with this bloc from the Deep South. California's delegates shunned Douglas and took part in the breakaway convention that nominated Breckinridge.

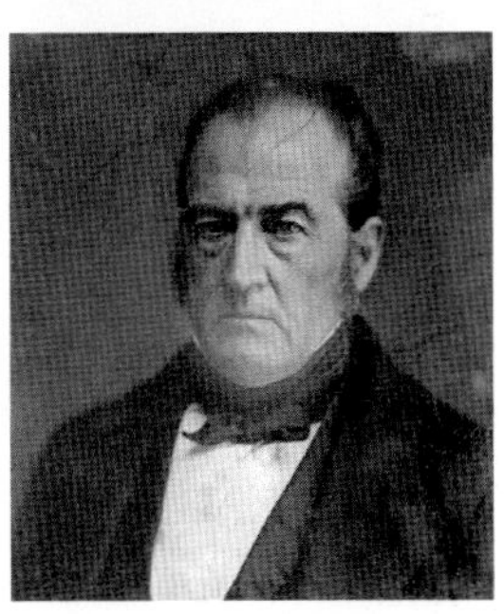

Images on this page courtesy of the Library of Congress.

Finally, there was the wild card, the **CONSTITUTIONAL UNION PARTY**, and its candidate, John Bell. Senator Bell believed that the political firestorm raging across the United States would die down if everyone—North and South—adhered strictly to the Constitution. Bell's position was popular in the Upper South, where both slavery and Union were held dear.

Here is the result of the election—as clear an expression of regional politics as the country has ever seen—in the East.

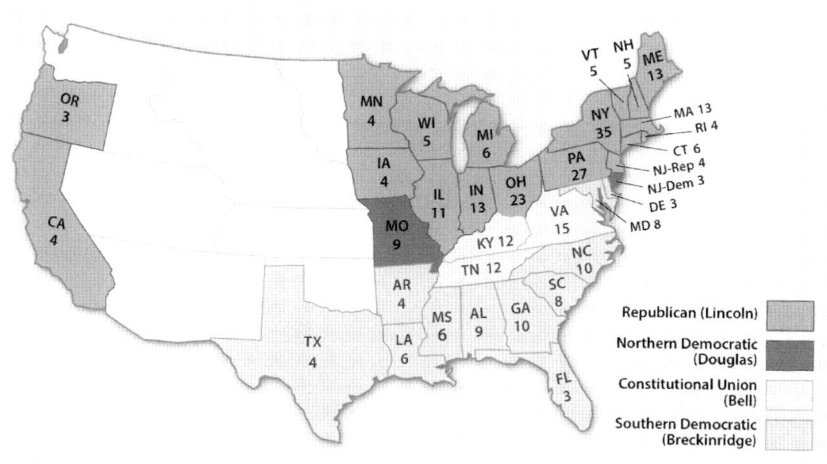

Election of 1860, electoral votes by state. *Map by the author.*

Looking at this map, you could easily infer that California was a Union state, just like any of the others that went for Lincoln. The truth is much more interesting.

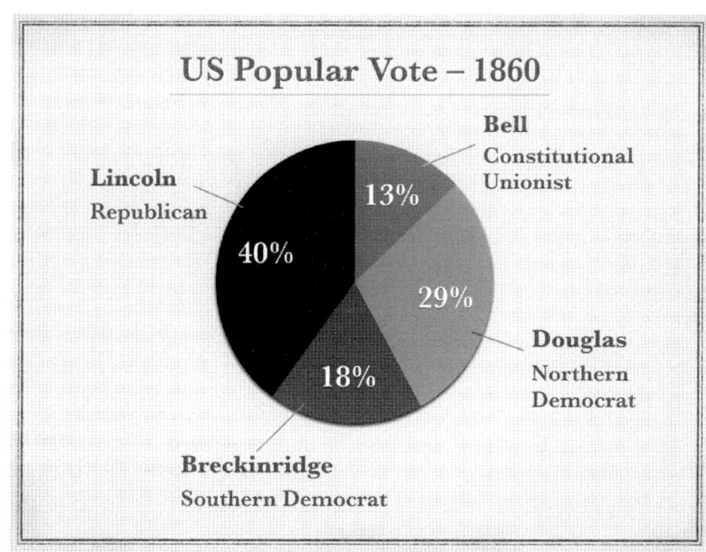

U.S. presidential election 1860, national results. *Chart by the author.*

Lincoln won the election with only 40 percent of the total. If he had been facing a united Democratic Party, Lincoln would have been buried. He truly was a sectional candidate whose name didn't even appear on ballots in the South.

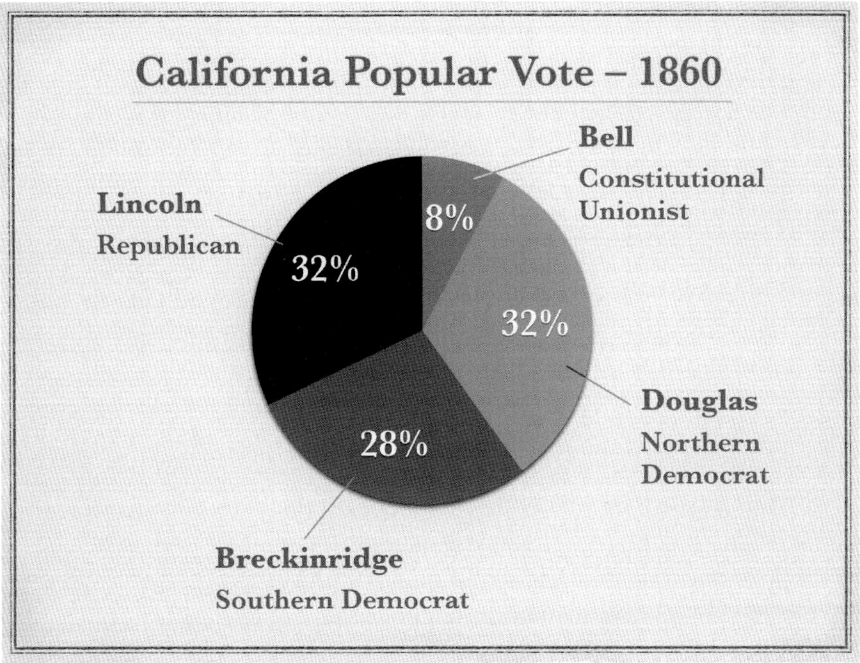

U.S. presidential election 1860, California results. *Chart by the author.*

Here is how California voted. Lincoln's portion shrinks; he runs eight points below where he did nationally. Breckinridge runs a whopping ten points better. California was decidedly more "Southern" than the nation as a whole. In the end, Lincoln won California by about seven hundred votes—roughly half a percentage point.

When the results of the presidential election are viewed county by county across the "old" states (i.e., excluding the Pacific coast), the regional nature of the contest becomes starkly obvious.[8] There is a near-perfect division between North and South—with Lincoln and Douglas on one side, Bell and Breckinridge on the other—until you get to Missouri, where order breaks down. The implications of this were dire. Missouri suffered the most vicious partisan fighting of the war because its people were divided in their allegiance. California was the same, only more so.

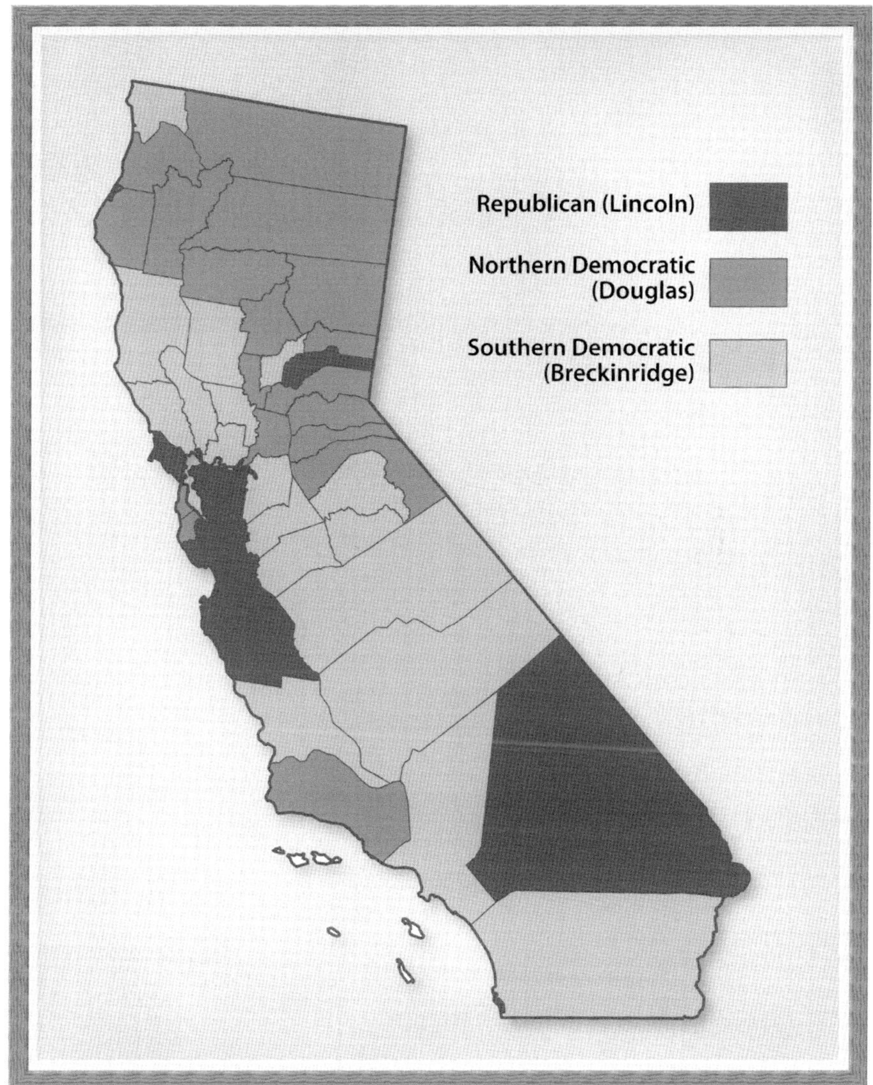

Presidential election of 1860, California results by county. *Map by the author.*

This map shows how scattered the political landscape of California really was. Lincoln won the Bay Area (except for the Peninsula) and San Bernardino and Nevada Counties. Douglas captured the top quarter of the state and Ventura and Santa Barbara Counties in the south. Breckinridge, the Southern candidate, won Los Angeles and a number of vast rural counties and swept the Southern Mines (the gold mining district supplied by the port of Stockton).

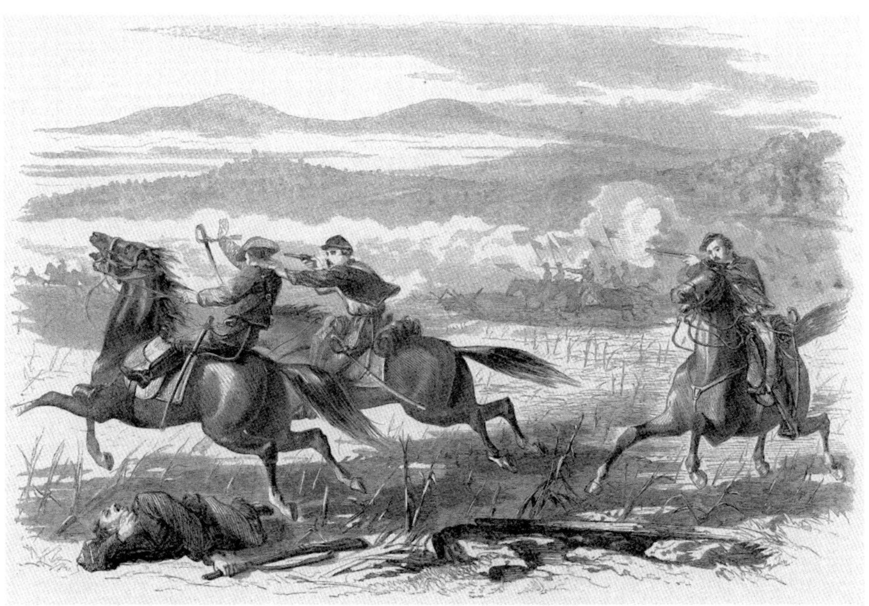

California would have been fertile ground for a Confederate partisan campaign, based in the Southern Mines. *From* Harper's Weekly, *November 29, 1862*.

The election of Abraham Lincoln led directly to the secession of South Carolina on December 20, 1860. Six more states from the Deep South withdrew before Lincoln assumed office. After the shelling of Fort Sumter on April 12, 1861, Lincoln called on the states to provide troops to put down the rebellion. Most of the Upper South ignored his request—and joined the Confederacy instead. Full-scale war was now a certainty.

Chapter 5

WHICH WAY CALIFORNIA?

Fear and confusion reigned throughout the United States in the period following Lincoln's election. Nothing like the Secession crisis had ever happened before; there was no precedent for the nation's leaders or citizens to turn to. Momentous questions hung unanswered in the air. *Will Lincoln try to force the departing states back into the Union when he takes office? If so, what chance will he have with the minuscule force at his command?*

The U.S. Army numbered around seventeen thousand men in 1861, and most of them were scattered across the West, protecting settlers and emigration routes. In effect, they were too few and too remote to matter, except as a source of officers for whatever volunteer forces might be raised. And it was far from clear which side would benefit most from this cadre of trained military leaders.

As far as California was concerned, no one knew if the state would stay in the Union. Jefferson Davis had high hopes the Golden State would join the exodus, a view that was shared by California's congressional delegation, who all belonged to the pro-Southern Chivalry faction of the Democratic Party. Abraham Lincoln, for his part, could take heart from the gathering strength of the Republican Party in the state and from the fact that immigrants from the Northern states outnumbered those from the South. There was latent Unionist potential in California, if it could be kept in the fold long enough for that potential to be expressed.

Adding to the general chaos was uncertainty over the intentions of California's governor, John Downey. Downey was an immigrant from

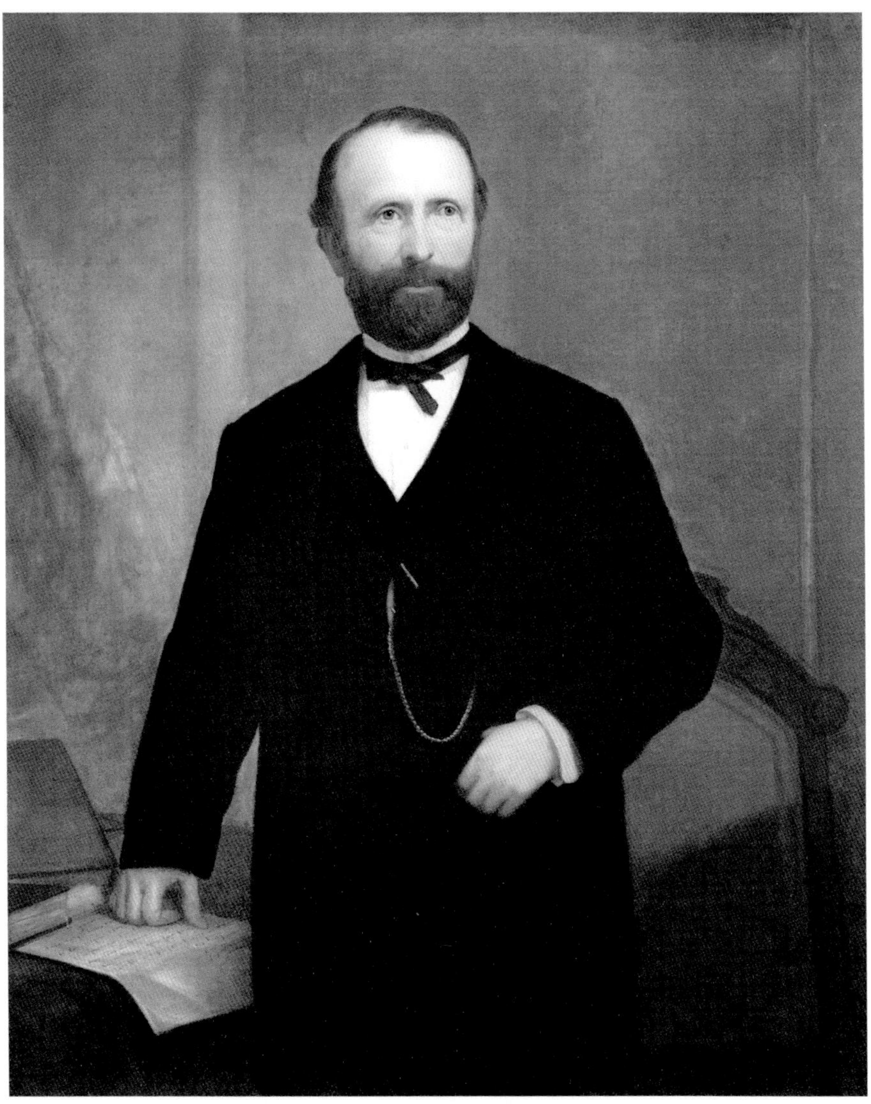

Governor John Downey, 1860–62. *Courtesy of the State of California, Department of General Services, Facilities Management Division, Capitol Historic Region.*

Ireland who arrived in Southern California at the age of twenty-one, during the gold rush. He was an able man and prospered there as an apothecary. Turning to politics, he rose swiftly under the aegis of the Chivalry, until he was elected lieutenant governor of California in 1859 as a "Lecompton" (i.e., proslavery) Democrat. Five days after his election, Downey's fellow

"Chiv," Milton Latham, resigned the governorship in order to assume the U.S. Senate seat left vacant by the death of Broderick. Thus, in January 1860, the thirty-two-year-old Downey found himself chief executive of a state that was set to fly apart at the seams.

Downey's term started well. In April 1860, he boldly vetoed a corrupt bill that would have handed over San Francisco's waterfront to a consortium of monopolists—an act that won him acclaim among voters and undying resentment from some very influential people in San Francisco.

Later that year, during the run-up to the critical presidential election of 1860, Downey parted ways with the Chivalry, who were openly touting Secession. Downey instead backed Stephen Douglas, the Northern Democratic candidate, who countenanced slavery but was firm for the Union. In the turmoil following Lincoln's election and South Carolina's secession, Downey made clear his own desire to keep California in the Union, but he left unanswered the question of whether he would support an attempt to bring back the departing states by force.

The first cannonball that arced over Charleston Harbor toward Fort Sumter changed political equations across the United States forever. The Lincoln administration's call for troops to suppress the rebellion left Border State leaders with no political cover at all. Would they accede to the federal government's request, or would they balk? Although California is not traditionally listed alongside Missouri, Kentucky, Maryland and Delaware in this category, the Golden State's dilemma was much the same.

Whatever Downey's innermost thoughts on Secession, his response to the Confederate attack on Sumter and to the Lincoln administration's subsequent requests for troops was prompt and unequivocal. In August 1861, the erstwhile Chiv from openly Secessionist Los Angeles set about to raise five regiments of infantry and one of cavalry to secure Southern California for the state, and the state for the Union.

General Johnston's Choice

In early 1861, one man had the potential to turn California's confusion and turmoil into open violence. That man was Albert Sidney Johnston, commanding officer of the U.S. Army Department of the Pacific.

Johnston was a Southerner, born in Kentucky, who graduated from West Point and served with distinction in the U.S. Army. He resigned his commission in 1834 to care for his ailing wife. After her death, Johnston moved to Texas and signed on as a private in the "Texian" army that won independence from Mexico. Johnston was swiftly promoted to major and headed Texas's armed forces in the early years of the republic. Johnston served ably in the Mexican-American War and resumed his career in the U.S. Army afterward. In December 1860, General Johnston was selected to take over the sprawling Department of the Pacific, which included all of California.

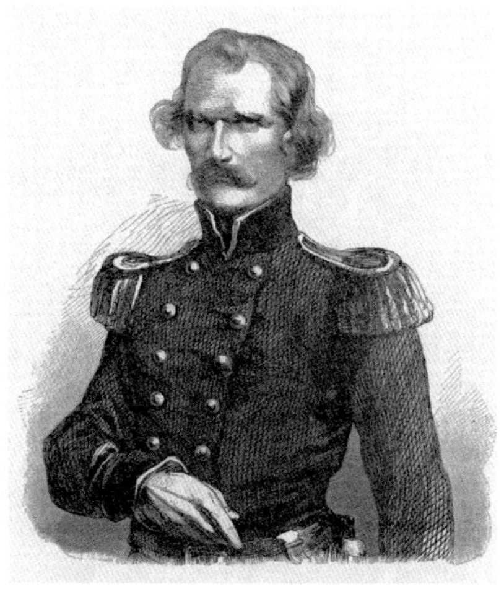

General Albert Sidney Johnston. *From* Harper's Weekly, *September 28, 1861.*

Johnston's appointment in the midst of the Secession crisis looked suspicious to many Unionists—especially in light of recent activity by John Floyd, secretary of war in the departing Buchanan administration. Floyd's orders for wholesale shipments of muskets and heavy guns to Southern arsenals (where they could be easily appropriated by state forces in rebellion) appeared to be treasonous in intent. In the charged atmosphere of the time, Johnston's appointment to the western command alarmed Republican partisans, and they made sure the incoming Lincoln administration heard their concerns. One of the new administration's first acts was to send out General Edwin V. Sumner, a rock-ribbed New Englander, to replace Johnston.

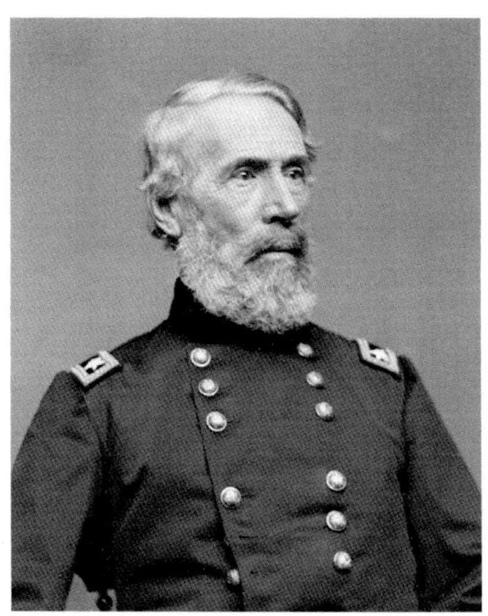

General Edwin Vose Sumner. *Library of Congress.*

In reality, Johnston's performance during his brief tenure of the Pacific command was exemplary. He worked closely with Governor Downey and bolstered the critical defenses of San Francisco. He also ordered weapons transferred to Fort Alcatraz from the more vulnerable arsenal at Benicia. Johnston, like many senior army officers from the South, was opposed to Secession and hoped to the very end that some peaceful resolution to the crisis might be found. But when his adopted home state of Texas left the Union, Johnston felt he had run out of options. He quietly sent his resignation back to Washington on April 9, 1861, but remained at his post, pending replacement.

Johnston was surprised by Sumner's arrival on the twenty-fourth. It was obvious that the Yankee general had been sent out to supersede Johnston before the resignation had been received in Washington. Johnston, a career officer, felt the implied lack of trust keenly. He left the Bay Area and headed for Los Angeles, where his brother and sister-in-law lived, to consider his options.

Sidney Johnston in retirement was still an important figure. Serving officers visited him frequently, seeking his counsel on what course to take as the nation unraveled. Johnston's advice was always the same: "If you sympathize with either side, and feel the call of duty to take part in a sectional war, go home, and fight there if necessary. But here there should be peace. Strife here would be civil war—not North against South—but neighbor against neighbor; and no one can imagine the horrors that would ensue."[9]

In the end, Johnston followed his own advice. He enlisted as a private in a Secessionist militia unit, the Los Angeles Mounted Rifles, and set out in June to cross the deserts of the Southwest and offer his sword to the Confederacy. Preston Johnston, in his biography of his father, describes the Rifles' experience along the way: "The route lay through one of the hottest regions in the world, where the thermometer often marked over 120° in the shade, when shade could be found…without a drop of water, or a sign of animal or vegetable life."[10]

The trip turned into a brutal ordeal, where life and death hung on reaching the next water hole. Johnston's party dodged Federal patrols and passed through the domain of the fierce Chiricahua Apache, passing en route the charred wreckage of two wagon trains. They arrived in Mesilla, New Mexico, at the end of July after an eight-hundred-mile journey. Another seven hundred arduous miles lay ahead of them to reach the safety of San Antonio.

Johnston's arrival in Texas caused rejoicing throughout the South. He proceeded in triumph to Richmond, where Jefferson Davis appointed him to command Confederate forces in the West (the region between the Appalachians and the Mississippi River). Eight months later, Johnston died at the head of his men in the Battle of Shiloh, after coming within a hair's breadth of tossing Grant's army into the Tennessee River. At the height of

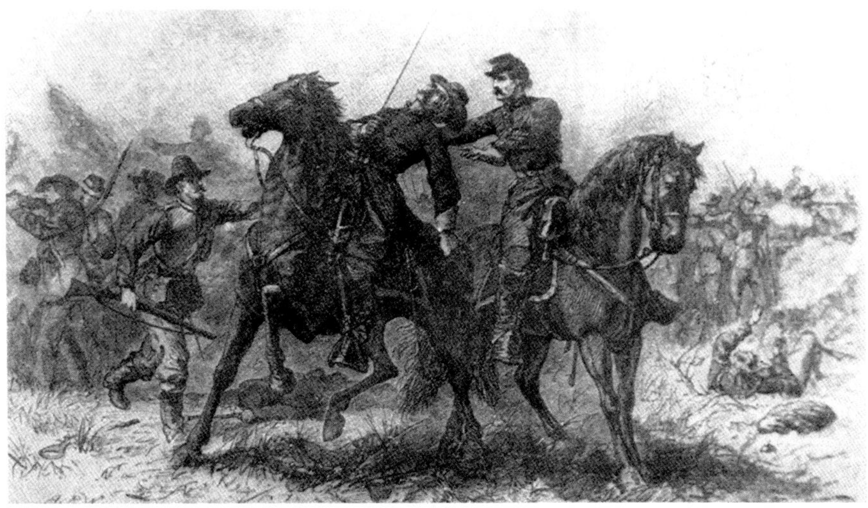

The death of Sidney Johnston at Shiloh, April 6, 1862. *From* The Great Battle of Shiloh *by Samuel Meek Howard (1921).*

the battle, Johnston was wounded in the leg. His life could have been saved by a simple tourniquet, but he had just sent his personal physician to care for a group of wounded Yankees.

Johnston was eulogized throughout the South and came to stand for the chivalric ideal that Southerners associate with their Cause. But it is California that owes the most to Johnston. His refusal to betray his officer's oath spared the state from war in 1861.

DANGEROUS TIMES

During the first months of 1861, it was unclear whether the nation would go to war over Secession. After the shelling of Fort Sumter on April 12, most Americans believed there was going to be a war, but they had no idea what kind of war it was going to be. The Union defeat at the Battle of Bull Run on July 21 answered that question. It was going to be a hard, serious war, and possibly a long one.

These were dangerous times for political leaders, who had to react quickly to changing circumstances and violent mood swings among their constituents. A politician who cried up peace to popular acclaim in March 1861 could easily find himself accused of treason in July.

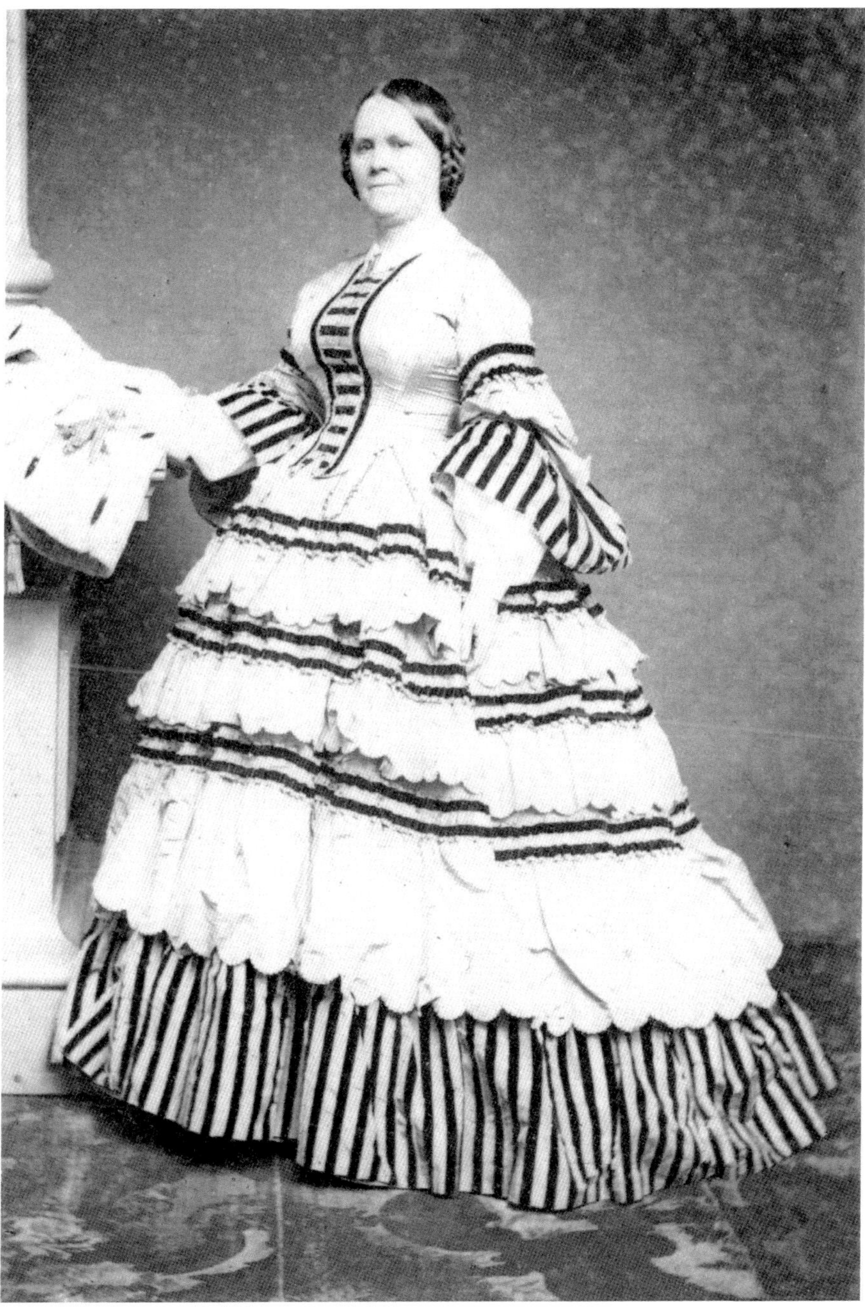

Mary Gwin was the premier Washington hostess during the Buchanan administration. Her lavish entertainments cost $75,000 in a single year (roughly $1.8 million in 2016 dollars). *David M. Rubenstein Rare Book & Manuscript Library at Duke University.*

California's congressional delegation (who were all Chivs) found themselves in a particularly awkward position. Despite their recent triumph at the polls, California's Southern Democrats could not hope to keep control of the state if their angry Northern Democratic brethren joined forces with the emerging Republican Party—and this is exactly what happened as the Secession crisis turned into a real shooting war. California's Chiv senators and representatives could feel the political ground heaving beneath their feet as they made their personal choices about staying in Washington or going south.

William Gwin, the leader of the California Chivalry, felt this dilemma most keenly. Though Southern by birth and inclination, Gwin had always been adept at reconciling contradictory forces for his own political advantage. His wife, Mary, was the premier hostess in Washington during the Buchanan administration. The dazzling (and stupendously expensive) parties she staged provided safe ground where politicians of different camps could meet. Gwin himself was on good terms with both Jefferson Davis and William Seward, secretary of state in the incoming Lincoln administration. It was only natural, then, that Gwin served as go-between during eleventh-hour peace negotiations between Seward and Davis. When these negotiations failed, Gwin was left with a stark and highly public decision to make about his own allegiance.

Gwin departed Washington, first for a visit to the South, where he saw all hope of reconciliation gone, and then on to California, where he confirmed his suspicion that his days as senator were numbered. (At this time, U.S. senators were elected by state legislatures, and it was clear to Gwin that his support in Sacramento was drying up.) Gwin left California by steamship and spent the war years at home in Mississippi and (after his plantation burned down during Grant's Vicksburg campaign) in Europe, promoting the Southern cause at the court of Napoleon III. Gwin returned to California after the war but never attempted to resurrect his political career in the Golden State.

Chapter 6

SPEAKING FOR THE UNION

As the Chivalry cast about for ways to keep its hold on California, pro-Union sentiment welled up across the state and found expression in a series of mass meetings. On May 11, 1861, a few weeks after the news of Fort Sumter, a diminutive preacher from Boston stood before a crowd in San Francisco that eventually numbered twenty-five thousand. The frail young man at the podium stood five feet, two inches tall and weighed 120 pounds. His name was Thomas Starr King, and his surprisingly deep, rich voice would soon be recognized as the most powerful weapon in the Union arsenal on the Pacific coast.

King grew up around Boston, with a family background that could hardly have been humbler. His father was a cobbler who turned in middle years to the ministry. Reverend King's death left young Starr (as he was known) the sole support of his mother and siblings. Starr's formal education ended at age fifteen, when he took on a full-time bookkeeping job at the Charlestown Navy Yard. Starr's engaging personality and astonishing aptitude drew help from many quarters. The list of his mentors is a roll call of New England's intellectual luminaries, whose kind efforts paid off. Dr. E.A. Chapin, King's father's successor at the First Universalist Church of Charlestown, described the young man in a letter to a colleague: "Thomas has never attended a Divinity School, but he is educated just the same. He speaks Greek, Hebrew, French, German, and fairly good English as you will see. He knows natural history and he knows humanity, and if one knows man and nature, he comes pretty close to knowing God."[11]

King was just twenty-two years old when he succeeded to the ministry at Charlestown. Two years later, he was called to the pulpit of the Hollis Street Unitarian Church in Boston. Thus, before he turned twenty-five, Starr King represented two of the most intellectually vibrant churches in New England, straddling their differences with characteristic grace and humor. (When asked to distinguish between the two denominations, King explained, "One thinks God is too good to damn them forever, the other thinks they are too good to be damned forever.")[12]

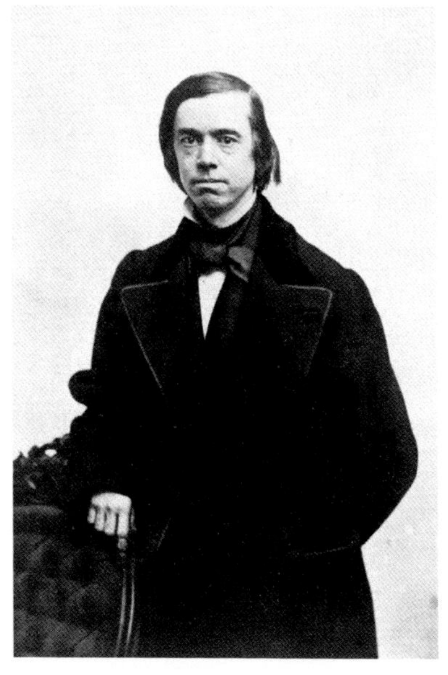

Thomas Starr King was undaunted by his small stature. As he put it, "Though I weigh only 120 pounds, when I'm mad, I weigh a ton!"[13] *National Portrait Gallery, Smithsonian Institution.*

King stayed at Hollis Street for eleven years. During that time, his responsibility for his family's finances weighed heavily, and he turned to the Lyceum lecture circuit to make ends meet. These popular lectures provided mid-nineteenth-century Americans of all classes access to university-level cultural and philosophical ideas. King's signature talks were "Goethe," "Socrates" and "Substance and Show," which he presented across the North, all the way to St. Louis and Chicago. King's time on the circuit was grueling and undermined his already frail health, but the experience he gained brought his gifts as a speaker to full fruition.

In 1860, King received an invitation from the First Unitarian Society of San Francisco to come west and lead its congregation. King accepted, hoping the new living would let him support his family without the exhausting grind of the Lyceum circuit.

STARR KING IN CALIFORNIA

Pro-Union sentiment was stirring when King arrived in April 1860 but lacked a voice. Former Illinois congressman Edward Baker, a close friend of Lincoln and Broderick, had spoken eloquently for the young Republican Party—his moving eulogy at Broderick's funeral did much to turn the tide of public opinion against the Chivalry. But Baker left in early 1860 to follow his political star to Oregon and was soon bound for Washington as a U.S. senator.

Baker's departure left Leland Stanford the ranking Republican in California, but Stanford was widely regarded as a pedestrian public speaker. Worse still, he had just been thrashed by the Chiv politician Milton Latham in the gubernatorial election of 1859 and was in political eclipse during the Secession crisis. In the tumult between Lincoln's election and the fall of Fort Sumter, it seemed as if pro-Union forces in California might lose their golden opportunity to unseat the Chivalry for want of a leader.

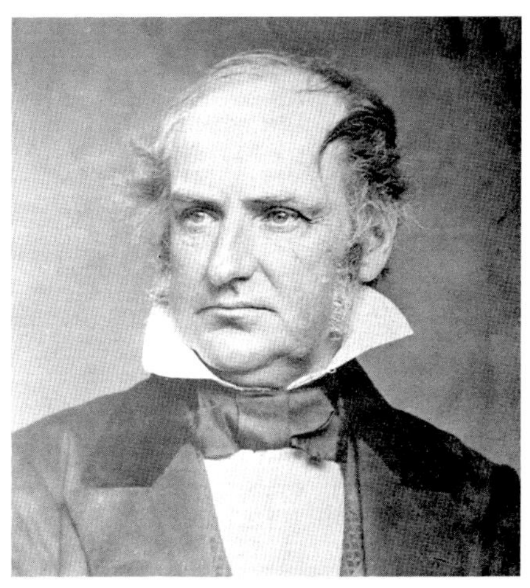

After Edward Baker defeated Abraham Lincoln in a congressional race in Illinois, the two became fast friends. Lincoln named a son after Baker. In 1861, Baker left the Senate to command a regiment and was killed at the Battle of Ball's Bluff. Lincoln was devastated. *Wikimedia Commons.*

Enter (miraculously) Starr King, one of the most gifted public speakers in the United States, with an array of beautifully written, field-tested lectures under his arm—including addresses on patriotic themes and pro-Union luminaries.

The effect of King's arrival in San Francisco was electric. He soon had the Unitarians digging out from under their debts and embarking on an ambitious building campaign for a new church. King's Sunday eloquence drew listeners from around the Bay Area, including Jessie Frémont, wife of the famed Pathfinder and 1856 Republican presidential candidate, John C. Frémont. Jessie promptly joined King's congregation, and he, in turn, joined hers, taking an honored place in her salon of notable men of arts and letters.

King's fame spread. Soon he was deluged with requests to take his lectures to venues throughout the state. This he did, with the same tireless energy and courage he brought to all his projects. King toured the inland valleys of California and the Sierra mining districts, many of which had strong Secessionist leanings—and all of which contributed to the appalling murder rate that made California notorious throughout the Union. Equally notorious was the rough humor of the miners, who enjoyed "snapping a pistol" at a visiting dignitary to test his nerve. (It was essential to show no reaction to this

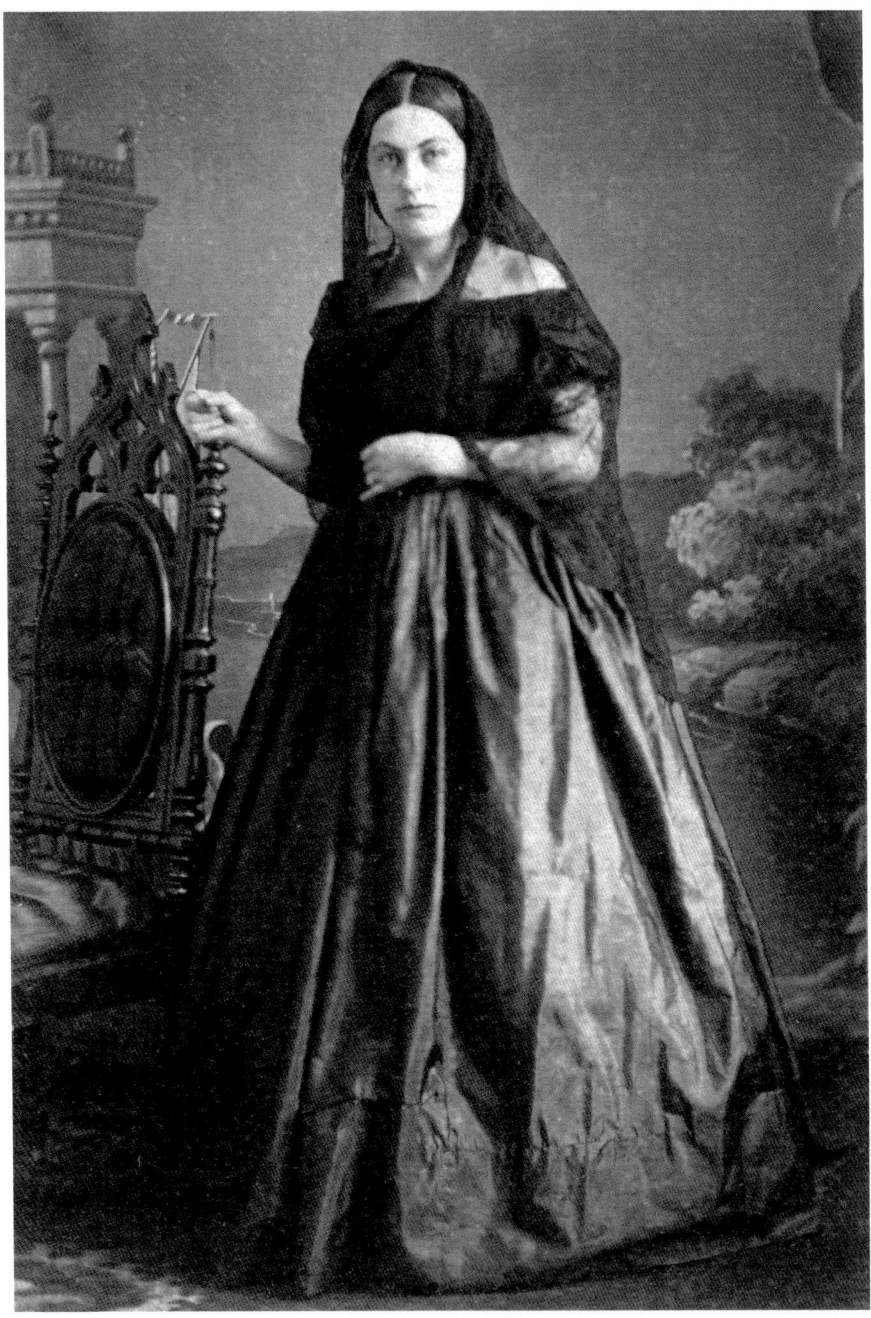

A presidential candidate's wife and a senator's daughter, Jessie Frémont knew the ways of power firsthand. She joined Starr King in advancing some of the first environmental legislation in U.S. history, aimed at preserving Yosemite as a national treasure. *Sharlot Hall Museum/John C. Frémont Family Papers/MS-55, Box 1, Folder 2.*

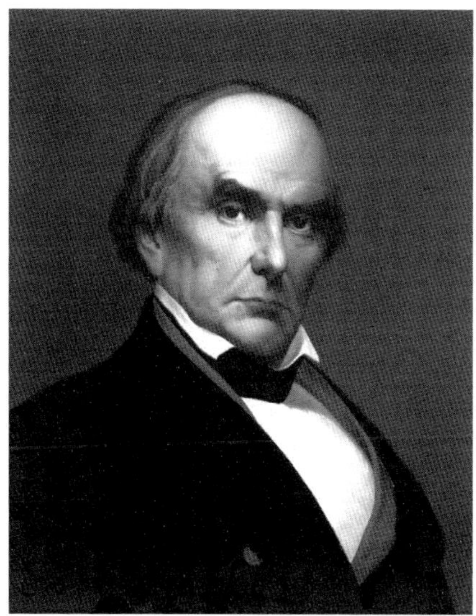

Daniel Webster was one of the outstanding lawyers of his day. He argued before the Supreme Court with unparalleled success. He won election to the House and the Senate and served twice as secretary of state. *Library of Congress.*

"jest," lest one be thought lacking in courage.) King passed this test but could not help but be aware that his life was in real danger. Typically, he made light of the matter, claiming that he "never knew the exhilaration of public oratory until I faced a front row of men armed with Bowie knives and revolvers."[14]

Remarkably, in a time marked by the bitterest sectional strife, King kept his tone firm but civil—never giving up on his Southern brethren, always hoping to draw them back into the fold through impassioned descriptions of the benefits of Union. In his lectures, King often evoked the natural beauty of the United States and showed how there is no natural feature of the country that could justify a division of the land into North and South. King's mystical evocation of common ground and shared heritage had tangible effect, even on Southerners who attended his talks. One observer of King's lectures remarked, "I am persuaded that, could he have gone through the Southern states, shaking hands with secessionists, he would have won them back to their allegiance by the mere magnetism of his touch."[15]

King's lecture on Daniel Webster was one of his most effective pleas for the Union. In it, he tells the tale of a frontier New Hampshire farm boy, tenth of ten children and the only one his father could afford to send to school. King artfully enlists his audience's sympathy as he describes young Daniel's steady rise through his own merit (Horatio Alger did not invent this form). King portrays Webster in his prime, as he wins a seat in the U.S. Senate after a brilliant career at the bar. Then we see Webster in middle age, donning the mantle of leadership for the cause of national Union.

The climax of King's story is the epic Senate debate of 1830, pitting Robert Hayne of South Carolina against Daniel Webster of Massachusetts. Hayne spoke for the doctrine of nullification, which claimed that a state could ignore any federal law it deemed unconstitutional. Webster defended the proposition that the Constitution is what it says it is, the supreme law of the land, established by the sovereign people of a united country.

King turns to the metaphor of jungle combat to describe the contest:

> [Hayne's] *speech made an immense and intense impression. Hundreds said that Mr. Webster was annihilated. A Senator from North Carolina, Mr. Iredell, observed to one of these jubilant friends of Mr. Hayne: "He has started the lion, but wait till we hear his roar or feel his claws."*
>
> *The roar and the stroke came the next day. Slim, agile, impetuous, fierce, in his intellectual assault, Mr. Hayne's attack was that of a leopard upon a good-natured, sluggish, sleepy lion in his prime.* [Webster's] *eyes opened; the mane bristled; the muscles swelled; he uttered his voice; he sprang; he struck.*

The result, as King describes it, is inevitable: Hayne's argument is demolished—to the relief and comfort of Union men everywhere.

> *The chord he* [Webster] *struck sounded rich and deep all over the land. It roused a new tone of patriotism. It called out a letter from the aged Madison, who endorsed his doctrine as the doctrine of the framers of the*

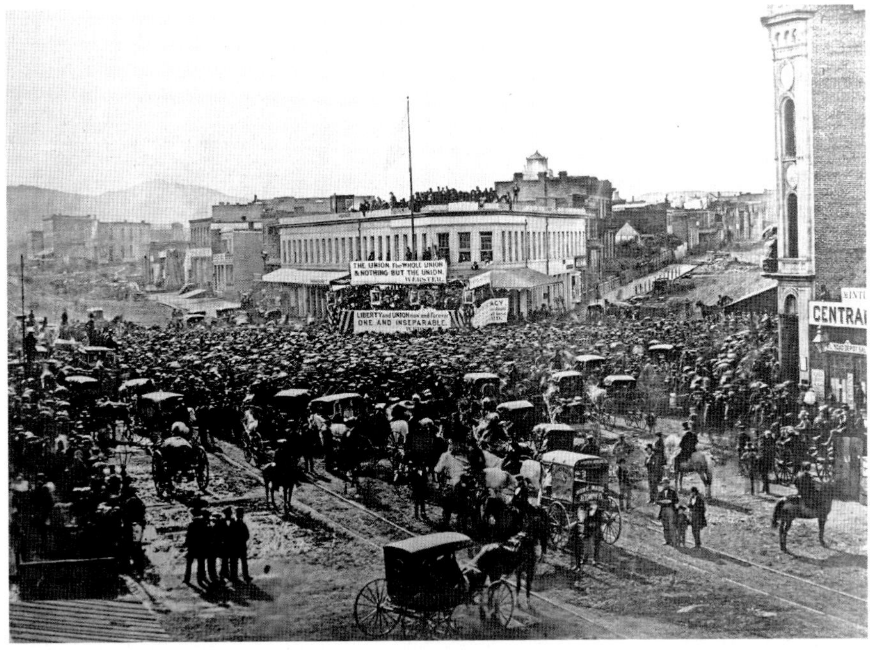

Starr King addressing a pro-Union rally on Market Street in San Francisco. *San Francisco History Center, San Francisco Public Library.*

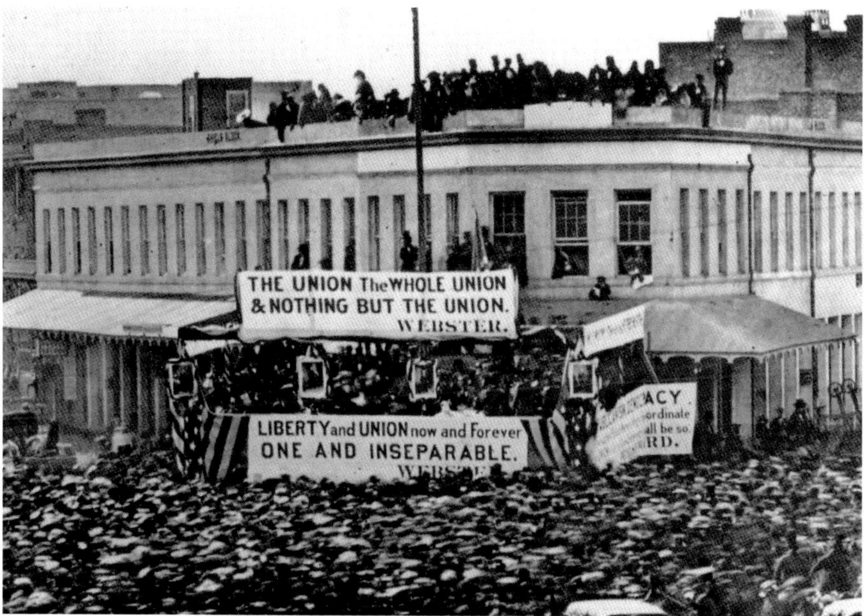

Enlargement of the speakers' platform, showing quotations from Daniel Webster. *San Francisco History Center, San Francisco Public Library.*

> *Constitution, and who said, "It crushes nullification, and must hasten the abandonment of secession."*

King goes on to liken Webster's speech to Fort Sumter,

> *which is built on courses of New Hampshire granite, frowning over his path with solemn muzzles, and bearing aloft, full high advanced, the gorgeous ensign of the republic, "its arms and trophies streaming in their original lustre, not a stripe erased or polluted, not a single star obscured, and bearing for its motto, in characters of living light, blazing on all its ample folds, the sentiment, dear to every true American heart, Liberty and Union, now and forever, one and inseparable!"*

Merging Webster's words with his own, King gave voice to the emotional wellsprings of American patriotism at a time when many Californians wavered. His impact in rallying the state for the Union is incalculable. His accomplishment was best summed up in the words of Abraham Lincoln, who dubbed King "the man who saved California for the Union."

Chapter 7

SECURING THE GOLDEN STATE

General Edwin Vose Sumner assumed command of the Department of the Pacific on April 25, 1861. His first report on the situation in California was on its way back to Washington three days later. After listing his efforts to "reinforce immediately and strongly" the fortifications of San Francisco Bay, Sumner offered his assessment of the political situation in the Golden State:

> *There is a strong Union feeling with the majority of the people of this State, but the Secessionists are much the most active and zealous party, which gives them more influence than they ought to have from their numbers.*
>
> *I have no doubt but there is some deep scheming to draw California into the secession movement; in the first place as the "Republic of the Pacific," expecting afterwards to induce her to join the Southern Confederacy.*
>
> *The troops now here will hold their positions and all the Government property, but if there should be a general uprising of the people, they could not, of course, put it down.*
>
> *I think the course of events at the East will control events here. So long as the General Government is sustained and holds the capital the Secessionists cannot carry this State out of the Union.*[16]

Sumner's initial concentration on securing the Golden Gate made sense. San Francisco was the only fortified port on the Pacific and the key to California's defense. The new commander soon learned, however, that his biggest danger lay in the south, where an ardently Secessionist populace was poised to rebel. As early as April 30, Sumner was shifting his forces to meet the threat:

> *I have found it necessary to withdraw the troops from Fort Mojave and place them at Los Angeles. There is more danger of disaffection at this place than any other in the State. There are a number of influential men there who are decided Secessionists, and if we should have any difficulty it will commence there.*[17]

Los Angeles was not the only trouble spot. Reports of Secessionist activity came from as far away as the Washoe Territory (now Nevada) and Sonora, Mexico. Adding to Sumner's burden in these early days was a scheme (floated by some eager soul back east in the War Department) to invade Texas from California via Mexico. Sumner was ordered to prepare the attack. Fortunately, sanity reasserted itself in the form of a report by the famed pioneer and surveyor General Edward F. Beale, who actually knew something about western geography. Beale's assessment of the plan was forwarded to Winfield Scott, general-in-chief of the U.S. Army, who quietly dropped the project.

Sumner's chief job was to secure California from insurrection, but his other tasks were formidable as well. Protection of the overland stage route was essential to maintaining California's communications with the national government in the East. Sumner was also responsible for protecting remote settlers along the entire Pacific, who were in a state of chronic warfare with the tribes whose lands they threatened. The existing force of regulars, some sixteen thousand men, were scattered over two million square miles and were barely adequate for the task at hand. Now these troops were being withdrawn to secure California and—the War Department hoped—be sent back east as soon as possible to help put down the rebellion.

Clearly, new troops would have to be raised in the West. On July 24, 1861, the War Department sent a request to Governor Downey to raise one regiment of infantry and five companies of cavalry to take over the defense of the overland mail route, which ran from the Carson Valley (in modern Nevada) to Salt Lake and Fort Laramie. This request was followed three weeks later by a call for four additional regiments of infantry and one of cavalry, all to be placed at General Sumner's disposal. Governor Downey, despite his mixed feelings about Secession, responded promptly. California mobilized for war.

THE CALIFORNIA VOLUNTEERS

The call for volunteers fell on willing ears. California in 1860 was a military recruiter's paradise. Out of an overwhelmingly male population of 380,000, fully 170,000—better than 46 percent—were young men of military age.[18] Furthermore, the men of the Golden State were by definition hardy physical adventurers, many of whom had just crossed a continent on foot to try to wrest riches from the earth. They made formidable soldiers, and they volunteered in large numbers. Despite its Border State demographics, California never had to call on the draft to raise troops. Indeed, the state sent extra soldiers back east to fill the quotas of other states.

Turning promising volunteers into effective soldiers was the next step, and California undertook it with customary enthusiasm. Training facilities were established in Sacramento, Stockton and around the Bay Area, but the largest camps were in the south, where new troops were most urgently needed.

Sumner was fortunate to have an ample supply of regular army officers to supervise the formation and training of the new regiments, which proceeded at a brisk pace. From this cadre of professionals came Sumner's own replacement, General George Wright, who took over the Pacific command in October 1861, when Sumner was recalled to the East. Sumner left behind an effective organization that had already deployed sufficient force to check any would-be insurrectionists in California. In military terms, California was secure—for the time being, at least.

THE STATE ELECTIONS OF 1861

As the Secession crisis deteriorated into open, bloody warfare back east, voters in California looked forward with trepidation to the statewide elections scheduled for September 1861, in which both the legislative and executive branches of California's government were up for grabs. The previous election had been a triumph for the Chivalry, who had swept statewide offices, dominated the legislature and returned a pro-Southern congressional delegation to Washington. The looming contest of 1861 would be a referendum on the Chivalry's ten-year hold on state government.

The Republicans ran Leland Stanford again for governor. Stanford was a spectacularly successful businessman who would do even better in

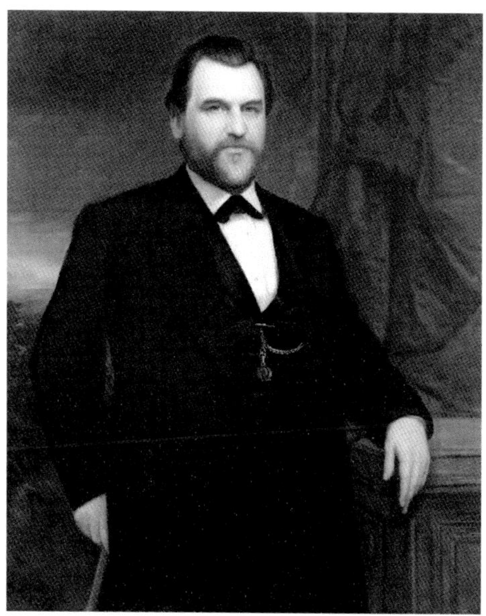

Governor Leland Stanford. *Courtesy of the State of California, Department of General Services, Facilities Management Division, Capitol Historic Region.*

years to come as a founder of the Central Pacific Railroad. He was not an effective campaigner, however. His speech was slow, and he always read from a prepared text. Worse still, he had been soundly thrashed in his prior attempt at the governorship in 1859, winning less than 10 percent of the vote that year.

The key difference in 1861 was the state of the Democratic Party. It was in no condition to fight anyone—inept speaker or not—because it was too busy tearing itself apart along the fault line exposed by the Broderick-Terry duel. By this point, Northern and Southern Democrats had become, in essence, two separate political parties, each fielding its own candidates. The result was a replay of the 1860 presidential contest, where the Democratic candidates canceled each other out, handing victory to their opponents. Leland Stanford became the first Republican governor of California with 46 percent of the vote. California's congressional delegation flipped from Southern Democratic to Unionist. Republican representation in the state legislature soared. By the beginning of 1862, California's state government lay firmly in Unionist hands—and would stay there for the rest of the war.

But just as the political situation inside California stabilized in the fall of 1861, new forces arose outside the state that threatened to drag it headfirst into the fighting.

Chapter 8

TURMOIL IN THE SOUTHWEST

From the very start of the war, it was evident to Confederate leaders that their greatest peril lay in the Virginia theater, where a military blunder could cost the new government its capital at Richmond in a matter of days. Jefferson Davis was trying to build a nation, however, and took the long view whenever possible. He valued Southern claims to the vast western territories seized from Mexico and thought them well worth defending—especially if a thrust in that direction could shake the Union's hold on California. Military success in the Southwest might well put California's fabulous gold resources in play and even secure a Confederate outpost on the Pacific—an essential goal in the formation of a new nation seeking to hold its own against the United States.

Confederate mobilization in the Southwest proceeded swiftly. As early as February 1861, U.S. forts and arsenals in Texas were handed over to state authorities by the department commander, General David Twiggs, who renounced the Union and went over to the South. In July, Colonel John Baylor led a battalion of Texas Mounted Rifles in a campaign in southern New Mexico that swiftly captured Mesilla and the garrison of nearby Fort Fillmore.

Baylor was buoyed by the fact that the citizens of Tucson and Mesilla had already declared for the South and were raising militia forces to help him. On August 1, 1861, he established the Confederate Territory of Arizona and appointed himself its first governor.

Serious problems confronted Baylor's régime from the start. Apache warriors controlled wide swaths of territory and took full advantage of the

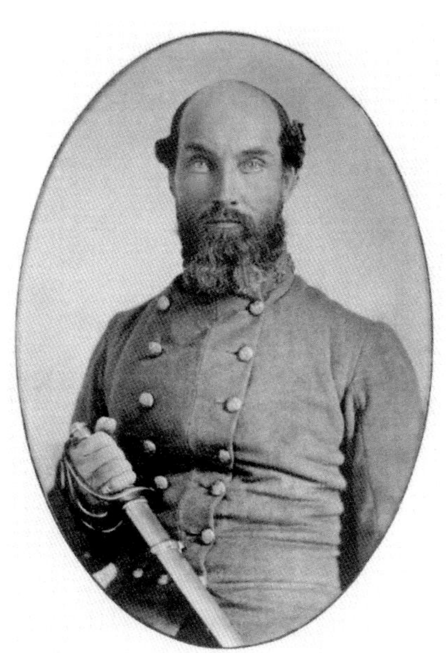

Baylor summed up his Indian policy in an order to one of his officers: "Use all means to persuade the Apaches or any tribe to come in for the purpose of making peace, and when you get them together kill all the grown Indians and take the children prisoners and sell them to defray the expense of killing the adult Indians." Jefferson Davis disapproved Baylor's tactics and eventually dismissed him from office.[19] *UNM Center for Southwest Research, William A. Keleher Pictorial Collection, N.H. Rose Collection of Old Time Photographs, San Antonio, Texas.*

quarrel among the whites to launch a series of deadly raids aimed at sweeping white settlers clean out of the country. Worse still, there were strong Federal garrisons at Fort Craig and Fort Union to Baylor's north and reports of a powerful Californian force gathering at Fort Yuma to his west. Baylor knew his small force was badly exposed, and he pleaded for reinforcement. After months of frantic worry, word came at last that help was on the way.

The Confederate Invasion of New Mexico

General Henry Hopkins Sibley was a former U.S. Army officer who had served in the New Mexico theater before the war. Sibley resigned his U.S. commission in May 1861 and journeyed to Richmond to sell his old friend Jefferson Davis on a plan to project Confederate power across the Southwest on the grandest possible scale. Best of all, Sibley maintained, the expedition would be largely self-funding. Morale among U.S. forces in the remote region was at rock bottom and the population disaffected. An invading Confederate force would be welcomed and could supply itself with captured provisions and arms. Davis approved the scheme, and by July, Sibley was back in Texas to raise an army.

By the time Sibley arrived, the most eager volunteers and best equipment in Texas had already been rounded up and sent east, and Sibley's recruitment

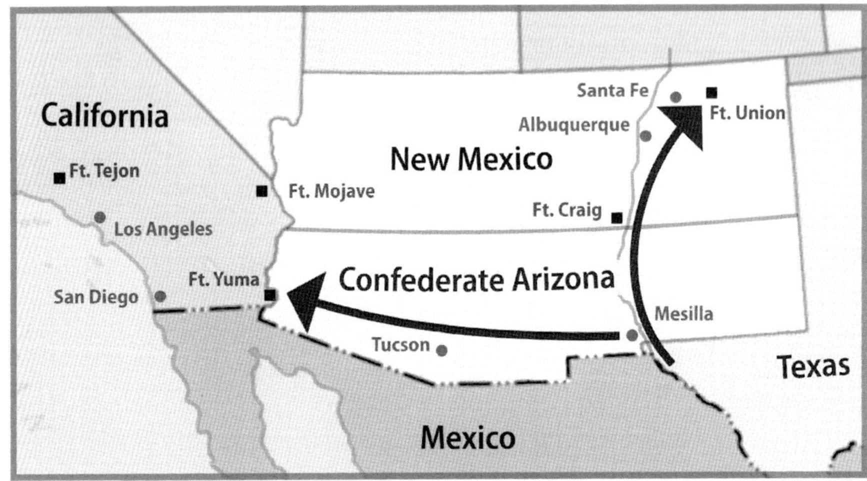

General Sibley's proposed campaign for the spring of 1862. *Map by the author.*

Confederate Arizona lay along the border of Mexico, stretching from Texas to California. The territory's northern border was the thirty-fourth parallel.

Sibley's plan was to strike north at Fort Union, the hub of the U.S. Army's supply system in the Southwest, causing Federal defenses in the area to wither on the vine. Other items on Sibley's to-do list included seizing Colorado's gold fields, invading Southern California, subduing the Southwest Indians and perhaps bagging a few provinces of Northern Mexico in his spare time. (Campaign planning at the beginning of the war tended to be optimistic.)

efforts suffered accordingly. When he finally launched his invasion in October 1861, Sibley's "Army of New Mexico" was undermanned, poorly armed and seriously short of money and supplies. When the last of his troops reached Mesilla in January 1862, Sibley's force numbered around 3,200 men, including Baylor's battalion and a few companies of Arizona volunteers.[20] Though a negligible quantity by eastern standards, Sibley's command constituted a powerful force in the Southwest. Sustaining it in the field would tax the resources of the country to the very limit.

Opposing Sibley were Federal troops under General Edward Canby, a regular army officer who had served in New Mexico before the war. Canby's forces included New Mexico militia, who felt no love for the Texan invaders but also had little stake in defending a U.S. government that had seized their land some sixteen years earlier. Canby's regular forces were also a doubtful quantity since many came from the South but (unlike their officers) could not resign without facing charges of desertion.

In early skirmishing, Sibley's Confederates consistently outfought their Union opponents. On February 21, 1862, his Texans won a dramatic,

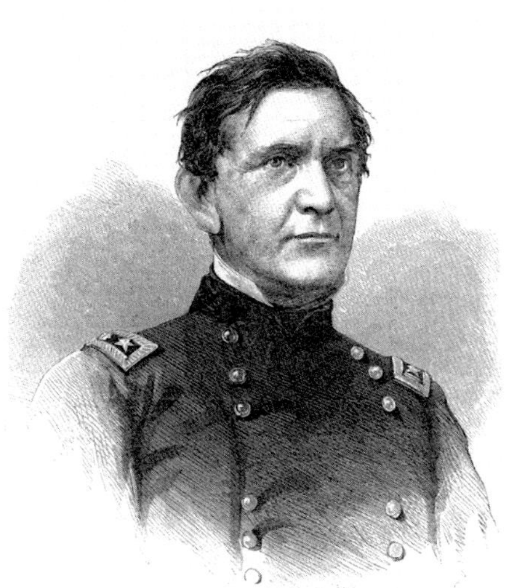

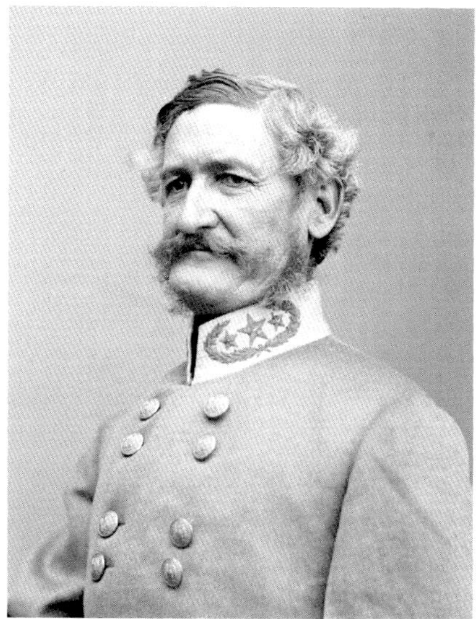

Left: A sober, cautious commander, Edward Canby held back from battle when he could beat his opponent by other means. A veteran campaigner in the Southwest, Canby knew that the killing terrain, relentless Indian opposition and desperate supply problems would plague his Confederate opponents every step of the way. Union forces, by contrast, could hunker down inside well-stocked forts when necessary. *From* Harper's Weekly, *April 15, 1865/Wikimedia Commons.*

Right: If ever a face was made to adorn a whiskey bottle label, it was Henry Hopkins Sibley's. He had a passion for powerful spirits and was frequently drunk while on campaign. His men referred to him as "the walking whiskey barrel." *Library of Congress.*

come-from-behind victory in a bloody action fought at Valverde Ford on the Rio Grande. Canby's men retreated to the safety of nearby Fort Craig, while the Texans marched north and seized Albuquerque and Santa Fe, brushing aside small Federal garrisons along the way. As these Union forces retreated, however, most took care to cart off or destroy their food stocks and ammunition. Soon the Confederate supply situation grew dangerous indeed, and Sibley took the only chance left open to him. He set his troops in motion against the great Federal supply hub at Fort Union.

On March 26, 1862, Sibley's advance forces pushed up the narrow confines of Glorieta Pass and ran headlong into an equivalent force of Colorado Volunteers—famously tough miners who had just marched four hundred miles in thirteen days through howling blizzards to beat Sibley to Fort Union. The ensuing action lasted two days, with heavy casualties on both sides. The Texans held the field at the end of the fight, but Union

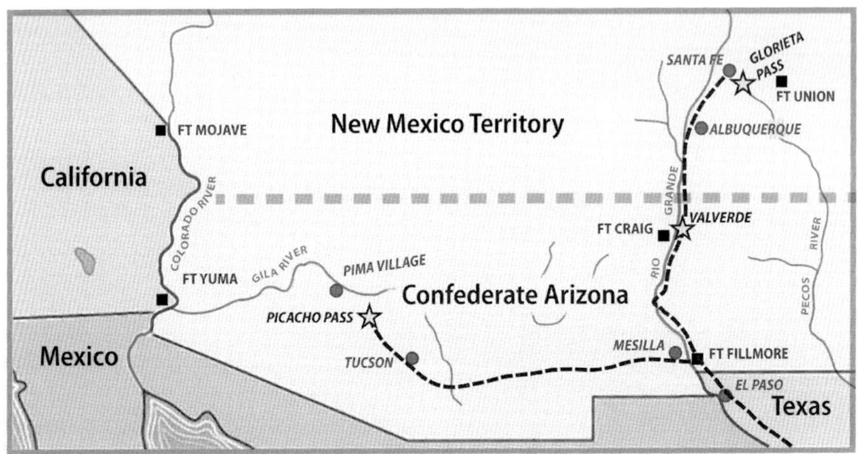

Confederate campaign in Arizona and New Mexico, October 1861 to April 1862. *Map by the author.*

Sibley's army won battles and occupied towns but never gained the strategic upper hand. Sibley's hopes rested on capturing large quantities of Union supplies and ammunition. Canby declined to provide them.

troopers seeking to flank the battlefield discovered the Confederate supply train and blew it up—after bayoneting the horses and mules for good measure. Sibley's supply situation, always perilous, now became desperate. On April 12, he turned his army south, seeking the relative safety of Mesilla and West Texas. Canby followed closely but did not press hard enough to bring on an engagement. He wanted the Texans out of New Mexico, with as few hungry prisoners left behind as humanly possible. In this, Canby was not being neglectful of his duty to weaken the Confederate war machine. As a seasoned campaigner in the Southwest, he knew that the job of killing Confederates could be safely entrusted to the desert.

Chapter 9

THE CALIFORNIA COLUMN

In February 1862, while his invasion of New Mexico was still prospering, General Sibley detached a company of cavalry under Captain Sherod Hunter to ride west and show the Rebel flag in Tucson, capital of the western district of Confederate Arizona.[21] Hunter's small command was composed of native Arizonans, and the tasks assigned to him and his men were daunting indeed.

Apache warriors had taken full advantage of the division among the whites, killing and driving off ranchers and miners and attacking wagon trains at will. Tucson itself was virtually besieged. This presented a serious political problem for the Baylor régime. Secessionist sentiment in the lower Southwest was fueled by the belief that Arizona had been neglected by a distant, uncaring Federal government. Now it was the Confederacy's turn to prove that it could support white settlement, and the results so far were not encouraging. Hunter's arrival provided a much-needed morale boost in Tucson, but in reality, his force was too small to affect the balance of power between whites and Indians. As far as the Apache were concerned, Hunter and his men were more prey.

Hunter's other duty was to scout for signs of the large Union force assembling at Fort Yuma, on the California-Arizona border. The most important of these signs, in Hunter's reckoning, were food and fodder caches, which not only showed that the Yankees were on the way but also offered a golden opportunity for stopping them. For weeks, Hunter and his men did a brisk business in burning hay caches and arresting Union scouts, agents and

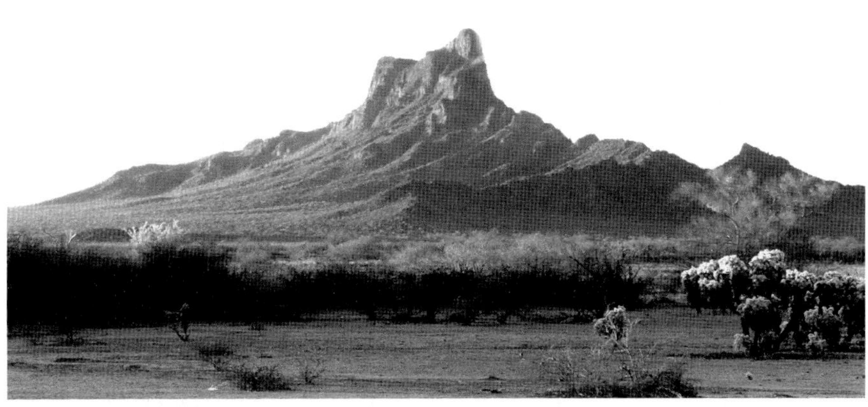

Picacho Peak, Arizona. Advancing California cavalry engaged Hunter's Arizonans here on April 15, 1862. *Photo by John Hunnicutt II.*

sympathizers in Arizona. They upended plans for the Union advance and set back its departure by weeks. On March 29, 1862, Hunter's roving Rebels ran into a Federal patrol at Stanwix station (an abandoned Butterfield stage depot near the Gila River). The resulting skirmish resulted in one casualty and is often cited as the "westernmost action of the Civil War."[22]

CALIFORNIANS ADVANCE

The Union officer whose plans Hunter upset was Colonel (soon to be Brevet General) James Carleton, who took General Wright's place at the head of U.S. forces in Southern California when Wright assumed the Pacific command in November 1861.

Carleton was a stern, competent career officer from Maine who fought well in Mexico and afterward served with the U.S. Dragoons in the West. Carleton's essential duties were to keep track of the restless Secesh of Southern California and to train volunteer regiments to replace the regulars, who were headed back east. He achieved both goals by building and maintaining large training camps around Los Angeles and stocking them with loyal recruits from the northern half of the state. As word of

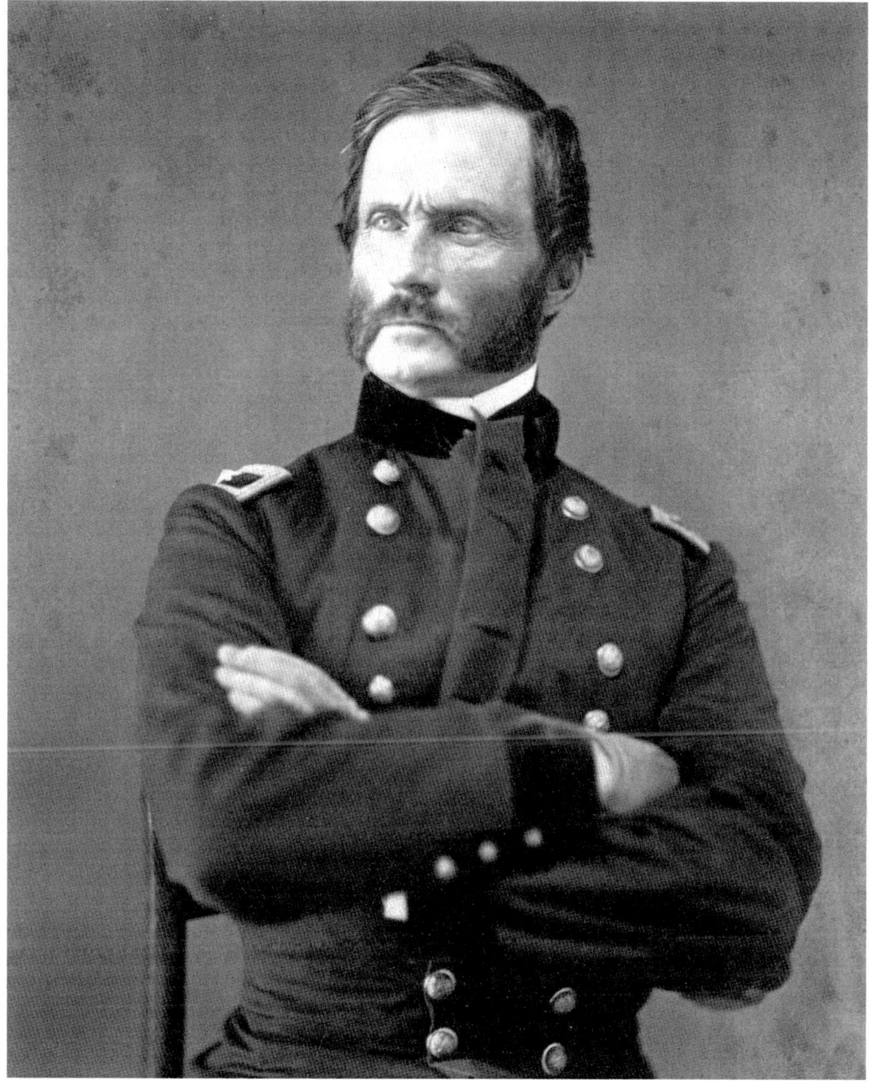

General James Carleton. *Courtesy Palace of the Governors Photo Archives (NMHM/DCA), 022938.*

Sibley's planned invasion of the Southwest leaked out, however, Carleton began transferring forces to Fort Yuma, on the border with Arizona. Their mission was to protect California and, as soon as possible, march out to confront the Confederate invaders of New Mexico.

This proposed march into the desert was a logistical nightmare of the first order. Bringing troops into action in the American Southwest during

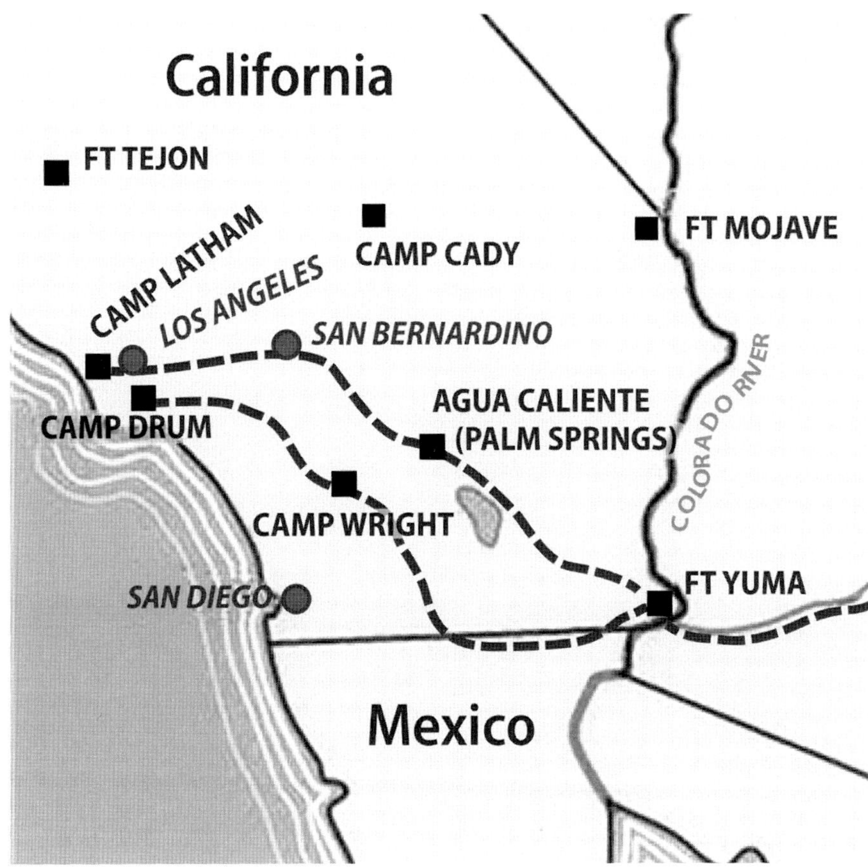

U.S. Army forts and training camps in Southern California, 1861–62. *Map by the author.*

Camps Latham and Drum trained recruits from Northern California, many of whom were sent on to Fort Yuma, the staging area for the California Column.

the Civil War era was a lot like fighting on the moon would be today. Carleton certainly had to plan for engaging the enemy, but his first and most difficult assignment was to get his men to the battlefield. Horse- and mule-drawn wagon trains required massive amounts of fodder when they couldn't forage, and few places on earth offered less forage than the Arizona desert. Substantial (and highly vulnerable) caches of food and fodder would be required along the route. Troop movements would have to be restricted to small parties, meticulously timed to the replenishment rate of water sources along the way. In sum, Carleton's force would of necessity enter the hostile desert as a long, thin column—a circumstance that would not escape the attention of the Apache warriors and Confederates awaiting them.

After repeated delays, Carleton began his piecemeal advance from Fort Yuma in April and May, wholly unaware that the Confederate invasion had already been checked at Glorieta Pass. General Canby, the Union commander in New Mexico, was equally in the dark about Carleton's motions, thanks to the vigilance of Apache war parties and Confederate patrols, who made communication between the Union generals virtually impossible.

Hunter's meager force was no match for the advancing Californians. He abandoned Tucson in stages, his last men leaving on May 14, never to return. The Apache bade the departing Confederates farewell by nearly annihilating a detachment of them at Dragoon Springs. The Confederates returned the compliment a few days later with a counterattack that retrieved their stolen livestock. Meanwhile, California troops began cautiously entering Tucson on May 20, 1862.

A Unionist Version of Arizona

It was a lucky thing for Edward Canby that he solved his Confederate problem in New Mexico on his own, because there was nothing in General Carleton's pace to suggest that he saw himself on a rescue mission. As California troops entered Tucson and regrouped, Carleton turned his attention to issuing decrees and establishing a government for the area, which the U.S. Congress had recently dubbed the Arizona Territory. This Federal territory of Arizona was divided from New Mexico by a line running north and south (today's alignment), thereby distinguishing it from the Confederate version, whose border ran east and west.

Carleton placed the new territory under martial law, on the commendable grounds that this was better than no law at all. He then proceeded to lay out the terms by which civilians could be prosecuted in military courts for the usual kinds of civic deficiencies—and also for a few new failings Carleton added to the list of proscribed behaviors:

> *I. No man who has arrived at lawful age shall be permitted to reside within this territory who does not, without delay, subscribe to the oath of allegiance to the United States.*

> *II. No words or acts calculated to impair that veneration which all good patriots should feel for our country and government will be tolerated within this territory or go unpunished if sufficient proof can be had of them.*
> *III. No man who does not pursue some lawful calling or have legitimate means of support shall be permitted to remain in this territory.*[23]

Carleton went on to establish modest taxes on the merchant community at large and highly immodest taxes on owners of bars and gaming houses. The funds were to be handed over to the medical director of the California Column for the benefit of sick and wounded soldiers.

It is evident in Carleton's correspondence and actions that he possessed a very strong sense of right and wrong, and he was not at all apologetic about trying to impose his values on a fallen world. (It is relevant to note that Carleton came from Calvinist stock and was a full-blooded New England Puritan on both sides.) Sin in the new territory of Arizona survived its encounter with Carleton largely intact, as students of the history of Tucson can attest. The same cannot be said for the Indian tribes who later fell under his authority. For them, Carleton's lethal mix of high idealism and granitic inflexibility would have disastrous consequences.

By mid-June, Carleton considered the situation in Tucson under control and was ready to move on. He sent three scouts to tell General Canby of his intentions. Two died at Apache hands; the third was captured by Confederates.[24]

Sibley hung on for a while along the Texas/New Mexico border as Carleton approached, hoping—like Dickens's Mr. McCawber—that "something would turn up." Sibley's officers, already furious at the "walking whiskey barrel" for botching the campaign, were convinced that the "something" on the way was a lot of Yankees, and they were not inclined to await their arrival. After a near-mutinous council of war, Sibley began withdrawing his troops. His shattered Army of New Mexico straggled back to San Antonio, leaving 40 percent of its number behind as prisoners or dead in shallow graves. The bones of many were left to bleach on the desert sands, marking the line of their retreat.

A WARM APACHE WELCOME

The Californians leaving Tucson were buoyed by the idea of coming to grips at last with the Confederates they had signed up to fight. The time had

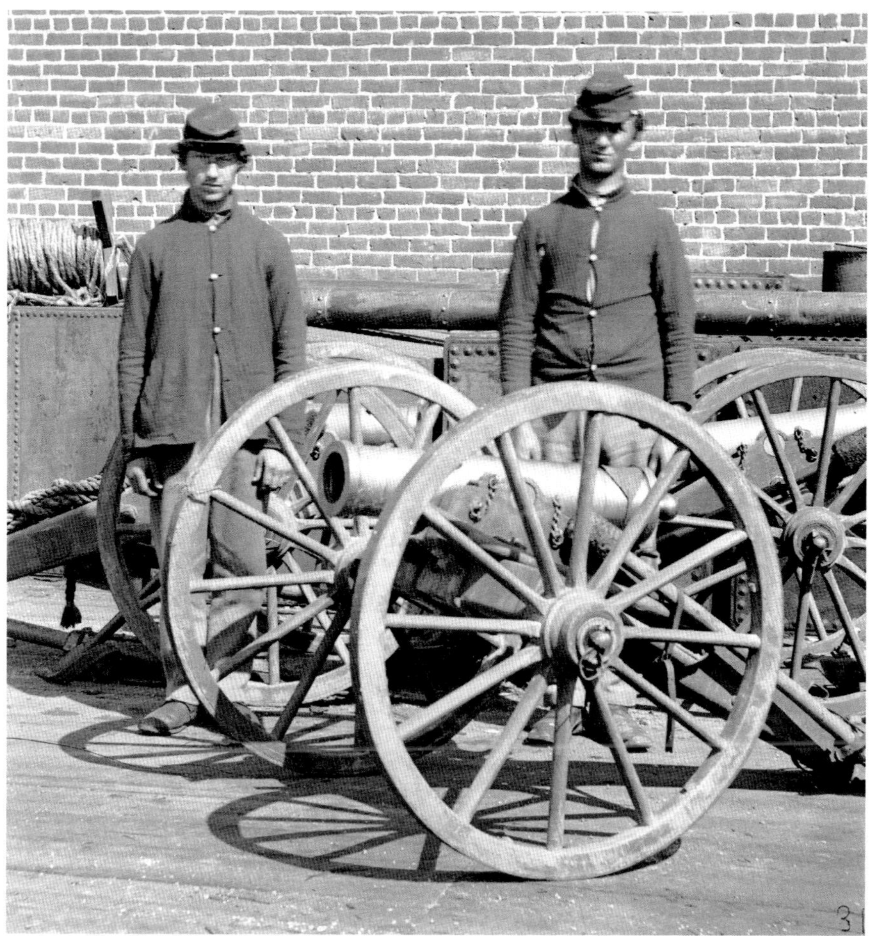

In the open spaces of the Southwest, light artillery gave U.S. troops a significant advantage over Apache and Comanche warriors. Shells thrown from guns like these saved Kit Carson and his New Mexico and California Volunteers from annihilation at the First Battle of Adobe Walls. *Library of Congress.*

not quite come, however; 270 arduous miles still lay between them and the Confederate force—miles that had to be traveled under the blazing July sun. Water and forage remained highly problematic, and advanced parties had to be kept small, since there was no assurance of enough water ahead to keep larger units alive.

At noon on July 15, 1862, two companies of scouts were approaching the critical watering hole at Apache Pass when hundreds of Chiricahua warriors opened up on them from ambush and sent the soldiers reeling back to the mouth of the pass.[25] Their commander, Captain Roberts, realized that retreat was not an option with his current water supplies; there was nothing to do but head back into the pass and capture the spring. Roberts unlimbered his two mountain howitzers, threw skirmishers out over the high ground lining the pass and advanced. The ensuing ferocious firefight lasted until nightfall, and it was only thanks to the howitzers that the Apache defenses were finally overcome. The Apache had built stone breastworks—impervious to rifle fire—on the hills overlooking the spring, but when Roberts's guns finally got in range and began lobbing shells up at them, the Apache warriors scattered. Roberts's men and animals drank their fill at the spring and then withdrew.

Roberts and his men could not know it, but they had just run headlong into the kind of warfare that would characterize the service of the California Volunteers in the West. There would be no set piece battles between Californians and massed Confederate troops (though there were occasional skirmishes with Southerners trying to keep alive their claims in the Southwest). Instead, the great majority of the Californians' fighting would be against native tribesmen, often in contests over water holes and mountain passes—the key choke points of travel across the immense Southwest.

Actions between California Volunteers and their Indian opponents were usually small-scale but deadly enough. Armament tended to be more equal than many might imagine today, especially when the tribes involved were practiced mounted raiders. Indian warriors often carried bows and arrows as

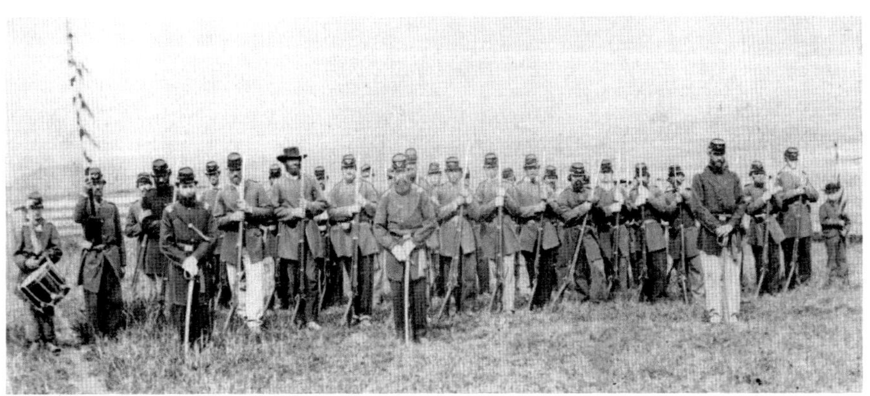

Union volunteers drilling in Hayward. *California State Library, California History Room.*

Most California Volunteers came from the northern half of the state, but even there, communities were sharply divided in their loyalties. In January 1865, the firmly Unionist mining town of Nevada City sent 252 volunteers to help form the Seventh California Infantry. The largely Secessionist town of Grass Valley, located just four miles away, sent 72.

supplemental arms, since they were light and efficient for hunting and saved precious ammunition. When they engaged white soldiers, however, many native warriors used carbines and six-shooters. California troops moving in significant numbers sometimes enjoyed the advantage of artillery and usually had better access to ammunition. Indians, for their part, possessed superior knowledge of the terrain, and each warrior possessed a lifetime's experience of desert fighting. There are a number of reports citing the Apache's wondrous ability to literally pop up out of the sands to ambush small parties.

In sum, there was nothing "soft" about the Californian Volunteers' service in the West. They faced the same paramount danger as the men back east: disease, which killed twice as many men in the Civil War as combat.[26] They also faced a danger unique to service in the West, namely the land itself. A California cavalryman on patrol in Arizona could die of heat stroke and dehydration in 120-degree Fahrenheit heat in the summer or freeze to death at negative-20-degree Fahrenheit in a New Mexican winter. Californians in the West had an additional burden to bear because surrender was rarely a viable option. Prisoners were sometimes kept alive for their hostage value, but usually they provided grisly entertainment at victory celebrations.

Chapter 10

THE DEPARTMENT OF NEW MEXICO

The arrival of Californian troops along the Rio Grande in July 1862 put an end to Southern hopes in the Southwest. Confederate troops who could still walk under their own flag began the long, harrowing trek from West Texas to San Antonio, where they had started the year before. Invalids left behind were cared for by Union medical personnel and then shipped by wagon to Texas as soon as they could stand the ride. This was done for practical reasons. Sibley's invasion of New Mexico had stripped the country bare, leaving Union commanders few enough rations for their own troops, let alone for prisoners.

Compounding the army's supply problems was an eruption of Indian raiding, made easy by the internal war that distracted the whites. The Comanche and their allies expanded beyond the already enormous bounds of their inland empire until the Santa Fe Trail became too dangerous for reliable army transport to and from the East. This pleased Confederate authorities, who encouraged Comanche harassment of Union supply lines. Less welcome to the Confederates was the surge of Comanche raiding aimed south and east, which rolled back white settlement in Texas more than one hundred miles during the war years.

Within New Mexico and Arizona, Apache tribes lashed out in a series of deadly raids on the white miners and farmers who were encroaching on their homelands. Navajo sheep- and slave-raiding also spiked. Added to this mayhem was a generous dose of brigandage, as men of various races and nationalities became outlaw plunderers, without any tribal or national allegiance to cramp their style.

The blood-soaked anarchy of the Southwest was well beyond the means of any civil government to control, and the attempt was not made. New Mexico and Arizona remained instead in the army's care, in an administrative unit known as the Department of New Mexico. Edward Canby served as head of the department until September 1862, when he was called back east to fight Confederates. James Carleton assumed the command after Canby's departure.

General Carleton's Indian Paradise

General Carleton felt a strong moral obligation to save the Southwest from disorder and lawlessness. The challenge before him was staggering. The immense, impoverished country was populated with fiercely antagonistic groups—Comanche, Navajo, Ute, Apache, Mexicans and Anglos, to name just the principals. All save the Anglos had been fighting one another for generations.

Carleton's trump card was the highly effective body of troops he commanded, the California Volunteers, whom Carleton himself had molded into savvy, well-disciplined desert fighters. He also commanded a force of New Mexico Volunteers who fought well against Indians but who, as long-term participants in the region's blood feuds, sometimes added to their general's headaches. Carleton's small force of U.S. Army regulars was a mixed blessing. The War Department tended to pull out good professional officers and send them back east. Those who remained behind were often left on the frontier for a reason.

As far as supplies were concerned, Carleton's situation ranged from poor to desperate. The Santa Fe Trail was often unusable, thanks to Comanche war parties, and the ravaged Southwest could barely raise enough food to sustain its own people, let alone supply hungry troops. Attempts to open up a supply line through Mexico foundered, due to the chaos prevailing in Sonora and Chihuahua, although wheat and beans could sometimes be procured from Mexican traders.[27]

A less determined and resourceful man would have sunk under such a burden, but not James Carleton. Carleton reoccupied abandoned forts to secure his line to California and then established new ones as needed (notably Fort Bowie, protecting the spring at Apache Pass). He then turned his attention to subduing the Indians who were busily dismantling the white settlement of New Mexico.[28] It was clear to Carleton that simple police work would not answer. He needed a comprehensive, game-changing strategy—and he was just the man to create one.

In his last posting in California, Carleton had observed firsthand General Edward Beale's ambitious attempt to solve the Golden State's "Indian problem." Beale's strategy consisted of relocating tribes away from the white population and sustaining and protecting them as they transitioned to full-time agriculture for their livelihood. Beale's intentions were humane—especially when compared to the other leading proposal of the day, which was simple extermination. Beale labored heroically to create a viable Indian community at Fort Tejon, and he came tantalizingly close to doing so. The project failed in the end because of funding shortfalls, political hostility and a disputed land claim. But it failed honorably—so much so that James Carleton felt sure he could apply a similar scheme to his own Indian problems in New Mexico.

Carleton's confidence rested in part on his special knowledge of the New Mexican landscape. In his prewar days as a dragoon, the army had sent him to survey a remote stretch of the Pecos River, not far from the Texas border. There Carleton discovered a natural garden spot—an American Eden—that roving Mexican fur traders had dubbed the *Bosque Redondo*, or "round wood" (so named for the shape of the forest there that graced a wide bend in the river). Carleton had grazed his horses on the Bosque's rich grasses and dined on its savory wild turkey. The soil was deep, dark and apparently rich. Carleton was smitten with the place and reported back that it was an excellent spot for a fort.

Visions of this enchanted Bosque filled Carleton's mind as he sought solutions to the horrific violence that plagued his department. What if the Navajo, whom Carleton saw as the most intractable threat to order, could be rounded up and sent to this wondrous garden spot? The Navajo, or Diné, as they called themselves, were experienced farmers. Surely they were the best candidates to put the site's agricultural potential to good use. There, far apart from white settlers and their tempting sheep herds, the older Diné would slowly abandon their war-like ways, while their children would be transformed by the Christian instruction offered to them free of charge.

It was a compelling vision, and Carleton pursued it for the rest of his tenure in New Mexico with Ahab-like determination. When reports came back from his surveyors that the waters of the Pecos were dangerously alkaline, Carleton brushed aside the objection. Hadn't he been to the

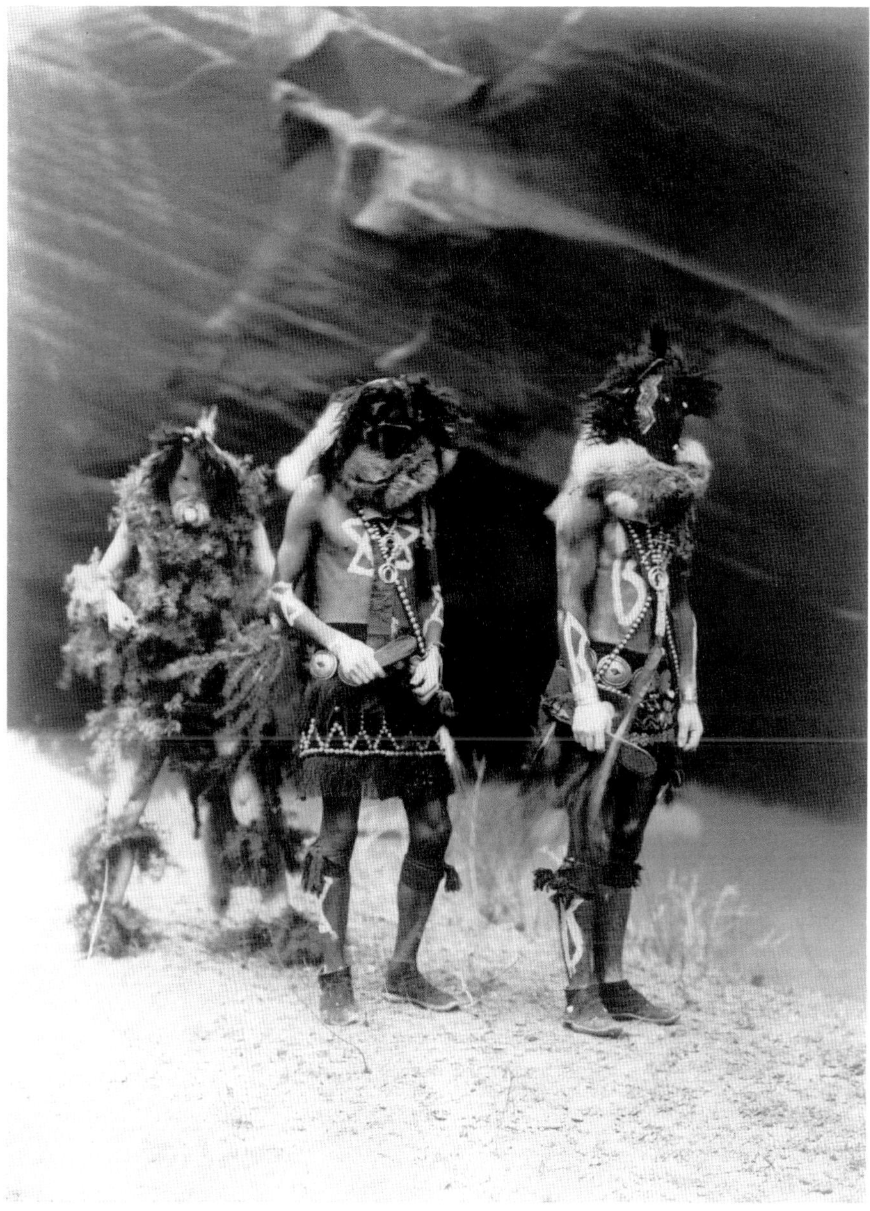

Yebichai (Navajo war gods) dancers. Raiding between the Navajo and New Mexicans went back generations. Sheep and slaves were the main booty. *Library of Congress.*

Bosque himself? Hadn't he fed his horses on the site's lush grass and dined on its abundant game?

To implement his scheme, Carleton drew on the military ace up his sleeve: the presence, close at hand, of his old friend Christopher "Kit" Carson, whose skills as a frontiersman were already a national legend. Carson lived in Taos and had married into a leading New Mexican family. He was an uncompromising (if soft-spoken) Unionist who had enlisted promptly when the Confederates threatened New Mexico. Carson raised a regiment of New Mexico Volunteers and led them with distinction at the bloody battle at Valverde. His success in that campaign proved that Carson was more than just a world-class scout; he was also an effective leader of troops in the field. So it was to Carson that Carleton turned when he needed a field commander to go out and gather up the Diné.

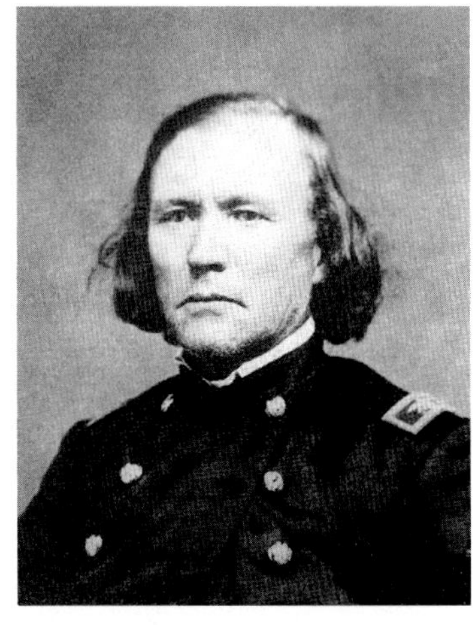

Colonel Christopher (Kit) Carson. *Courtesy Palace of the Governors Photo Archives (NMHM/DCA), 007151.*

Carson's life didn't leave much time for education. (He had to dictate his official reports while serving in the army.) He was, however, an accomplished linguist, fluent in Spanish and a number of Indian languages. It is a great loss that he was unable to record his astonishing life in his own words.

Kit Carson was old by frontier standards and far from well. All he wanted at this stage of his life was to spend more time with his wife and children, but James Carleton would have none of it. He applied relentless pressure, appealing repeatedly to his friend's sense of duty, until Carson finally gave in and took the command.

First on the list to enjoy the new Indian paradise were not the Navajo, however. That honor belonged to the Mescalero Apache, a small but determined tribe whose remarkable violence earned them special attention. Carleton, who could be bloody-minded enough when he chose, ordered Carson to kill all the adult male Mescalero and send the women and children to the Bosque. Carson ignored the order and deported the entire tribe.

Next came the Navajo, who presented an altogether different scale of challenge. Their homeland, the Dinétah, was immense, comprising large areas of New Mexico and Arizona, along with smaller portions of Utah and Colorado. The whole tribe numbered something on the order of twelve thousand souls and possessed a formidable military capacity. Decision-

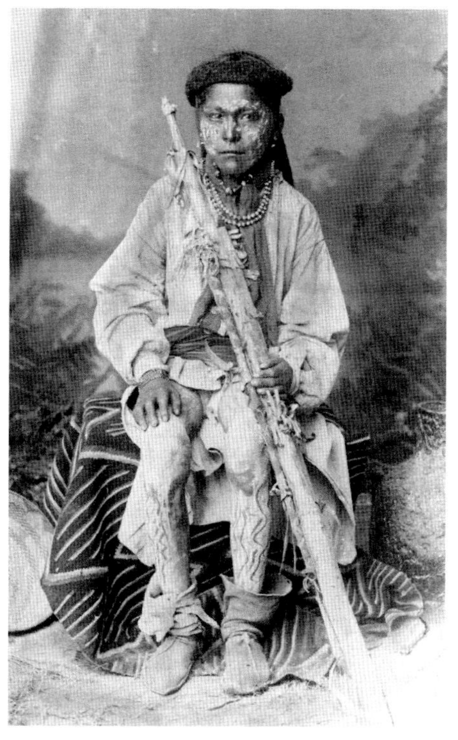

Right: Mescalero Apache boy. *Wikimedia Commons.*

The Mescalero were the first tribe rounded up and sent to Bosque Redondo. They were also the first to flee the reservation when conditions there proved unbearable.

Below: Canyon De Chelly, the heart of Dinétah, was a natural fortress of enormous strength. Earlier Mexican and American expeditions failed to reduce it. *Photo by Timothy O'Sullivan (circa 1870)/ Wikimedia Commons.*

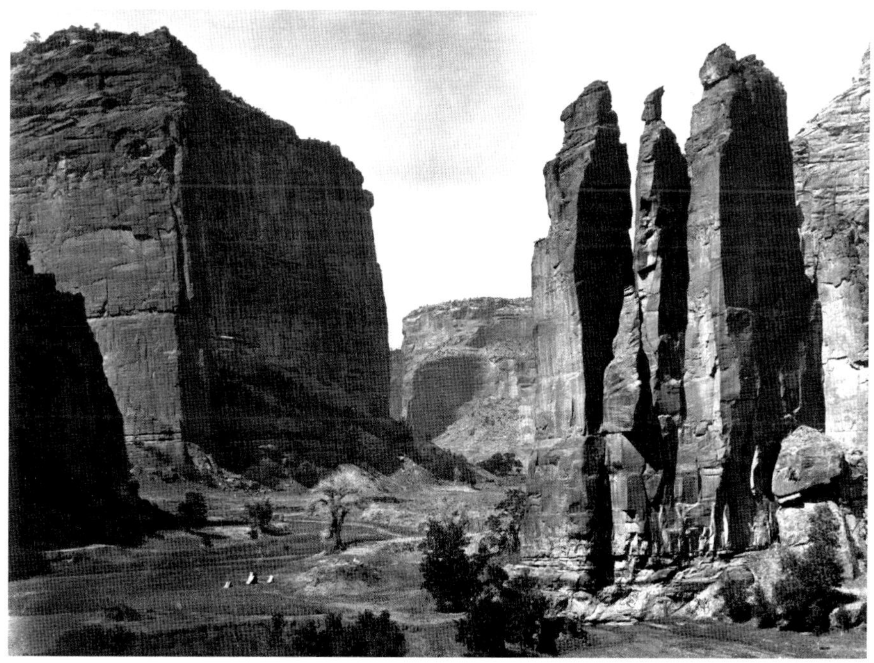

making in the Diné world was extremely diffuse, however, and was often exercised on a band-by-band basis, if not warrior-by-warrior. This made coordinated action—either military or diplomatic—hard to achieve.

To subdue the Navajo, Carson could draw on the services of about one thousand soldiers—a mixed force of California and New Mexico Volunteers, regulars and Ute scouts.[29] The expedition took the field in July 1863 and for six months relentlessly hunted the Navajo—but almost never found them in the vast, broken terrain of Dinétah. The soldiers did find the Diné's ripening cornfields, their fruit orchards and much of their livestock, and these they appropriated or destroyed utterly. It was a grim, dispiriting campaign, devoid of anything like glory and conducted under conditions of intense physical hardship.

The climax of the expedition occurred in January 1864, when Carson and his men set out in bitter cold for the fabled Canyon De Chelly, a wonderland of dramatic interlocking canyons that served as chief sanctuary and spiritual homeland of the Diné. Again, Carson and his men found few Indians, but those they did find bore unmistakable marks of extreme deprivation. Some were found dead of starvation.

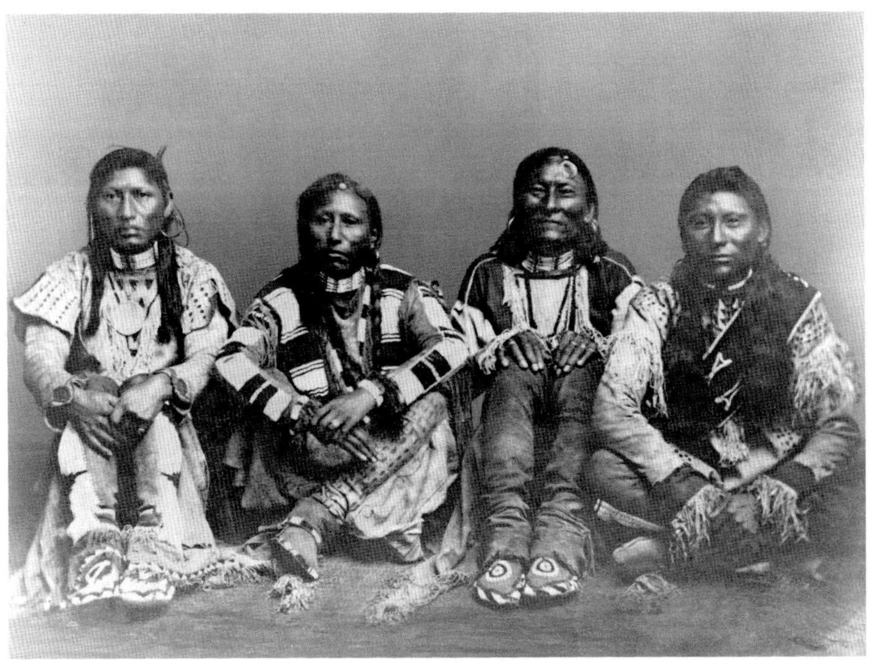

Ute warriors. California Volunteers fought alongside Carson's Ute scouts in campaigns against the Navajo, Comanche and Kiowa. *Utah State Historical Society.*

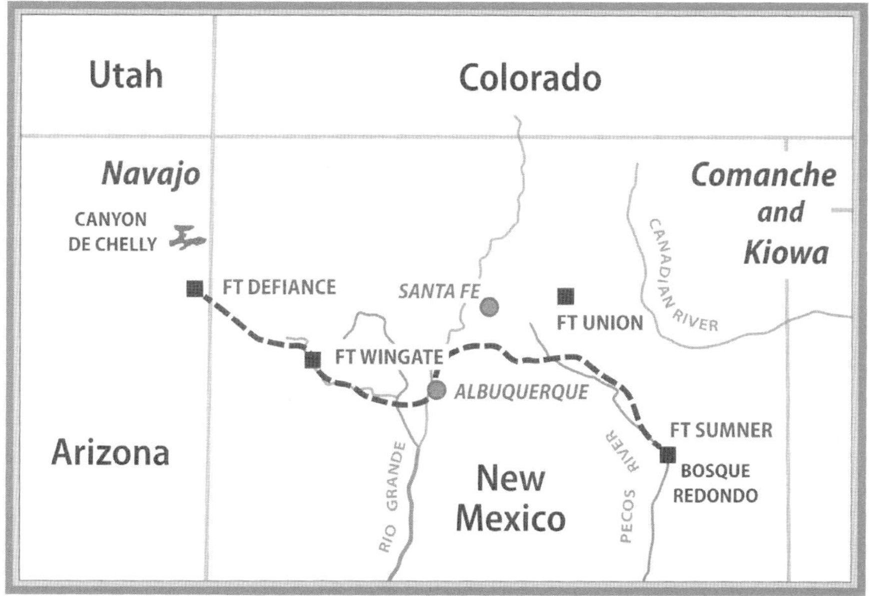

Navajo removal, 1864 (the Long Walk). Carson's scorched-earth campaign and four years at Bosque Redondo reduced Navajo numbers by a third. *Map by the author.*

Over the rest of the winter, thousands of weak and hungry Navajo gave themselves up. Carson did what he could to feed and clothe them and then sent them in batches to the Bosque. Many of the soldiers who herded the Navajo along were New Mexicans, pleased to see their ancestral enemies humbled and anxious to do what they could to increase their suffering. The terrible, 280-mile forced march remains seared in Navajo tribal memory as the Long Walk. It is estimated that over two hundred Diné perished on the way to Bosque Redondo. Others were kidnapped and sold into slavery by New Mexico Volunteers.

When the Navajo arrived at their new home, they were dismayed. The new land was foreign, bearing no part in the rich mythology that shaped their lives in the Dinétah. Nor were the Mescalero Apache the companions the Diné would have chosen to share their new home. Nonetheless, the tribe set about building the extensive irrigation network required to plant corn, the staple crop that sustained them through hard times. Hope grew as acres and acres of green corn stalks rose, tall and lush. It wasn't until a few weeks before harvest that a soldier discovered that cutworms had invaded the fields and eaten out the kernels inside the healthy-looking ears. The crop was a complete loss.

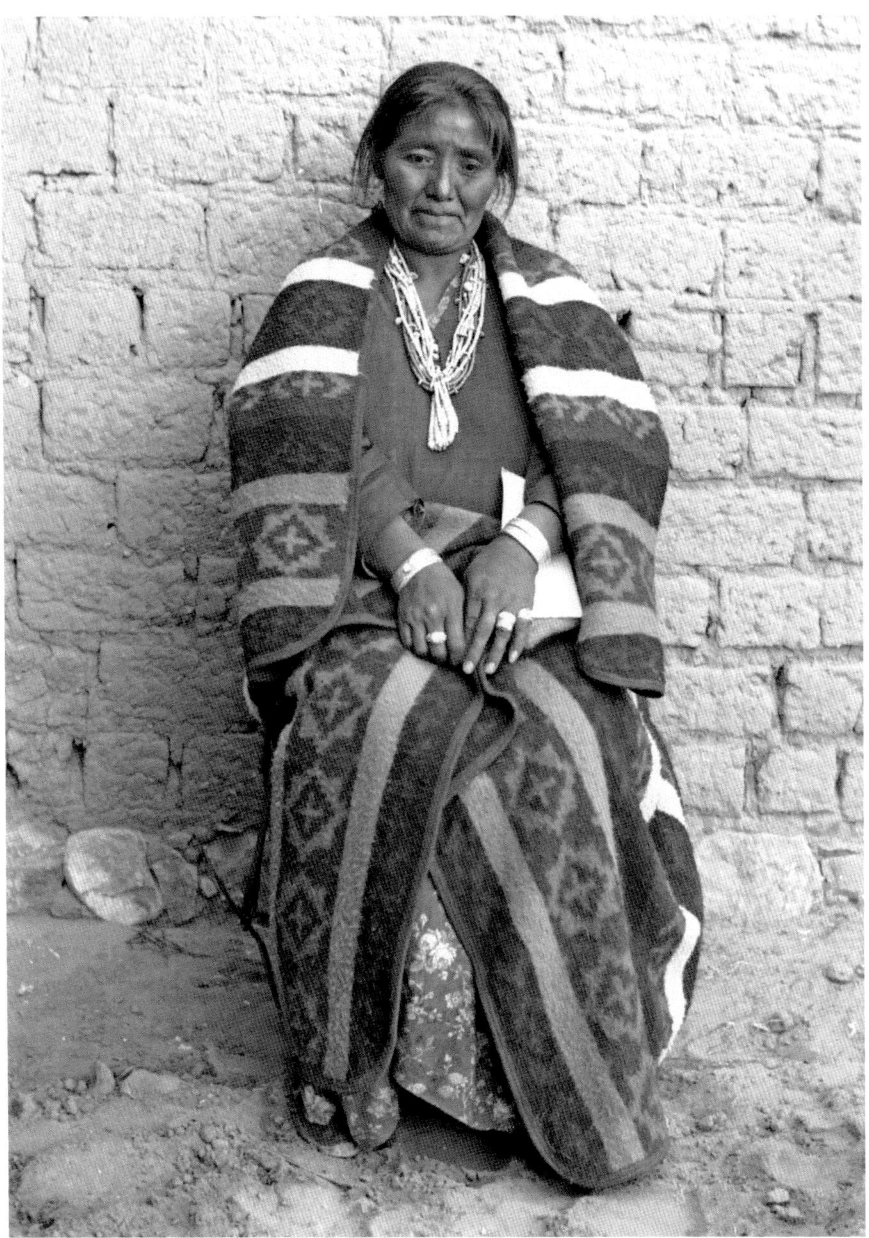

Rosa, daughter of Chief Manuelito, circa 1905. *Wikimedia Commons/C.C. Pierce Photography Collection, California Historical Society Collection.*

The miseries endured by the Navajo in the first year at Bosque Redondo were repeated in one form or another for the rest of their stay there. In 1868, General William Sherman inspected the reservation and heard testimony about conditions. Sherman let the surviving Diné return to their ancestral lands.

Carleton was horrified. He moved heaven and earth to bring in supplies to his faltering project. He ordered his own men onto half rations to spread food stocks further. But he could not overcome the basic facts of the situation; the Bosque's alkaline water was unhealthy for humans, and the settlement was terrifically overcrowded, housing multiples of the number of people originally anticipated. Nor could Carleton summon help from a distant War Department, whose attention was absorbed by the crisis of the war back east.

Disease, hunger and social dislocation were the Navajo's lot at the Bosque, but that was not the sum of their suffering. By moving the Diné to eastern New Mexico, Carleton had placed them well within range of the Comanche and Kiowa war parties that were wreaking bloody havoc all along the borders of Comancheria. In a series of lightning strikes, Navajo men were murdered, women and children seized as slaves and livestock stolen. Fort Sumner, the military post that supervised life in the Bosque, could not defend adequately against the raiders, much less hunt them down and retrieve their booty and prisoners.

Carleton's solution to the security problem at the Bosque was to take the war to the Comanche, to strike them deep in their homeland and convince them that attacking New Mexico was a losing proposition. It was a bold plan, involving terrible risks to the soldiers who undertook it. No U.S. Army force had ever campaigned in the heart of Comancheria before. If the soldiers actually succeeded in finding the Comanche, they could count on being vastly outnumbered and being far, far from rescue. It was a desperately dangerous assignment, and in General Carleton's eyes, there was only one man in the department who was qualified to undertake it.

The Battle of Adobe Walls

On November 12, 1864, Colonel Kit Carson left Fort Bascom, a distant outpost near the Texas border, with two companies of cavalry, one of infantry and a large party of Ute scouts. The force comprised about four hundred men in all, most of them California Volunteers.[30] Their objective was to locate the winter encampments of the Comanche along the Canadian River and attack them.

Carson was fortunate in his subordinates. Major William McCleave, who commanded his cavalry, came to California from Northern Ireland in

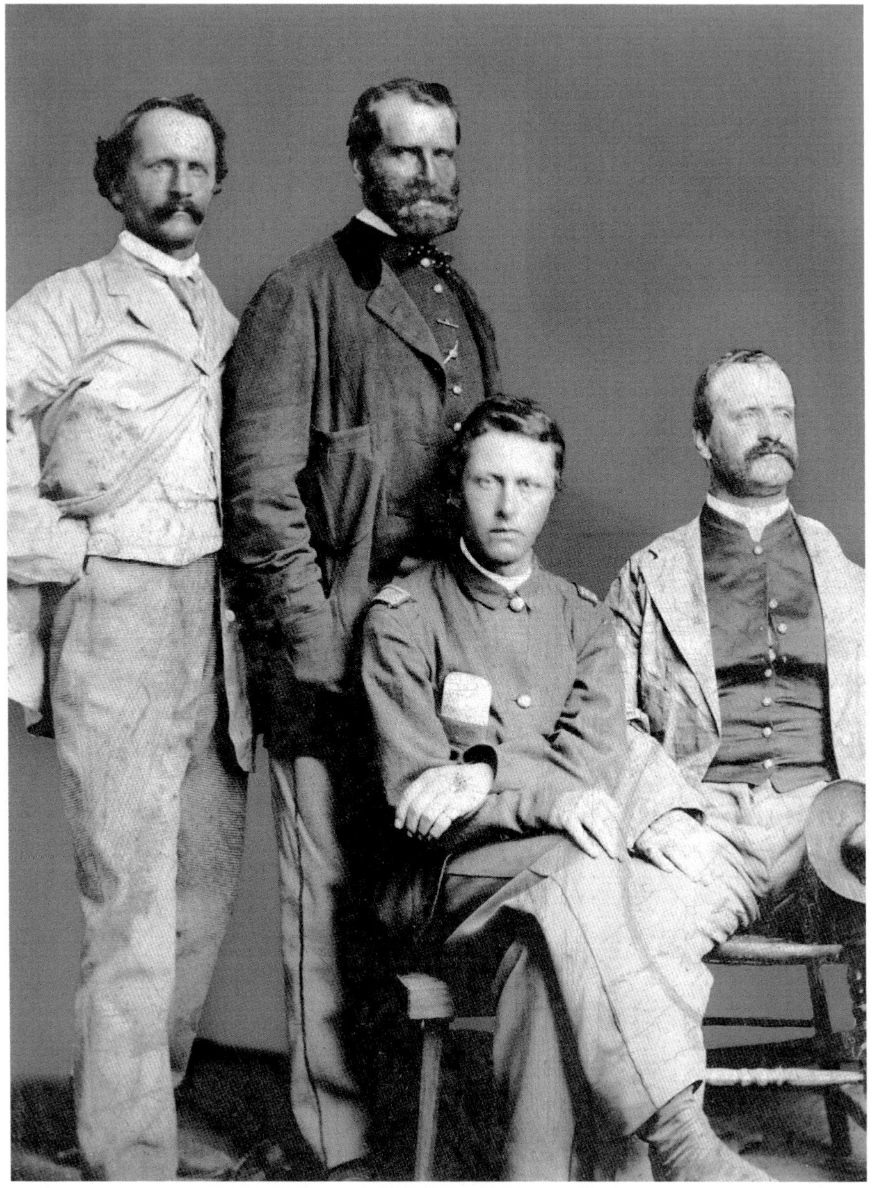

Officers of the California Column. *Courtesy of the Bancroft Library, University of California, Berkeley.*

Major William McCleave (*center, standing*) and Captain George Pettis (*seated, far right*) were exceptional officers who played key roles in Carson's campaign against the Comanche.

1850 and enlisted in the dragoons. He rose to sergeant and was the army's chief camel herder when the war broke out—rescuing McCleave from the camels.[31] He was breveted captain of volunteers and helped organize the First California Cavalry.

McCleave was captured by Confederates in March 1862 while setting up supply depots in Arizona for the California Column. His Southern captors, however, recognized a belligerent Scotch-Irishman when they saw one and were heartily glad to exchange him for two Confederate lieutenants. (McCleave refused back pay for the time spent as a prisoner, on the grounds that he had done nothing useful for the Union cause during his captivity.) After his release, McCleave hunted down and destroyed several Apache raiding parties before being selected by Carson for the Comanche expedition.

Captain George Pettis enlisted in the first call for troops and was elected second lieutenant of Company K, First California Volunteer Infantry, an outfit composed of Sacramento-area printers who felt that the sword was, in this instance, mightier than the pen. Pettis rose to command of the company and was also in charge of a pair of mountain howitzers that were to play a key role in the crisis of the campaign.

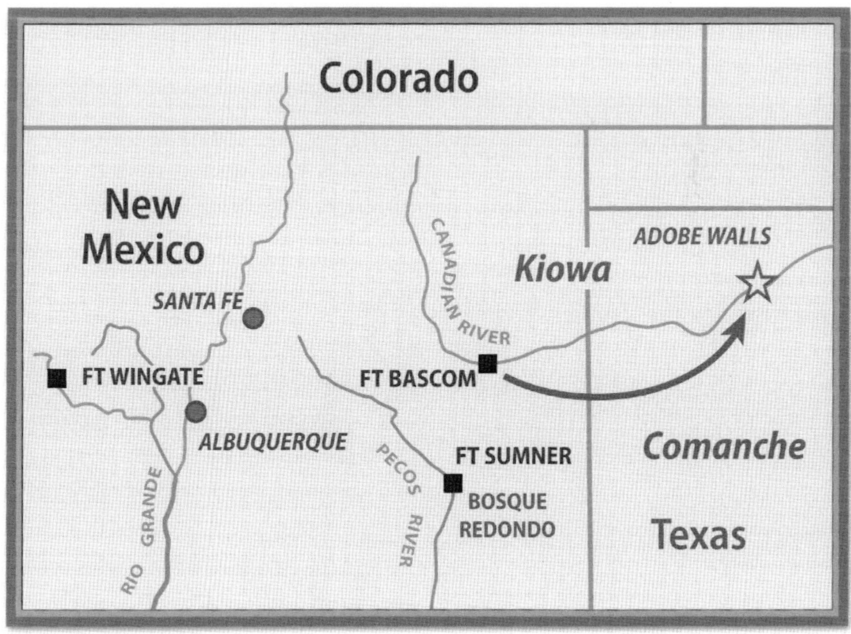

Carson's small force pushed deep into Comancheria. In the event of mishap, there was no chance of rescue. He and his men were on their own. *Map by the author.*

For twelve days, the expedition pushed out onto the *Llano Estacado* (Staked Plains), a vast, featureless tableland where few whites had ever ventured. On the afternoon of November 24, 1864, Carson's Ute scouts discovered a cluster of Kiowa and Comanche villages in the valley of the Canadian River. Carson listened to the scouts' report and summed it up in English for his white troops. "We will have no difficulty," he assured them, "finding all the Indians we desire."[32]

Carson left some of his infantry behind with the wagon train and advanced with his cavalry and remaining infantry by moonlight, with strict orders against smoking or talking. The column dropped down into the river bottomland and halted near the enemy villages, each trooper holding his horse's reins until first light. Then they resumed their advance—and were soon challenged by Kiowa pickets. Carson's Utes tore off after the pickets, while McCleave's cavalry charged the Kiowa encampment. Carson followed with Pettis and the battery, which made poor time over the narrow, sandy trails of the river bottomland.

McCleave knew he was headed for a fight. There were around 175 teepees in the Kiowa camp, which, by frontier reckoning, meant that he and his troopers would soon be trading lead at close quarters with about 350 warriors. But luck was with him—most of the Kiowa warriors were off on a raid, with only a small force left behind to protect the camp. These guards held off McCleave's troopers long enough for the women and children to flee. Then the guards fled in turn, making for a large Comanche village just visible in the distance. McCleave's men searched the Kiowa camp and discovered evidence of white hostages. They also found a government wagon and ambulance and piles of excellent buffalo robes.

Meanwhile, the fleeing Kiowa spread the alarm. Mounted warriors approached in ever-increasing numbers and began trading fire with the soldiers. McCleave's position in the camp was badly exposed. He ordered his men forward to the relative safety of a ruined trading post known as the Adobe Walls, which was just a few hundred yards away. There, the rest of the command caught up with McCleave—except for the lumbering howitzers, which trailed behind. As soon as Carson arrived, he took charge of the defense. He ordered the troopers' horses to be led inside the crumbling walls of the fort, which were still high enough to shield them from the hot incoming fire. A hospital was set up inside as well. Carson threw out his dismounted troopers as skirmishers in the tall grass around the fort, where they returned the hot incoming fire.

It was then that Carson discovered just how big a hornet's nest he had kicked over. Lifting his field glasses, he spotted in the distance one of the largest Indian forces ever assembled in North America—some 1,400 warriors—with more arriving every minute from Comanche villages downstream and out of sight. The Indians were massing for the charge that would sweep the soldiers off the plain and into the history books as Carson's Last Stand.

In his memoirs, Captain Pettis describes what happened next: "This was the prospect when the battery came on the ground. A finer sight I never saw before, and probably shall never see again. The Indians seemed to be astonished when the pieces came up at a gallop and were being unlimbered."[33]

Carson ordered Pettis to place the guns atop a low knoll outside the fort. "Throw a few shell into that crowd over thar," ordered Carson. Pettis obliged.

> *At the first discharge, every one of the enemy, those that were charging backwards and forwards on their horses but a moment before as well as those that were standing in line, rose high in their stirrups and gazed, for a single moment, with astonishment, then guiding their horses' heads away from us, and giving one concerted, prolonged yell, they started in a dead run for their village. In fact, when the fourth shot was fired, there was not a single enemy within the extreme range of the howitzers.*

Carson reckoned that the howitzers, which were evidently a complete surprise to the Indians, had ended the contest. He ordered his men to eat and drink and get ready to move out. For once, the legendary scout was mistaken.

> *Less than half an hour had elapsed, and Carson had not, as yet, given the order to saddle up, when the enemy were returning and seemed to be anxious to renew the conflict. Presently…the sharp, quick whiz of the Indians' rifle balls was again heard, the cavalrymen were deployed as before, and the fight was going on again in earnest.*

The Kiowa and Comanche had come to a quick decision about how to deal with the whites' terrifying new weapon. "The howitzers were fired but a few times, as the enemy were shrewd enough to know that their policy was to act singly and avoid getting into masses, although the detachments were kept on the field in the most exposed situations."

The Indians countered the effects of what they called "the gun that shoots twice" with remarkable skill.[34]

> *At one of the discharges, the shell passed directly through the body of a horse on which was a Comanche riding at a full run, and went some two or three hundred yards further on before it exploded. The horse, on being struck, went head-foremost to earth, throwing his rider, as it seemed, twenty feet into the air with his hands and feet sprawling in all directions, and as he struck the earth, apparently senseless, two other Indians who were near by, proceeded to him, one on each side, and throwing themselves over on the sides of their horses, seized each an arm and dragged him from the field between them, amid a shower of rifle balls from our skirmishers.*

One resourceful Kiowa warrior named Satanta brought special talents to the contest:

> *About two hundred yards in rear of their line, all through the fighting at the Adobe Walls, was stationed one of the enemy who had a cavalry bugle, and during the entire day he would blow the opposite call that was used by the officer in our line of skirmishers. For instance, when our bugles sounded the "advance," he would blow "retreat"; and when ours sounded the "retreat," he would follow with the "advance"; ours would signal "halt"; he would follow suit. So he kept it up all the day, blowing as shrill and clearly as our very best buglers.*

After initial confusion, Carson's men came to appreciate the humor in the situation. "He [the Indian bugler] would answer our signals each time they were sounded, to the infinite merriment of our men, who would respond with shouts of laughter each time he sounded his horn."

A steady stream of reinforcements from nearby Comanche villages raised the count of Indian warriors to something like three thousand, leaving the troopers outnumbered ten to one. Carson, unlike George Custer, knew when enough was enough. At 3:30 p.m., he rejected his officers' pleas to attack the Comanche village in their front and instead ordered a retreat. The soldiers withdrew under heavy fire to the Kiowa village they had overrun that morning. There they drove out the Indians who had reoccupied it and burned the place down, along with its food caches and stacks of first-rate buffalo robes (after the soldiers helped themselves to one apiece). Night fell as they destroyed the village, and the Comanche and Kiowa disengaged. Carson's exhausted men left the river valley and rode out onto the plains by moonlight. Three hours later, they spotted campfires and rejoiced to hear the challenge of the sentries guarding the wagon train—proof that

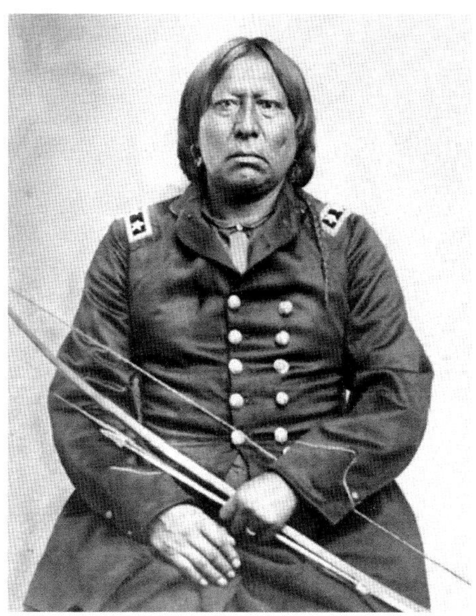

The Kiowa warrior Stumbling Bear made so many reckless charges that his small daughter's shawl, which he wore for good luck, was pierced by a dozen bullets. Stumbling Bear was not wounded. *Beineke Rare Book and Manuscript Library, Yale University.*

their companions were safe and that they would have food and ammunition for the 250-mile ride back to Fort Bascom.

The Kiowa and Comanche resistance had been impassioned, and they had indeed driven off the soldiers. Summing up the Indians' conduct that day, Carson later said, "They acted with more daring and bravery than I have ever before witnessed." But to use the Indians' own idiom, Carson had "counted coup" on them. He had invaded the heart of Comancheria, destroyed an important village and inflicted heavy casualties on his enemies, while suffering few losses of his own. The implications were clear enough. The destruction of the Comanche empire was now only a matter of time, and not much time at that.

The Battle of Adobe Walls took place in late 1864, the year that marked the end of most Californians' service in New Mexico. Their three-year enlistments were running out, and most returned to the Golden State. About five hundred Californians chose to remain in the Southwest, with many marrying into Hispanic families and serving in prominent positions in civil society. Their presence did much to impart an American cast on the emerging territories of New Mexico and Arizona.[35]

Kit Carson survived the war but died of an aneurism three years later at the age of fifty-eight. James Carleton clung to his plan of transforming Indian hearts and minds at Bosque Redondo, but conditions grew so terrible there that many fled and returned to their homelands, regardless of consequences. By 1866, Carleton's authoritarian manner had worn out his welcome among the civilian population of New Mexico, and he was relieved of command. He served out the remainder of his days as a cavalry officer, dying in San Antonio, Texas, in 1873 at the age of fifty-nine.

Chapter 11

LIFE IN WARTIME CALIFORNIA

The failure of the Confederate invasion of the Southwest was a severe blow to Southern sympathizers on the Pacific coast. Sibley's defeat and withdrawal meant that the nearest organized Confederate force lay 1,500 miles east, in San Antonio, Texas. The possibility of direct support for Rebel activity in the West disappeared with the last shattered remnants of Sibley's Army of New Mexico. California's Secessionists were on their own.

Pro-Southern citizens still composed a majority in a number of communities, especially in Southern California and in the Southern Mines (the gold-mining communities in the Sierra foothills that were supplied from Stockton). But their influence in statewide politics declined in the first year of the war and never fully recovered.

Civil and military authorities kept a close eye on Secesh communities. Both General Sumner and his successor, General Wright, monitored elements they deemed disloyal and did not hesitate to station California Volunteers (drawn mainly from Northern California) in hotspots where pro-Southern rhetoric threatened to spill over into pro-Southern action.

The town of Visalia, county seat of Tulare County, was an example. Situated on the eastern side of the southern San Joaquin Valley, the town was a stop on the Butterfield Overland Stage line, which carried immigrants across the Southwest and Southern California and up into the gold country. Visalia's population was predominantly Secesh, but the town also contained a determined pro-Union party. Tensions between the two groups were acute.

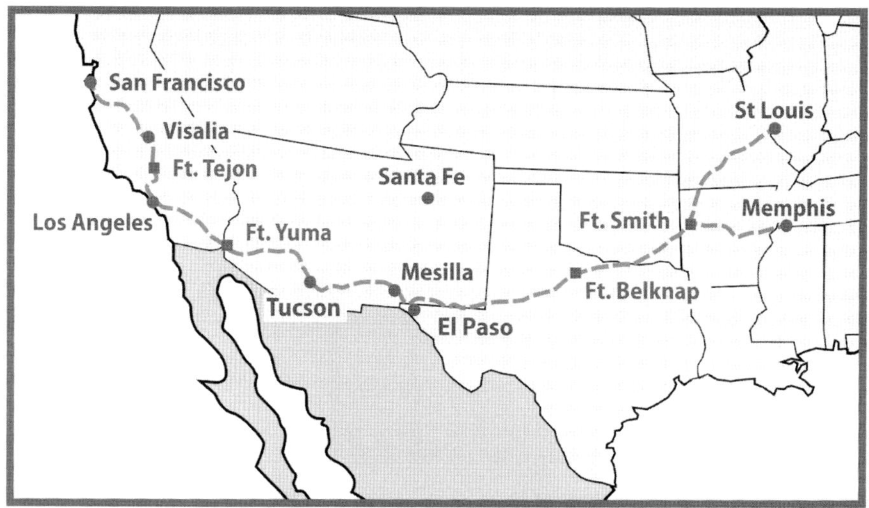

The Butterfield Overland stage brought Southern immigrants to California in the late 1850s. As the Civil War broke out, U.S. troops were withdrawn from key forts guarding the route, rendering it too dangerous for commercial use. It was superseded in 1861 by the Central Overland route and then by the transcontinental railroad in 1869. *Map by the author.*

Both factions enjoyed the services of newspapers that catered to their political tastes in the approved manner of nineteenth-century journalism, in which news and editorial content mingled freely to produce cataracts of partisan abuse. Thus, Visalia's *Equal Rights Expositor*, the pro-Southern paper, presented President Lincoln to its readers as a "cadaverous, long shanked, mule-countenanced rail splitter from Illinois."[36]

Newspapers of the period often contained literary flights aimed at refining the sentiments of their readers (while conveniently filling up pages on slow news days). Uplifting compositions of this sort could also be used to promote political ends. Here, for instance, is the editor of the *Expositor* expressing his gratitude to his female readership, who raised money to ensure the paper's survival:

Their soft cheeks, how they glow when the news it doth come,
Of all the brave deeds that our heroes hath done.
For the cause, all they have, they would freely bestow
And nightly they pray for old Abe's overthrow.
Oh may all the blessings that Heaven can spare,
Be theirs, the brave wives and maidens of Tulare.[37]

General Wright, commander of Union forces on the Pacific, refrained from censoring Secesh newspapers on literary grounds, but he did take notice of open and consistently advocated treason. In September 1862, after the *Expositor* declared that "the south stands justified before God and before the world for the position she has assumed," Wright invoked new powers granted him by the War Department. He asked the San Francisco postmaster to ban the *Expositor* and four other Secesh papers from the U.S. mail.[38] To emphasize his point, he also detached two companies of the Second California Volunteer Cavalry and ordered them to establish camp outside Visalia.

Relations between the soldiers and Visalia's Southern sympathizers began badly and ran sharply downhill. Two editors of the *Expositor* were jailed and then released after taking the loyalty oath—whereupon they immediately resumed blackguarding the soldiers. On March 5, 1863, the editors referred to some Union cavalrymen fighting back east as "California Cossacks" who "hire out their service." The Cossacks' comrades replied that night by demolishing the *Expositor*'s office and throwing its type, paper and ink out into the street.

In the following weeks, the cavalrymen set up special patrols in Visalia and provided pro-Union men with guns and ammunition so they could help out in the event of open fighting. A series of ugly incidents peaked in August 1863, when a Secessionist named James Wells shot and killed an off-duty cavalryman in a street altercation. Wells's home mysteriously burned to the ground that evening. Wells himself was spirited out of the county by friends and never stood trial for the killing.

Variations on Visalia's experience occurred around the state. Viewed collectively, a consistent pattern emerges. General Wright did occasionally interfere with Secessionist newspapers, but he did not find the strategy useful and generally allowed publishers to resume use of the mails fairly quickly—after taking a loyalty oath and, in some cases, posting a bond. Some Secesh editors complied with Wright's terms; others did not. Wright evidently felt that heavy-handed suppression was ultimately counterproductive. He was rewarded for his restraint by streams of censure from ardent Unionists, who regarded him as too lenient.

Union newspapers, in turn, did not lack for partisan spirit. The *American Flag* provides many stirring examples, such as this description of a Democratic Party meeting that took place in November 1864:

> *The Last Grand Scramble of the Gorillas!—Howls, Roars, Groans, Yelps, Yells, Red Fire, Rages, and Blue Blazes!—The Species on Horseback, on Foot, in Buggies, in Hacks, on Drays, in Swill Carts and Mud Boxes!—Broom Rangers, Steamship Rioters, Aliens and Reprobates Howl Themselves Hoarse!—Death on a Pale Horse, and All Hell Following Him!*[39]

The *American Flag* began life in 1860 in the gold rush town of Sonora, in Tuolumne County. Its editor was Daniel O. McCarthy, who became an impassioned abolitionist after watching the abuse of a slave in his home state of Mississippi. Most of McCarthy's fellow Sonorans were also Southerners—but of a very different political cast. His neighbors eventually convinced McCarthy that his physical health and financial prospects would be better served if he and his newspaper moved to some other part of the state. McCarthy (with financial assistance from Leland Stanford) obliged, and in April 1864, firmly Unionist San Francisco became the new home of the self-proclaimed "Slasher of the Press."

In San Francisco, McCarthy was seconded in his work by a writer named Calvin McDonald (better known as "the Triple Thunderer"). Between them, they caused a remarkable amount of grief in political circles. Their investigative efforts led to the arrest of a prominent local Democrat, John Chipman, for sedition. This coup was repeated with interest on July

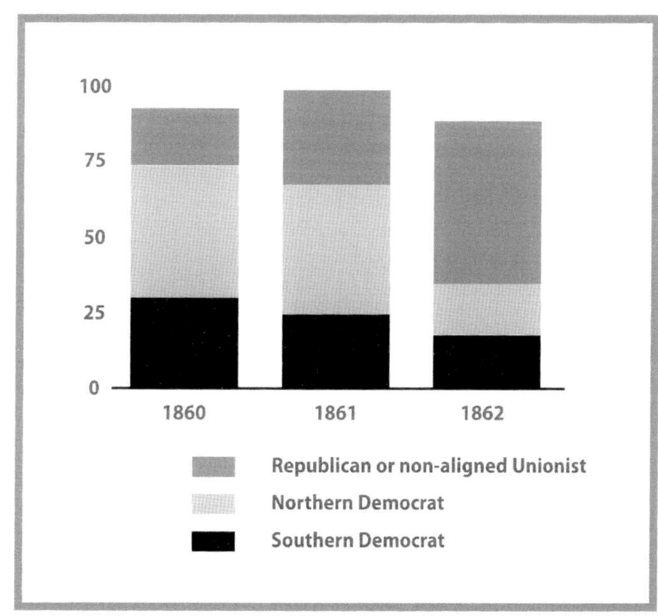

Southern Democratic newspaper ownership declined steadily over the first years of the war, while Republican and "decline-to-state" Unionist papers surged. Many Northern Democratic papers moved to the Republican or general Unionist camp. *Figures from Chandler, "Fighting Words." Chart by the author.*

25, 1864, when the *Flag*'s reporting led to the arrest of Charles Weller, chairman of the Democratic state committee, for treasonous remarks addressed to an Irish political club. Chipman and Weller spent some weeks in Federal custody on Alcatraz Island before being released. McCarthy and his *Flag* eventually came to grief after he expanded his crusading efforts and started attacking political corruption in Sacramento. By 1866, McCarthy's accusations had outrun his ability to substantiate his claims, and he ended up serving some time in jail.

From the earliest days of statehood, Californians cherished their newspapers and supported a remarkable number of them. Publishing was, however, a high-risk, high-turnover business. During the war years, papers changed hands frequently, with a steady migration of ownership away from Southern Democrats and Northern Democrats toward Republicans and publishers who lacked party affiliation but favored the Union cause.

Ultimately, the most serious threat to pro-Southern Democratic newspapers in California was not government repression but shifting public opinion. Widespread belief that the South was responsible for starting the war alienated Northern Democrats and even many former Breckinridge men. As the war progressed, it became harder and harder to sell anti-Union newspapers outside of Secessionist strongholds.

Political Tides

Northern Democrats and Republicans worked together in 1861 to wrest control of California from the pro-Southern Chivalry. The two groups officially joined forces and presented a fusion Union ticket in the election of 1862.

Deep divisions between the new allies over public policy remained. Most Northern Democrats were uncomfortable with the idea of blacks acquiring rights of any kind, much less becoming full participants in civic life. And as the war ground on for year after bloody, unrelenting year, many Union-leaning Democrats lost faith in the enterprise and came to favor a peaceful settlement—even if it meant Southern independence.

Democratic war-weariness was a national phenomenon, given impetus in March 1863 by institution of the nation's first military draft, which was undertaken to shore up Union armies that had suffered terrible punishment the preceding year.[40] Opposition to the draft was led by Representative

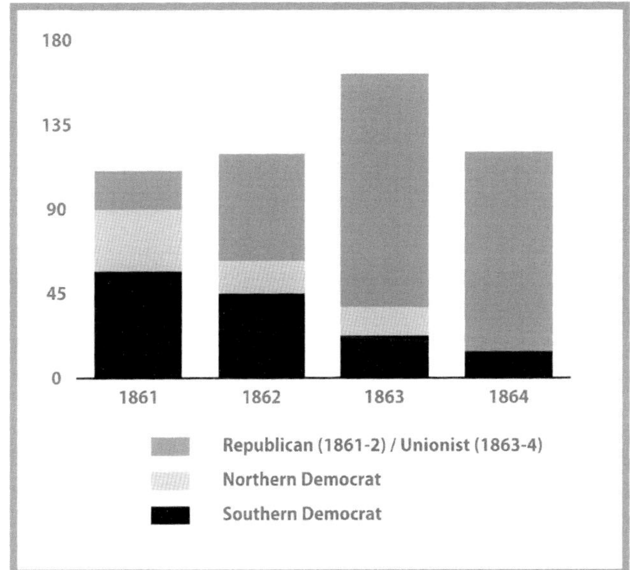

This graph shows the number of legislators (including both Senate and Assembly) belonging to individual parties during the war. Southern Democratic numbers declined steadily. In 1863, most Northern Democrats officially joined forces with the Republicans under the new Union Party banner. By 1864, Union Party control of the state legislature was complete. *Chart by the author.*

Clement Vallandigham of Ohio and presented a serious political challenge to the Lincoln administration in the Midwest and in New York City, where bloody riots had to be put down by Union troops freshly arrived from the field at Gettysburg. The administration responded by jailing Vallandigham and closing down Copperhead newspapers that advocated resistance to the draft.[41]

The draft issue never played a significant role in California politics, since the state met its troop quotas easily through volunteer enlistments. But the related issues of arrest for sedition, denial of habeas corpus and newspaper censorship became hot buttons in state elections. California Democrats were also unhappy about new state laws that went well beyond what the Lincoln administration advocated at the national level. California laws enacted in 1862 and 1863 allocated significant state funds to supplement the Volunteers' pay and provide for their families. Loyalty oaths were required of people wishing to teach, practice law or engage in other sensitive occupations. Secessionists were theoretically barred from courts of justice. Violently anti-government speech could net the offender a $1,000 fine and a year in county jail. And finally, in an unbearable affront to the Chivalry, the state legislature endorsed Lincoln's Emancipation Proclamation and pledged full support for the measure.

This last resolution technically put an end to Indian slavery in California, but the system of "servitude" for young Indian captives continued unofficially for years. Similarly, provisions for legal restraint on

Secessionist speech and writing were rarely enforced. A handful of high-profile Secesh politicians and editors spent a few weeks under lock and key on Alcatraz Island, but that was the extent of the matter. Californians have long enjoyed a certain informality in their relationship to the law when they deem it expedient. In the case of Secessionist opinion, most loyal Californians were willing to let their erring brethren say and write what they chose so long as the sentiments expressed didn't ripen into tangible action.

The statewide election of 1863 provides a snapshot of mid-war political opinion in the Golden State. John Downey, whom we last saw in 1861 serving dutifully as governor and raising troops at the War Department's request, typifies Democrats who embraced the Union cause in response to Fort Sumter but then lost enthusiasm. Downey did not like the look of Republican California. He loathed Republican initiatives for racial equality and bitterly resented General Wright's suppression of free speech. Downey came out of political retirement in 1863 and ran for governor as a peace Democrat. His opponent was Frederick Low, a Republican representing the combined forces of the Union Party. Low won the governorship handily, and Downey's political career died with this defeat. But the steady undercurrent of white supremacism Downey represented survived intact, only to surface with renewed force after the war.

The presidential election of 1864 was the supreme test of Northern will. The horrendous casualty lists produced by Grant's Wilderness Campaign brought agony to households across the North that spring and summer. Lincoln himself thought he would be defeated by his opponent, General George McClellan, who found himself in the odd position of being a pro-war Democrat nominated to represent a party with an adamantly anti-war platform. We will never know how McClellan would have attempted to square that particular circle. Eleventh-hour battlefield successes—notably the capture of Atlanta by General William Sherman—shifted public feeling and led to a solid Union victory at the polls. Lincoln's vote tally in California must have been especially gratifying to the embattled president. He carried the state with 58.6 percent of the vote—up an astonishing 26.3 points from his 1860 total of 32.2 percent.

Lincoln's triumph in 1864 marked the high water of Unionism in California. His stunning victory showed that voters in the Golden State were willing to stand resolutely behind the national administration—at least until the war was won.

Chapter 12

CONFEDERATE PARTISANS

Californians who wanted to fight for the South headed back east at the start of the war, either by steamship or by land. Both routes became steadily more difficult as a system of passports was implemented for sea passage and the buildup of Union troops at Fort Yuma soon allowed for more effective patrolling of land routes from Southern California. General Carleton's assumption of command in the Department of New Mexico brought added danger to would-be Southern recruits crossing the Southwest, as that implacable general favored hanging Confederates found not wearing uniform.

What about fighting at home? Throughout the war, Confederate authorities in Richmond were regaled with stories of thousands of eager young men in California yearning to take up arms for the South. Whether there was any truth to these claims we can never know. What we can say is that, after an initial rush by enthusiasts to go east and fight, few Southerners in California took direct action for the Confederacy.

It was not that conditions for guerrilla warfare in California were lacking. In 1860, Breckinridge voters composed 28 percent of the state's electorate and constituted a majority in a number of localities—most notably in the Southern Mines and Los Angeles County. Any Rebel partisan force raised in those areas could count on local civilian support, as Colonel John Mosby famously did in the northernmost counties of Virginia. But there was an essential difference between Mosby's situation and that of potential Rebels in California: Mosby's men (or Quantrill's or Morgan's, for that matter) could take refuge in times of need in nearby areas under Confederate military control. There they could tend their wounded, give their healthy soldiers a rest and resupply themselves with vital munitions. By contrast, men undertaking to fight Union troops in the Golden State would have no secure safe zone. And after the fall of 1861, they would face large numbers of well-trained, highly motivated, physically robust California Volunteers. It was a daunting military challenge, and few undertook it. For the most part, Confederate sympathizers in the Golden State contented themselves with railing against the iniquitous Yankees—even as they got on with their mining or farming.

There were exceptions. Partisan bands did form—most notably in the rugged Santa Cruz Mountains—and they did carry out actions. But the first and most dramatic attempt to strike a blow for the South in California did not take place on land at all. Instead, it was a bold—some historians say wildly reckless—attempt to sail a ninety-ton privateer schooner, the *J.M. Chapman*, from San Francisco Bay.[42] The *Chapman*'s intended quarry were the Pacific Mail Steamships that plied the route from San Francisco to New York, carrying California's seemingly endless supply of gold back east.[43]

The conspirators' means of attack was well chosen. Southern commerce raiders—armed merchant ships under Confederate navy command—caused massive damage to the Northern merchant marine during the war. The *Chapman* was smaller than the typical Southern raider, but it was fast and nimble and, when properly armed, could deliver enough punch to send an unarmed merchantman to the bottom. This, of course, was not the objective, but the threat was necessary to make a potential prize stand to. Then, the *Chapman*'s numerous crew would swarm aboard, armed to the teeth, and seize control of the steamer and its cargo.

The conspirators' target was equally well chosen. As the war widened and deepened, the financial burden of sustaining the conflict drove leaders on both sides to despair. Purchasing arms, medicines and munitions on the international market required ample credit, and credit, in turn, depended on possessing hard currency reserves, which in those days meant gold.

The Confederacy's natural source of hard currency was its cotton crop, which could be easily converted into gold in England or France, where hungry fabric mills depended on Southern cotton. But the Union naval blockade, set in place at the very start of the conflict, kept most of the South's cotton rotting in warehouses throughout the war.[44]

The North, on the other hand, was blessed with one of the greatest sources of gold on the planet, namely the mines of California. General

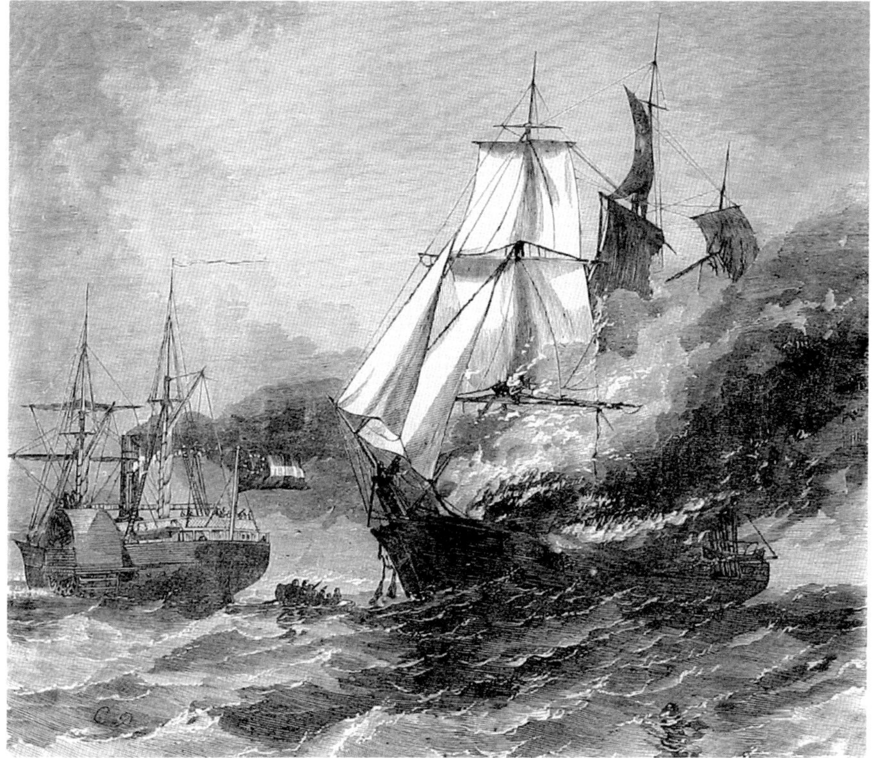

CSS *Nashville* burning a Northern merchant ship. *U.S. Naval Historical Center Photograph, Photo #NH 59350.*

Individual Confederate commerce raiders inflicted devastating losses on the Union merchant marine during the war, but their numbers were never great enough to affect the strategic balance.

Grant himself summed up the importance of this asset when he wrote, "I do not know what we should do in this great national emergency were it not for the gold sent from California."[45]

Since gold shipments were critical to the Northern war effort, stopping that gold ranked high in Southern war aims. Confederate hopes of seizing California's treasure by land faded with the retreat of General Sibley's men back into Texas. The next best thing, in the eyes of the *Chapman* conspirators, was to seize the gold at sea.

The three ringleaders of the plot were Ridgley Greathouse, Asbury Harpending and Alfred Rubery. The first two were wealthy young Kentuckians who had come to California in search of adventure and riches. The last was an Englishman who traveled around the United States and

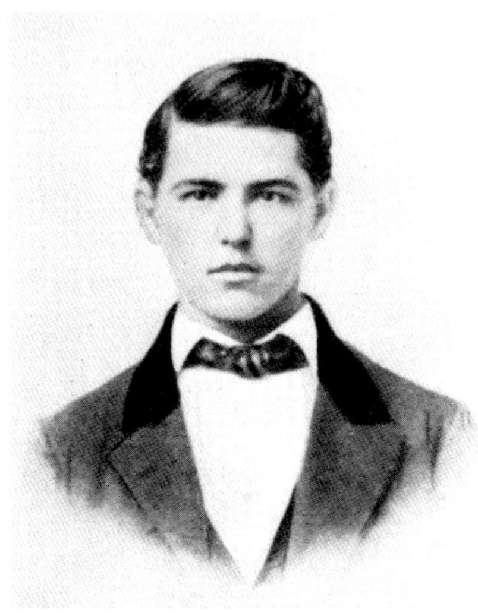

At age fifteen, Harpending ran off to join a proslavery revolution in Nicaragua. Thwarted by U.S. authorities, he headed west to California's gold fields—and to his destiny as a Confederate conspirator. *From* The Great Diamond Hoax, *James H. Wilkins, 1913.*

became enamored of the Southern planter aristocracy.[46] Most of what we know about the inner workings of the plot comes from Harpending's memoirs, which are wonderfully well written and entertaining but need to be approached with a certain degree of care.[47]

The basic idea was to buy and provision a suitable craft, load it with committed Southern fighting men and sail it down to the island of Guadalupe, off Baja California. There, the vessel would be fitted out as a privateer and then sailed on to Manzanillo, to lie in wait for the next Pacific Mail Steamship. That ship, when taken, would then be converted into an additional armed raider and turned against its sister ships of the Pacific Mail. There were further plans from there, but they diverge with ever-increasing speed from the plausible.

Oddly enough, the plan proceeded fairly well. In early 1862, Harpending (the instigator of the plot) steamed down to Acapulco and crossed Mexico to Vera Cruz—a highly dangerous passage, since Mexico was on the verge of civil war and always subject to wholesale brigandage. Harpending recounts that he then sailed on a blockade runner north to Charleston and journeyed overland to Richmond, where he obtained a letter of marque and a captain's commission in the Confederate navy from Jefferson Davis.[48] Harpending needed these documents to avoid being hanged as a pirate in the event of capture.

In late 1862, the conspirators began looking in earnest for a vessel. Their search ended in February 1863, when they discovered the *J.M. Chapman* for sale. Events moved swiftly from there. Two rifled, twelve-pounder brass cannons were smuggled on board in crates labeled "machinery," along with a generous supply of firearms and cutlasses.[49] Fifteen fighting men, the essential ingredient of a privateer, had been enlisted, probably through the offices of a nearby "castle" of the Knights of the Golden Circle, a secret Secessionist organization with branches throughout the state.[50] These men came aboard on the evening of March 14, 1863, and hid themselves below decks.

All that remained was the arrival of the navigator, William Law, whose pro-Southern sympathies and extensive knowledge of Mexican waters led the conspirators to hire him for the cruise. Hours passed, and Law's continued absence became more and more ominous in the minds of the plotters. Harpending later described their dilemma: "The suggestion of treachery could not be avoided. We cast loose from the wharf and anchored in the stream. But we were helpless. We could not sail without our navigator. We had nothing to do but wait."

Morning came, accompanied by two boats of sailors and marines from the U.S. warship *Cyane* and a tugboat full of San Francisco policemen. The *Chapman* was boarded and searched, but not before Rubery and Harpending had a chance to burn and eat sheaves of incriminating papers in the cabin. What they failed to destroy was damning enough, however, and worse was to come in the form of testimony by William Law, the navigator, who had developed cold feet and given the conspirators away to authorities.[51]

Harpending, Greathouse and Rubery were all convicted and sentenced to ten years in jail and fined $10,000. A general amnesty issued by Lincoln freed Harpending and Greathouse after some months in jail. President Lincoln directly pardoned Rubery as a favor to his uncle, John Bright, a British statesman whose devoted advocacy of the Union before Parliament more than merited the release of a wayward nephew.

Captain Ingram's Partisan Rangers

Southern attempts to seize Union gold had better luck by land. Stagecoach robbery in California's Mother Lode country had developed into a thriving trade by the 1860s; it was only natural for underfunded Southern partisans to try their hand at it.

It is difficult, at this remove, to distinguish genuine partisan activity from garden-variety stickups. Indeed, the distinction may not have been entirely clear in the minds of the participants. But the spectacular Bullion Bend Robbery of June 30, 1864, offers an example of stagecoach robbery that was clearly undertaken to further Confederate war aims. The robbery took place near Placerville, a small town in the Sierra Gold Country, but its origins lay farther west.

Santa Clara County, at the base of the San Francisco peninsula, was home to a large number of Secessionists, including an active "castle" of the Knights of the Golden Circle. These men began training themselves as partisan rangers in remote hideaways in the rugged Santa Cruz Mountains. Whether or not they would have progressed to overt action on their own is uncertain, but the arrival of an experienced Confederate partisan officer in their midst in 1864 changed the group's tone dramatically.

The officer in question was Rufus Henry Ingram, who earned the sobriquet of the "Red Fox" in the vicious guerrilla warfare that plagued Missouri and Kansas throughout the war. In August 1863, Ingram was among the Rebel partisans who rode with William Quantrill on the infamous raid on Lawrence, Kansas. After four hours of merciless butchery, the partisans left almost all the town's male population dead and the commercial district in ashes.

After the Lawrence raid, Ingram fled to Mexico, where he encountered a young farmer named George Baker, who was traveling east to volunteer his services to the Confederacy. Baker told Ingram of partisans back in California who lacked only trained leadership to get their fighting underway. Ingram decided to head west, accompanied by Baker, to try his hand at stirring up rebellion in California. The pair joined up with partisans in the

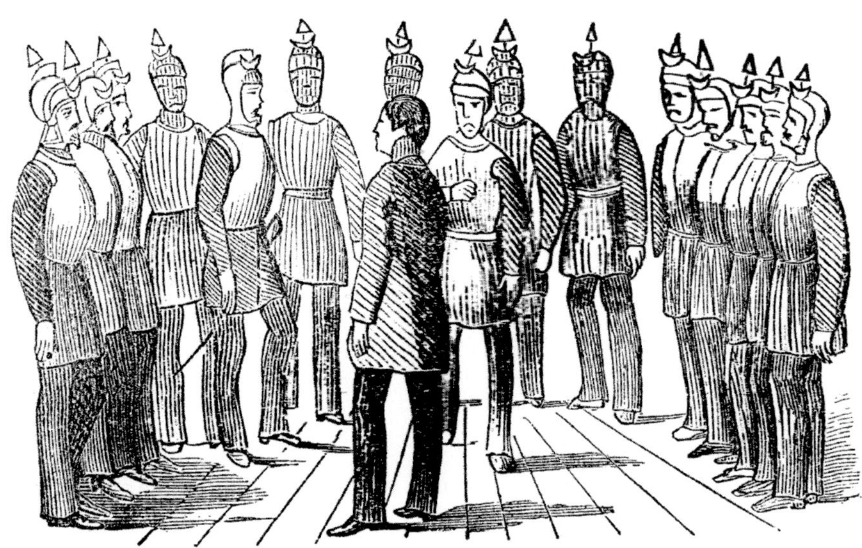

The hidden core of rebellion in California was the Knights of the Golden Circle, a secret society formed to support Southern ideals and expansionism. *From* An Authentic Exposition of the K.G.C.—Knights of the Golden Circle, *C.O. Perrine, publisher (1861).*

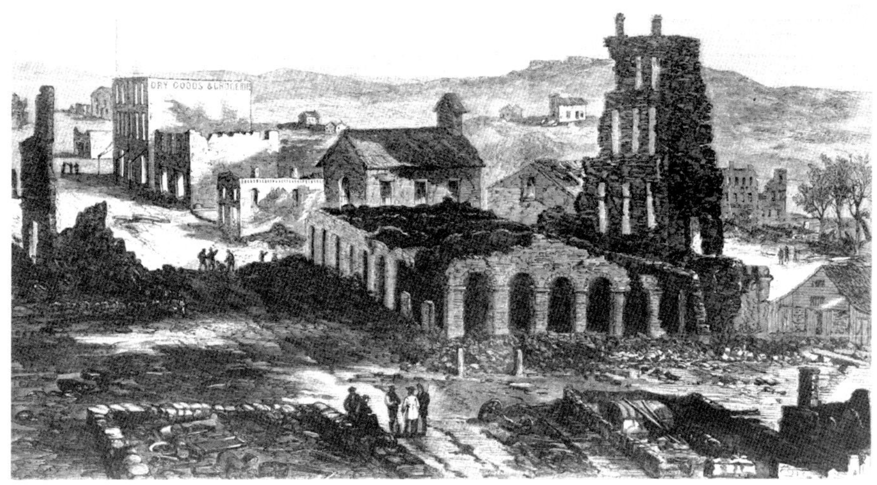

Lawrence, Kansas, after Quantrill's Raid. Ingram's partisans planned a similar raid on San José. Banks and stores were the main objectives. *Library of Congress.*

Santa Cruz Mountains in the early spring of 1864. Ingram presented his commission and assumed leadership of the group, who dubbed themselves Captain Ingram's Partisan Rangers.

The Rangers' goal was to head back east to fight, but this required money for arms and transport. Naturally, their thoughts turned to stagecoach robbery, and they sent men to scope out the stage route from Virginia City to Sacramento, which was known to carry large shipments of silver and gold from the Comstock Lode. Loose talk by one of the scouts caused the mission to be aborted, so the partisans set about planning a Lawrence-style raid on nearby San José, whose banks and stores could provide the needed funds. Here, too, the partisans were stymied—in this case by alert lawmen who got wind of their plans.

The Rangers' thoughts turned back again to those heavily laden stagecoaches, and this time they succeeded. On the night of June 30, 1864, Ingram and five of his Rangers held up a Pioneer Line stagecoach outside Placerville. Then, to their surprise, a second stage rolled up in the darkness. The driver, assuming the first stage was experiencing mechanical problems, stopped his team, got down, approached and inquired if he could be of assistance. He was at once assured by Ingram and his men that he could.

Estimates of the haul vary (as they usually do in these affairs), but all sources agree that the take was spectacular—something between $26,500 and $52,000 in silver and gold (the equivalent of roughly $750,000 to $1,500,000 today). The other striking feature of the heist was the punctiliousness of the chief highwayman, who offered his victims a blank receipt, to be filled in at their leisure:

> *June, 1864.*
> *This is to certify that I have received from Wells Fargo & Co. the sum of $______ cash, for the purpose of outfitting recruits in California for the Confederate States Army.*
> *R. Henry Ingram, Captain, Commanding Co., C.S.A.*

The considerably lightened coaches reached Placerville after midnight, and the El Dorado County sheriff immediately sent out teams of deputies to hunt for the robbers. A party of three deputies found Ingram's trail and followed him to a boardinghouse, where the tired partisans had decided to put up for the night.

One of the deputies turned back to inform the sheriff of the robbers' whereabouts. The other two rode up to the boardinghouse and asked the proprietress if she had seen any strangers about. The woman nodded in the affirmative and pointed to the side door of her establishment. One deputy, George Ranney, strode through the door, only to find himself surrounded by Ingram and his men, who promptly reached for their guns. Ranney, sizing up the situation with commendable coolness, inquired politely if the gentlemen had noticed any horsemen passing that way during the night. The gentlemen, it turned out, had not.

Ranney smiled and walked back out the door. On the porch, he met his companion, Deputy Joseph Staples, and warned him about the gunmen inside. Staples pushed past Ranney and entered the room with his shotgun leveled. Ingram raised his hand in surrender, but two of his men opened up on Staples with six-shooters. Staples got off one round from his shotgun, badly wounding one of the partisans, and then collapsed, mortally wounded. The remaining partisans sprang out of the room and gunned down Ranney, whom they left for dead. They then fled, leaving their injured companion behind.

The wounded Rebel turned out to be Tom Poole, a former Monterey County sheriff's deputy of ardently Secessionist conviction. Poole had volunteered earlier for service on board the *J.M. Chapman* and had been arrested along with the other participants in that ill-fated venture. After a short stretch in custody, Poole had taken an oath of loyalty to the Union and been released. This must have counted against him when he was tried in August for the murder of Deputy Staples. Even though Poole had not fired his weapon at Staples (being preoccupied, at the moment, with a load of buckshot in his face), he was nonetheless convicted of murder and sentenced to hang. Appeals and legal maneuvers stretched out the execution date. Poole was an affable man who engaged the sympathy of his jailers. In the end, sheriffs from three counties wrote to the governor, begging mercy for Poole—but to no avail. In October 1865, six months after Lee's surrender, Poole was hanged.

Most of the other conspirators also paid a heavy price. After hiding out in their Santa Cruz mountain fastness for two weeks, Ingram and the remaining Partisan Rangers moved out again, this time to rob a stage carrying the New Almaden quicksilver mine's payroll. While staying at a farmhouse near the planned holdup site, the men's loose talk betrayed their intentions to their host, who dispatched a neighbor to alert the authorities in nearby San José. Sheriff John Hicks Adams rode out with a posse and surrounded the small house where the Rangers were staying. Adams approached the front door and called on the partisans to surrender. They replied by charging out of the house, guns blazing. Two Rangers were killed outright and one wounded. But Ingram and Baker, the two men who had met in Mexico and started it all, escaped and made their way back to Missouri.

One of Adams's men was wounded. The sheriff himself escaped serious injury when a bullet struck him in the chest—only to be deflected by the heavy gold watch he was wearing.

The idea of robbing stagecoaches for the Confederacy did not disappear with the passing of Ingram's Rangers. A new crop of self-proclaimed partisans, the Mason-Henry gang, sprang up in the Santa Cruz Mountains, but their tale belongs more properly to the history of law enforcement in California. The Mason-Henry gang never had any intention of sharing their proceeds with the Confederacy. They did succeed in murdering a few civilians of Unionist persuasion, but they never undertook any action that benefited the Southern cause.

Chapter 13

WITH CONNOR IN UTAH

The California Column's push into the Southwest was the most extensive and most strategically important campaign conducted by California Volunteers during the war—but it was far from the only one. At the same time that Colonel Carleton was assembling his men in Southern California, another regiment, the Third California Volunteer Infantry, was taking shape in Stockton, the bustling port city on the San Joaquin River that served as transportation hub for the gold mining communities of the Sierra foothills to the east.

The Third California Infantry formed in September 1861 under the leadership of Colonel Patrick Edward Connor. Connor was born in 1820 in County Kerry, Ireland, and immigrated to New York as a youth. He joined the First Dragoons in 1839 and served for five years as a private, first at Fort Leavenworth in Kansas and then in the Iowa Territory (both of which were frontier postings at the time). When his enlistment expired, Connor returned to New York and civilian life, but not for long. The looming war with Mexico drew him southward. In 1846, he enlisted in the Texas Volunteers and then transferred to the U.S. Army as a lieutenant when the war began in earnest. Connor won promotion to captain and fought with distinction at the Battle of Buena Vista, where he was wounded in the hand. When peace came, he resigned his commission and—like so many other veterans—headed to California to find his fortune.

His life as a civilian in California was no less eventful. He served as a lieutenant in the militia that hunted down and killed Joaquin Murrieta, the

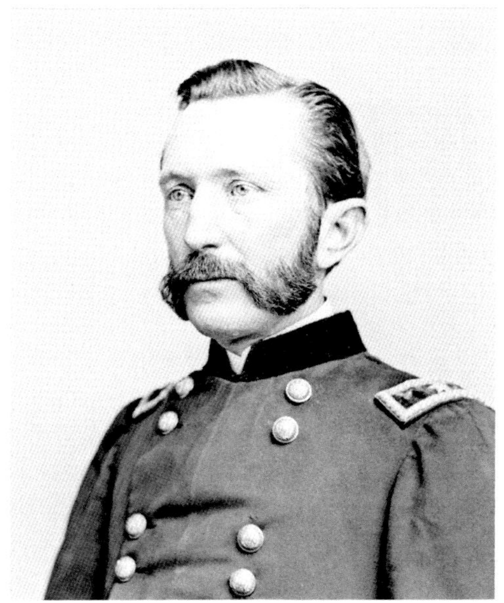

Connor's resemblance to the affable crooner Bing Crosby is entirely misleading. Connor was an exceptionally gifted but merciless officer who presided over one of the worst Indian massacres in U.S. history. *Library of Congress.*

notorious Sonoran bandit (or Mexican resistance leader in some versions of the story). Connor kept up his connection with the military and was an officer in the Stockton Blues, a militia unit that broke up during the Secession crisis due to the varying political loyalties of its members.

Connor's commitment to the Union was never in doubt. He helped form the Third California Infantry from Unionist members of the Blues, and he was colonel of the new regiment when it was ordered to the Utah Territory to guard the critical Central Overland Mail route from Indian attack. A less publicized assignment given to Connor and his men was to keep a sharp eye on the Mormons, whose loyalty to the United States was very much in doubt.[52]

Protecting the mail and watching Mormons was not what Connor and his men signed up for. They wanted to fight Rebels, and they lobbied vigorously to go east and do just that. At one point, Connor offered the War Department $30,000 from the regiment's payroll to defray the costs of sending the Third back east. The offer was declined. The reality was that California troops were urgently needed in the West, where they replaced the entire prewar army of the United States. (This occurred despite California's relatively small population, which ranked twenty-sixth out of thirty-four states at the start of the war.)

Connor and seven companies of the Third California Infantry set off for Utah in July 1862.[53] Mormon leaders weren't particularly glad to see them.

Brigham Young and his associates had already offered to guard the U.S. mail route with their own troops, and they saw no reason why they needed a regiment of Californians to help with the job. Mormon suspicions were heightened when Connor chose to build his new home for the Third, Fort Douglas, on a site immediately overlooking Salt Lake City.

The Mormons were right to be worried. Connor's feelings about the faith were clearly expressed in a report to his superiors at the Pacific command, dated September 14, 1862:

> *It will be impossible for me to describe what I saw and heard in Salt Lake, so as to make you realize the enormity of Mormonism; suffice it, that I found them a community of traitors, murderers, fanatics, and whores. The people publicly rejoice at reverses to our arms, and thank God that the American Government is gone, as they term it, while their prophet and bishops preach treason from the pulpit. The Federal officers* [i.e., the civilian governor and other officials sent out from Washington] *are entirely powerless, and talk in whispers, for fear of being overheard by Brigham's spies. Brigham Young rules with despotic sway, and death by assassination is the penalty of disobedience to his commands.*[54]

In his report, Connor was completely open about why he wanted to position the Third's new home where he did: the regiment could seize Salt Lake City in a matter of hours. The Pacific command made no objection.

Connor's posting to Salt Lake made him the ranking U.S. officer in a vast swath of the West, and his duties were many.[55] In addition to watching the mails and the Mormons, it was his responsibility to protect settlers from attacks by hostile Indians, a practice that had picked up considerably across the West after regular U.S. troops were withdrawn in 1861 to cope with the rebellion.

The tribe of greatest concern to Connor and the Third were the Shoshone, who lived across substantial portions of the present-day states of Nevada, Utah, Idaho and Wyoming. Four to seven main bands are cited by modern writers, with the bands acting in concert or independently as occasion required.[56] The Northwestern Shoshone lived in closest proximity to the Mormon settlers and enjoyed an unusual relationship with the church. Mormon belief held that America's native peoples were in fact "Lamanites," one of the lost tribes of Israel, who should be cultivated for conversion back to their "original" faith. On a more earthly level,

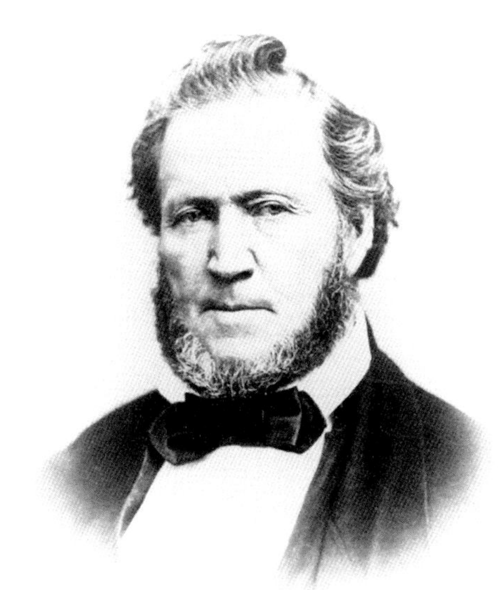

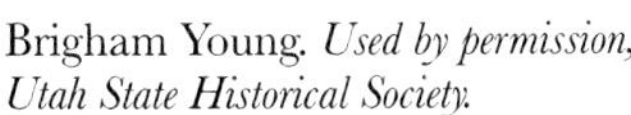

Brigham Young. *Used by permission, Utah State Historical Society.*

Connor and Young disliked and distrusted each other. In the end, however, both realized that fighting between their followers would be foolish. Connor maintained rigid control over his men to forestall potential conflict with local civilians.

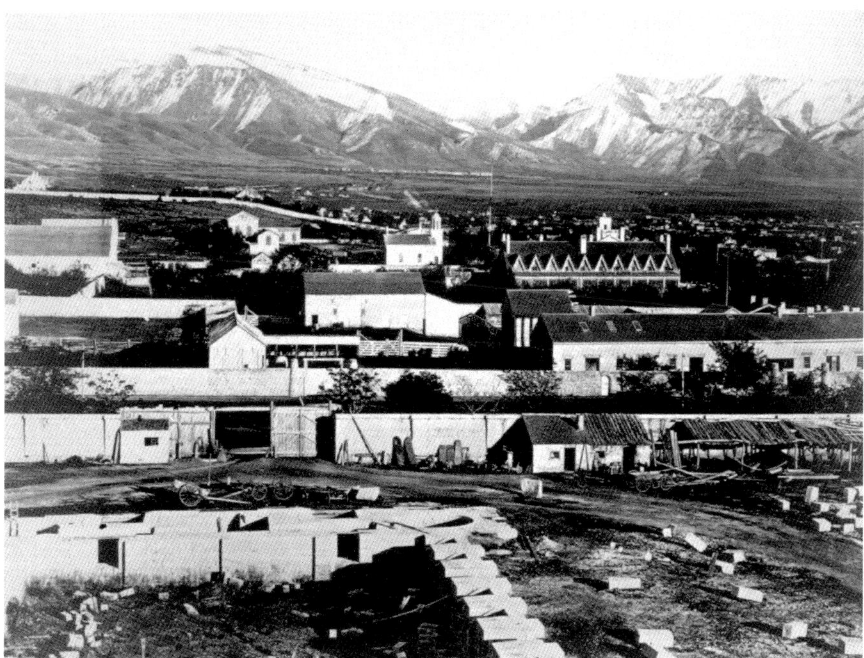

Salt Lake City from the top of the Tabernacle (1868). *Library of Congress.*

Brigham Young's house is the many-gabled structure in the mid-ground. Camp Douglas is visible at the base of the mountains in the distance. Connor's siting of the camp was meant to send a message to the Mormon leadership.

Brigham Young determined very early that it was "better and cheaper to feed and clothe the Indians, than to fight them" and followed his own advice whenever possible.[57]

Nevertheless, Mormon relations with their Shoshone neighbors were tense and sometimes violent. As Mormon numbers kept growing, farmers and ranchers pushed out from early settlements and began to appropriate resources the Shoshone people counted on for survival. Mormon farmers rounded out their diets with the same game animals the Shoshone hunted; the cows of Mormon ranchers ate and trampled the grass whose seed was an essential food source for the Indians. Unsurprisingly, cattle rustling came to be seen by some Shoshone as a reasonable way of collecting rent for the land and resources expropriated by their white neighbors.

With the arrival of the troops from California, the politics of the Utah District devolved into a three-way struggle among the Mormons, the Shoshone and the Federal government, as represented by Colonel Connor. Relations among these groups were bad and trust hard to come by. But for pure, murderous violence, the interaction between the army and the Indians was in a league of its own.

The trouble started early—even before the Third reached Salt Lake City—when Connor received word of the massacre of a wagon train at Gravelly Ford on the Humboldt River in central Nevada. He detached a force under Major Edward F. McGarry to find the Indians responsible and then "immediately hang them, and leave their bodies thus exposed as an example of what evildoers might expect while I command this district." Connor also authorized McGarry to "destroy every male Indian you find whom you may encounter in the vicinity of the late massacres."[58]

McGarry followed his instructions to the letter—or at least tried to. (The absence of trees of sufficient height and strength led him to shoot the Shoshone men he captured, rather than hang them.) Three sets of captives were taken. Most of them were gunned down "attempt[ing] to escape." Two men were released from the last batch of captives so they could arrange for the surrender of the perpetrators of the Gravelly Ford massacre. Since the men did not return within the prescribed time limit (i.e., later that evening), the remaining hostages were shot.[59]

Connor thus made clear his message to potential "evildoers," right from the start. In the event of attacks on whites, any Indians discovered in the area would be killed, with no attempt made to distinguish innocent from guilty. The Shoshone responded by looting wagon trains and stealing livestock. Then, in early January 1863, Shoshone warriors fell

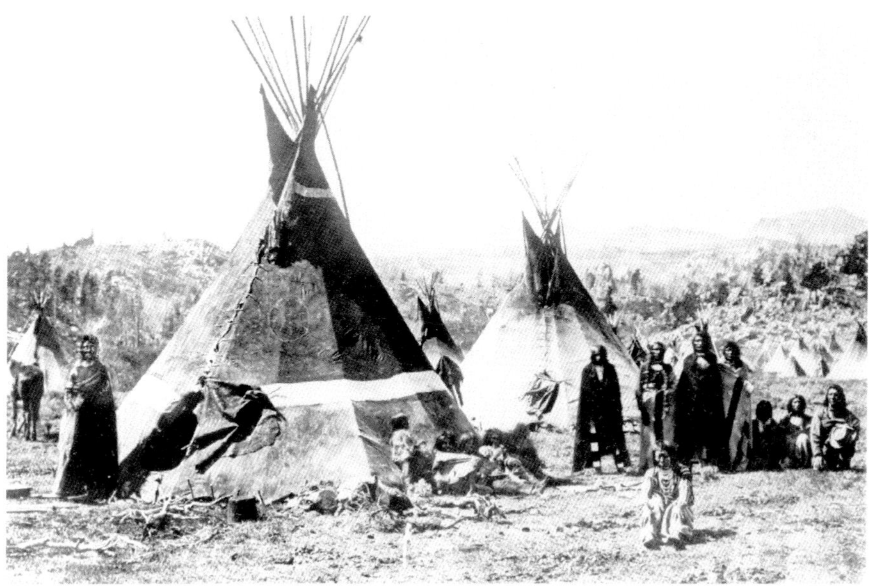

The Shoshone were a semi-nomadic people whose homeland lay squarely across the main route of white settlers traveling to the Pacific coast. Something like 400,000 immigrants passed through Shoshone lands before the Civil War, with devastating impact on game and grasslands. The most severely affected bands were reduced to near-starvation. *Library of Congress.*

upon a party of eight miners traveling through the Cache Valley. The Indians "robbed their [the miners'] wagons, drove off their stock, and behaved very discourteously to the…men." The next day, by way of an afterthought, the Indians set upon the miners again, firing at them from across a river and killing one of the party.

The surviving miners proceeded to Salt Lake City, where a judge—not knowing the names of the Indians involved—issued a warrant for the arrest of three headmen of the Shoshone bands known to be in the area. A territorial marshal took the warrant to Third Infantry headquarters at Camp Douglas and asked for Connor's help in serving it. As it happened, Connor was already well advanced in preparations for an expedition against the Shoshone. The marshal was welcome to come along with his warrant, but he must do so without expectation of bringing any Indians back, since the colonel did not intend to take prisoners.

The Battle of Bear River

Connor knew that relations between the Mormons and the Shoshone were tense, but he also knew that individual Mormons were friendly with the tribe and might warn them of any punitive action contemplated by the soldiers. To forestall possible breaches of security, Connor marched a small force of infantry out of Fort Douglas on January 22, after putting out a cover story that they were on their way to escort a grain shipment in the Cache Valley, which lies to the northeast of Salt Lake City. Traveling with the infantry were fifteen supply wagons, laden with food and munitions—including a pair of disassembled howitzers and one hundred shells. Rumors that the foot soldiers were on a punitive expedition against the Shoshone surfaced in the press, but the size of the force (seventy men) did not present a credible threat to the Indians, who were gathered in large numbers for a Warm Dance (a mid-winter festival meant to hasten the arrival of spring). The celebration was held at the mouth of Beaver Creek, where it joined the Bear River, and had drawn together a number of bands, with more than enough warriors to resist a company of infantry. If word of the troops' presence reached the Indians, Connor's sortie would appear to be an exercise aimed at "showing the flag" along the border of Shoshone country.

Two days after the infantry left, Connor himself set out at night with the business end of the strike force: four companies of troopers from the Second California Volunteer Cavalry, some 220 men in all. The brutal pace Connor set pressed man and horse to the limits. The column covered sixty-eight miles in their first night out, riding straight into a howling north wind that covered the trail with a foot of snow.[60] Standard-issue cold-weather gear wouldn't come into play for the cavalry for another generation; the California Volunteers of 1863 made do by wrapping themselves in extra blankets.

Faces and ears went numb almost at once. Hands and toes soon followed. Once numb, the heavily swathed riders had little chance to check for frostbite, which is detected by visual inspection. Troopers looking for solace from their whiskey-filled canteens found them frozen solid.[61]

Men and animals who broke down were left at Mormon farms along the way. The appalling human cost of the march did not become clear until the column stopped the next day for rest near Brigham City. By the time the last frostbite welt was tallied, seventy-five men—more than a third of Connor's cavalry—were judged unfit for action and had to be left behind.

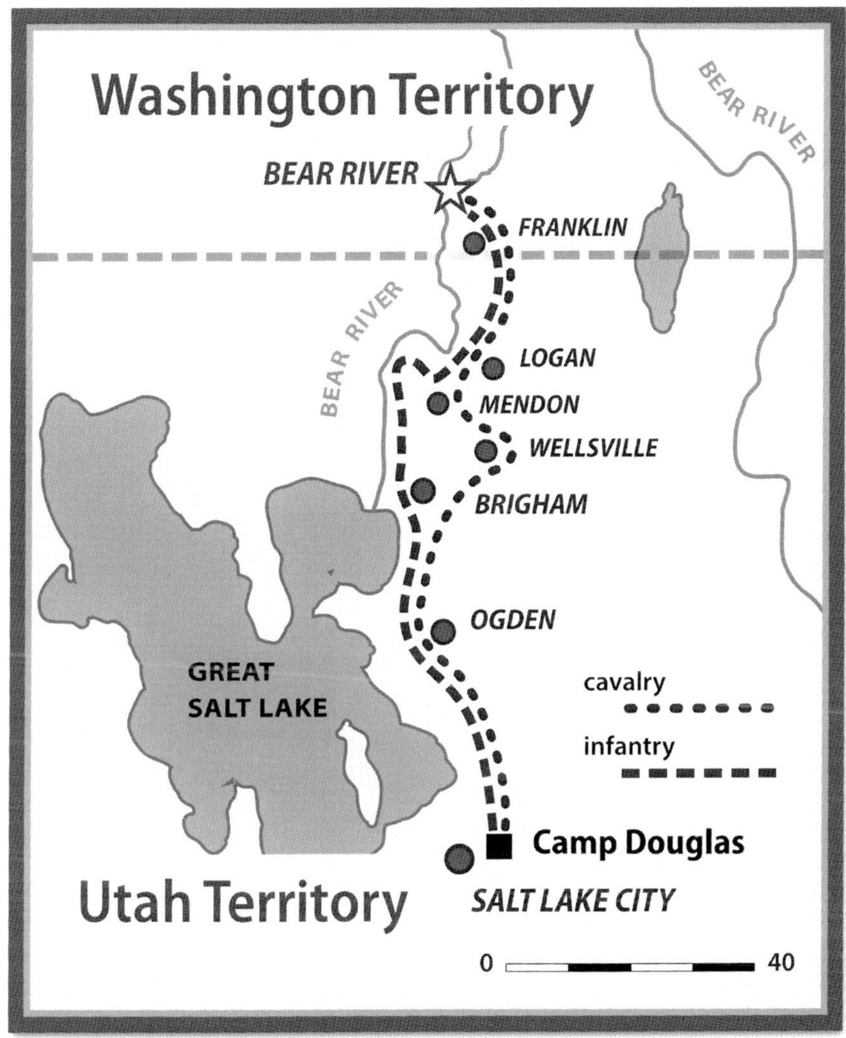

Connor's march to Bear River. *Map by the author.*

Connor's infantry marched seven days to reach their destination. His cavalry, moving secretly by night, took four. The deception worked. The Shoshone had no idea of the weight of the hammer that was about to fall on them.

The second stage of the troopers' journey, also undertaken at night, was shorter but even more challenging in terms of terrain. The weary column pushed over into the Cache Valley through four-foot snowdrifts to join the infantry near Mendon. After the rendezvous, Connor sent his infantry on to

Franklin, the northernmost Mormon settlement, where they were spotted by three Shoshone men who had come into town to pick up a grain shipment. The Indians hastened away to inform their people of the soldiers' arrival, but the consensus at the Bear River camp was that the foot soldiers were too few to constitute a threat.

Other Shoshone felt a deep sense of unease. Word had already reached the tribe through a friendly Mormon that the soldiers were out to crush the Indians. Pocatello, chief of a peripatetic band who was present at the Warm Dance, had taken the warning seriously and decamped the day before, taking his people with him.

Connor's cavalry followed the infantry toward Franklin at a discreet distance and halted twelve miles out of town, where they waited out the remaining daylight hours. They then advanced and rode into Franklin a little after midnight.

Connor's plan hit a snag at this point, when he failed to find locals willing to guide him to a critical ford on the approach to the Shoshone village. A pair of brothers was finally pressed into service, but the delay upset Connor's plans to advance his cavalry and infantry together. Fearing that the Indians would get away, Connor ordered his cavalry forward under Major McGarry.

McGarry's men drew near the village at first light. The final approach to the battlefield required the California troopers to ford fifty yards of the strongly flowing Bear River through broken ice that covered their boots. The horses balked, and two troopers went down for a total immersion in ice water.

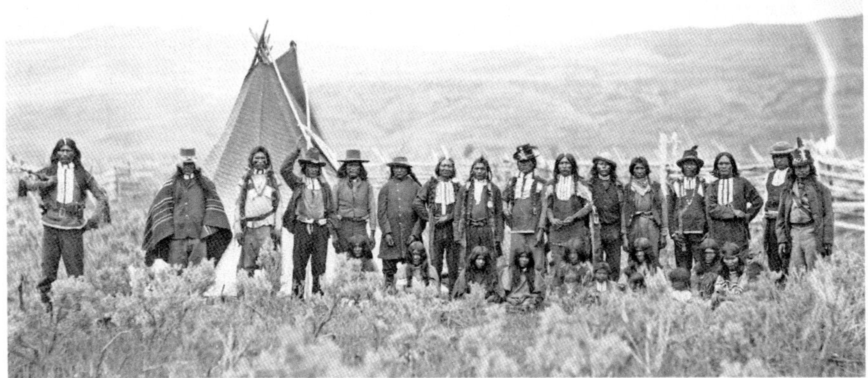

Tribal history maintains that the warriors who attacked the miners in the Cache Valley were from Pocatello's band (shown here), who left the Bear River encampment the day before Connor's attack. *Princeton University Library. Department of Rare Books and Special Collections, (WA) WC064, S1552.*

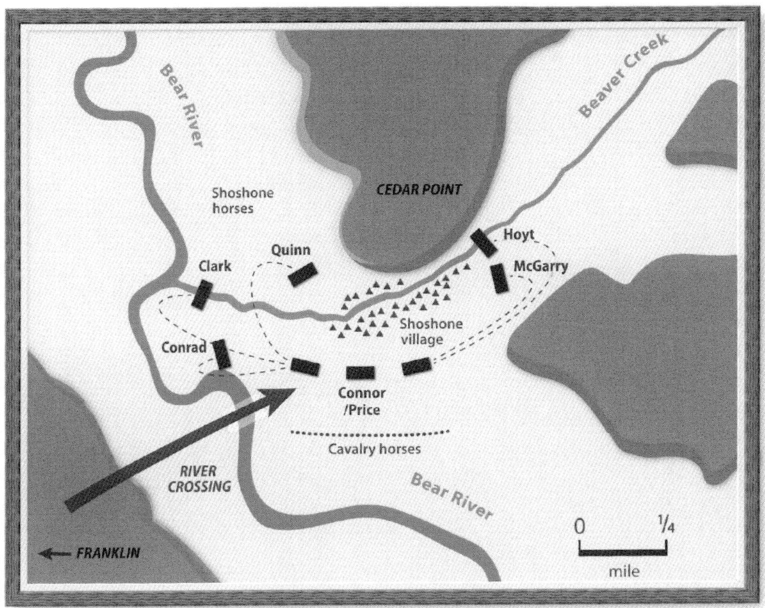

After a futile frontal assault, Connor sent men to both flanks of the Shoshone position. This ringed the Indians' defensive works and blocked off escape routes. Once the Shoshone ran low on ammunition, the warriors were doomed. Not shown in this map is the willow thicket that screened the Shoshone village. *Map data after Masden,* The Shoshoni Frontier and the Bear River Massacre, *p. 184. Map by the author.*

Meanwhile, the soldiers had been spotted from the Shoshone camp. Warriors seized their weapons and deployed in defensive positions. What happened next varies from account to account. Bear Hunter, chief of the encamped Indians, is said by most sources to have advanced to the river bottom and waved his buffalo robe at the soldiers, yelling, "Come on, you California sons of bitches! We're ready for you!"

If this was a taunt to provoke the Californians into a charge, it worked (though one newspaper account attributed the swift attack to the bitter cold, which made inactivity unbearable). Without artillery, without Connor and the infantry, McGarry ordered his men forward. As the troopers grew close to effective range, McGarry ordered his men to dismount. One man in four held the reins of the cavalry horses. The rest advanced.

The Shoshone made their stand near the mouth of the Beaver Creek ravine. Protected by bluffs on both flanks and screened by willow trees, the Indians waited until the soldiers were within range and then opened up a

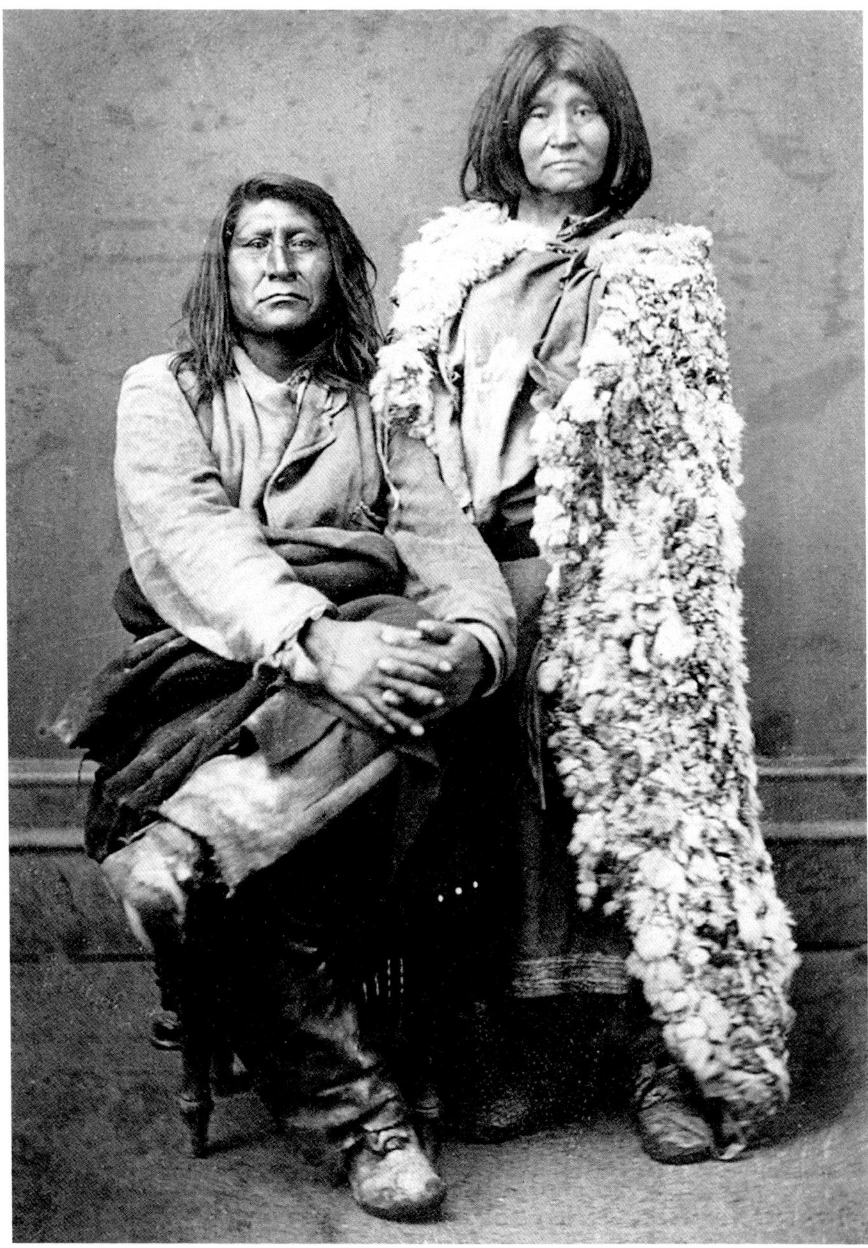

Sagwitch was the first Shoshone to spot the approaching troopers. He had two horses shot out from under him and was wounded in the hand. He escaped at the end of the fight by riding a horse across the Bear River. The woman standing next to him, Bia-Wu-Utsee, was Bear Hunter's wife at the time of the massacre. She married Sagwitch after her first husband was killed by Connor's soldiers. *Courtesy Church History Collections, the Church of Jesus Christ of Latter-day Saints.*

devastating fire from their concealed positions. Troopers dropped. Around twenty men fell dead or wounded in the opening volleys.

Connor arrived at this point, with the infantry close behind. Seeing the futility of approaching the Shoshone across open bottomland, Connor ordered flanking movements against both wings of the Indian defensive line. The soldiers worked their way up the faces of the bluffs on both sides of the village and then began to move side-hill, closing in on their opponents and laying down a deadly enfilading fire. The tide of battle turned as the Shoshone found themselves running short of ammunition. Their well-sited defense turned into a death trap as California troops pressed forward along the slopes and began firing down on the village from the sides and rear. A modern member of the tribe describes the scene: "Arrows and tomahawks did little against the rifles and side arms of the soldiers. The Shoshone men, women, children and babies were being slaughtered like rabbits, butchered by Colonel Connor and his troops."[62]

The Californians fought their way into the camp, and the killing went on and on. Cries for mercy went unheeded. Shoshone warriors battled with whatever weapons remained to them and succumbed only after being repeatedly wounded.

With the village overrun and retreat up Beaver Creek cut off, the only chance of escape lay in the freezing waters of the Bear River in front of the camp. Fleeing Shoshone were shot as they broke for the water or floated downstream. Tribal accounts and Mormon witnesses paint a terrible picture of rape and murder in the village after the battle.

When the killing finally stopped, the troopers removed everything of value from the village and burned the rest. Connor's account states that he left "a small quantity of wheat" for the surviving women and children. Shoshone tribal accounts say nothing was left behind.

The Reckoning

Connor's men paid a high price for their part in the fight. Of the 270 Californians who set out from Camp Douglas, 22 died, either on the field or later; 49 soldiers were wounded; and 79 were incapacitated by frostbite or hypothermia. Accounts of Indian fatalities vary dramatically but probably were between 250 and 350, out of an original camp population of around 500. There are no tallies of the injured, but anecdotal evidence suggests that a high proportion of the survivors were wounded.

Colonel Connor's conduct of the campaign was much praised at the time and earned him a promotion to brigadier general.[63] He was put in command of the newly constituted Department of the Plains (which included his old Department of Utah). In the fall of 1865, Connor led a complex campaign, known as the Powder River Expedition, against the Arapaho, Cheyenne and Sioux in what is now Montana and Wyoming. The plan called for three independent columns, comprising a total of 2,500 men, to invade the Indians' homeland. The orders Connor issued to his commanders became known to the public and stirred controversy even before the campaign was underway: "You will not receive overtures of peace or submission from Indians, but will attack and kill every male Indian over twelve years of age."[64]

Connor's part of the plan was successful, and his own personal heroics won victory in battle, but the other two columns involved in the campaign floundered badly. They were severely harassed, fought largely on the defensive and were reduced to eating their own horses to survive.

The mixed success of the expedition tarnished Connor's star, as did the harsh orders he issued. The earlier (November 1864) slaughter by Colorado militia of peaceful Cheyenne and Arapaho at Sand Creek had raised an outcry that was still reverberating around the country. Indian policy was being hotly debated in Congress and in the press, and demands for a more humane approach were beginning to be heard.

Connor retired from the army in 1866 after receiving an honorary brevet promotion to major general of volunteers. He had long harbored a keen interest in Utah's mineral resources, so he returned to Salt Lake to pursue his mining schemes—and, incidentally, to continue his feud with Brigham Young. Connor remained to the end an unrelenting foe of the Prophet and did whatever he could to break the Mormon hold on the territory.

Patrick Edward Connor died in 1891, after a long, exciting but ultimately unsuccessful career as a mining baron. He was an extraordinarily brave man, a superb leader of men—a natural soldier. The tragedy of his life was that he was not permitted to bring that talent to bear on the foe he wished to fight but ended up squandering it instead on a brutal campaign of dispossession that made no distinction between guilty and innocent.

The California Volunteers he commanded never did get to fight any Confederates. Ironically, many of them found themselves fighting alongside former Rebels who opted to escape prisoner of war camps by enlisting to fight Indians in the West. These "galvanized Yankees" proved highly effective soldiers and formed, along with the Californian cavalrymen, the most dependable units Connor led in his last campaign.[65]

Chapter 14

CALIFORNIANS FIGHT BACK EAST

The men who answered the first call to arms in California did so in the belief that they would soon be defending the state against Rebels, either at home or back east. Many were keenly disappointed when the reality of their situation set in: the War Department was not going to ship California Volunteers across the continent when there was urgent work for them to do in the West. It was no consolation that they were taking over the role of the entire prewar U.S. Army, protecting hundreds of thousands of settlers and securing a desperately exposed transportation network from the depredations of angry native peoples. With the Union itself in mortal danger, it was Rebels these men wanted to fight—not Indians.

Some ardent spirits found the situation intolerable and came up with an ingenious solution. They petitioned Governor John Andrew of Massachusetts to take into his state's service a company of cavalry to be raised and equipped in San Francisco. If Massachusetts would assume the cost of shipping the men back to Boston, they could be counted against the Bay State's recruiting quota. Governor Andrew approved the idea, and neither Wright of the Pacific command nor Henry Halleck, general-in-chief of the Union armies, was in a position to argue with the governor of Massachusetts, whose support was vital to the Lincoln administration. Thus was born the "California Hundred" (subsequently expanded into a full battalion), whose adventures while serving with the Second Massachusetts Cavalry form the most dramatic story of California's Civil War.[66]

The moving spirit of the California Hundred was J. Sewall Reed, a Massachusetts man by birth, who had gone west in 1849 and lived the life of wild outdoor adventure so typical of that pioneer generation. Reed's mining efforts took him up into the Sierra foothills and as far afield as British Columbia; other commercial ventures drew him to Southern California, Mexico and South America. He returned to visit Massachusetts in 1859, met and married a local girl and sailed with her back to San Francisco, determined to settle down and raise a family.

Reed had long been active in California militia companies, in a variety of ranks. When the scheme was hatched to raise a cavalry company for service in the East, Reed was a natural choice to lead the effort. He was commissioned as captain and supervised the selection and training of the men who answered the call. In the first days, five hundred restless, patriotic Californians applied for the job. The Hundred who were chosen were a handpicked force, with outstanding horsemanship their distinguishing characteristic. Forty-two of these idealistic young men also took the "dashaway" pledge, forswearing hard liquor. Just one was married.

The Hundred sailed east via Panama in December 1862 and were enthusiastically received in New York and Boston in early January 1863.

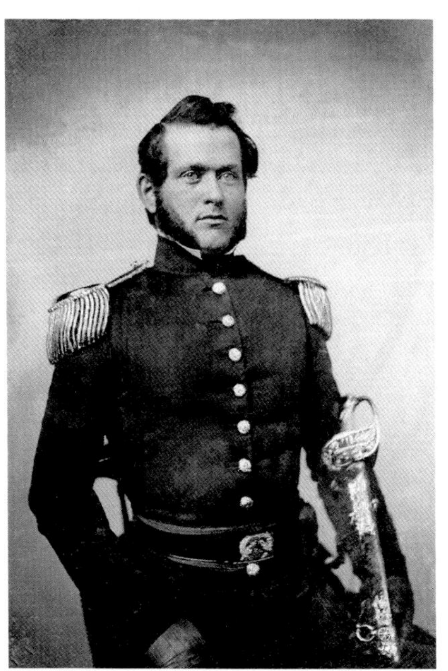

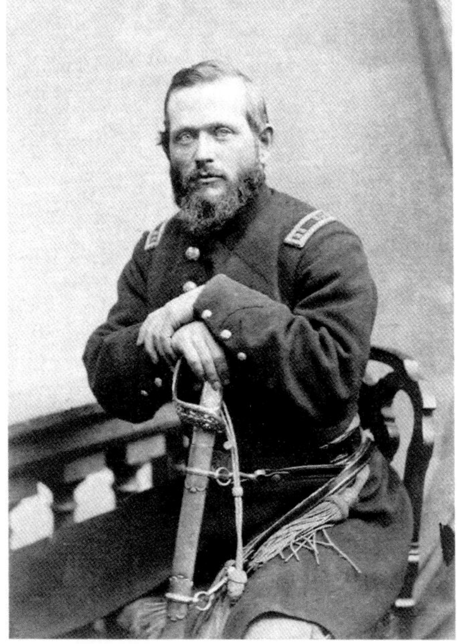

Captain J. Sewall Reed as a California militiaman in 1859 (*left*) and as a serving officer in Virginia in 1863 (*right*). *Michael K. Sorenson Collection.*

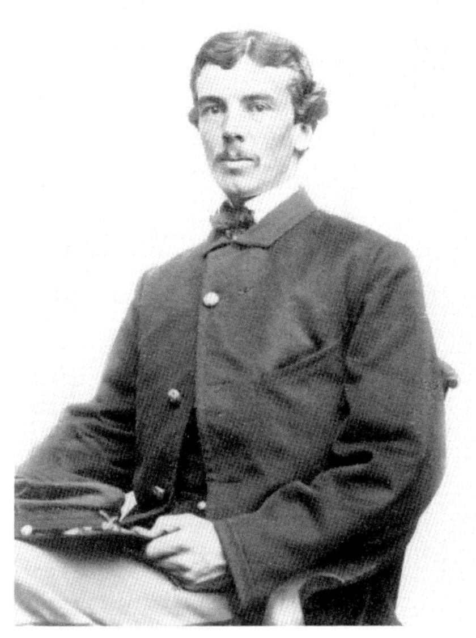

Charles Lowell commanded the Second Massachusetts Cavalry, home to the California troopers who went back east to fight. Lowell was the scion of a prominent Boston family. He was valedictorian of his class at Harvard and afterward pursued a career in metal manufacturing. Signs of tuberculosis forced him to give up his career but did not stop him from enlisting at the start of the war.

Lowell rose on merit and was very much a "lead from the front" officer. In September 1863, he married Josephine Shaw, sister of Colonel Robert Gould Shaw, whose death at the head of the Fifty-Fourth Massachusetts is chronicled in the film *Glory*. *Library of Congress.*

They went by train to Camp Meigs (near Boston), where they formed Company A of the first battalion of the Second Massachusetts Cavalry.[67] Meanwhile, back on the West Coast, four more companies of cavalrymen were raised to go east under the command of Major D.W.C. Thompson, another California militiaman with a long history of service. This second component shipped out for the East a few months after the Hundred, tracing their steps through Panama, New York and Boston to Camp Meigs. There they found that the first battalion had already left for the front. After a brief period of training, the second battalion also headed south to join the rest of the regiment in Virginia.[68]

Many letters from the Californian troopers survive, alongside a steady flow of reports written by a correspondent of the *Alta California* (the state's leading newspaper).[69] The war they describe in the summer of 1863 was one of picketing (guarding key points like river crossings) and patrol (looking for enemy forces), with occasional larger-scale raids against enemy railroads carried out in cooperation with other units. All were dangerous undertakings, since the local people were solidly Secesh and more than happy to relay the location and movement of Union troops to Southern commanders. Ambush was a constant danger; many Californians' first experiences of combat took the form of violent surprise attacks, followed by desperate flight or pursuit on horseback. This was a style of warfare in which the healthy, hard-riding, highly motivated Californians excelled, and their exploits soon began appearing in army reports and press clippings.

The Rebels they faced were fearsome opponents, fighting on home ground with the confidence of Southern cavalry, who were widely held to be superior to their Yankee counterparts at this stage of the war. The employment of skilled California horsemen was, in fact, a conscious effort to offset this Confederate advantage. By contrast, the men who enlisted in Massachusetts were indeed unpromising horse soldiers, a fact that led Colonel James R. Lowell to distribute his California companies throughout his regiment.[70] In the end, Lowell's strategy proved correct. The Second Massachusetts eventually became known as one of the best cavalry units in the Union army.[71]

Toe to Toe with the Gray Ghost

In June 1863, the focus of the regiment's operations shifted from the Tidewater area near the York River to the northernmost counties of Virginia, which border the District of Columbia. Though nominally behind Union lines, this area was also perilous for detached service, since the population was decidedly pro-Secesh in its sympathies. Worse still, these counties were the field of operations of John Singleton Mosby, arguably the most dangerous and effective partisan leader our country has ever produced.

John Mosby was actively pro-Union in the run-up to the war—just a young lawyer with no military experience, whose decision to don gray came as a surprise to his friends and family. He enlisted as a private and fought at Bull Run, the first major battle of the war. His military gifts were unmistakable, and he rose swiftly through the ranks. In January 1863, J.E.B. Stuart, Lee's cavalry commander, authorized Mosby to form an independent command, the Forty-Third Virginia Cavalry Battalion. This unit eventually grew into a feared, regiment-sized force of partisan rangers that kept Northern Virginia in turmoil for the rest of the war.[72]

Mosby's boldness, imagination and speed of decision-making made him a nightmare to pursue. Expeditions sent out to kill or capture him often became targets themselves, suffering high casualties and ignominious defeat at the hands of the guerrillas. Mosby's chief stock-in-trade was surprise. His men spent their days as civilian farmers and then assembled at prearranged locations by night to strike where least expected. Mosby once

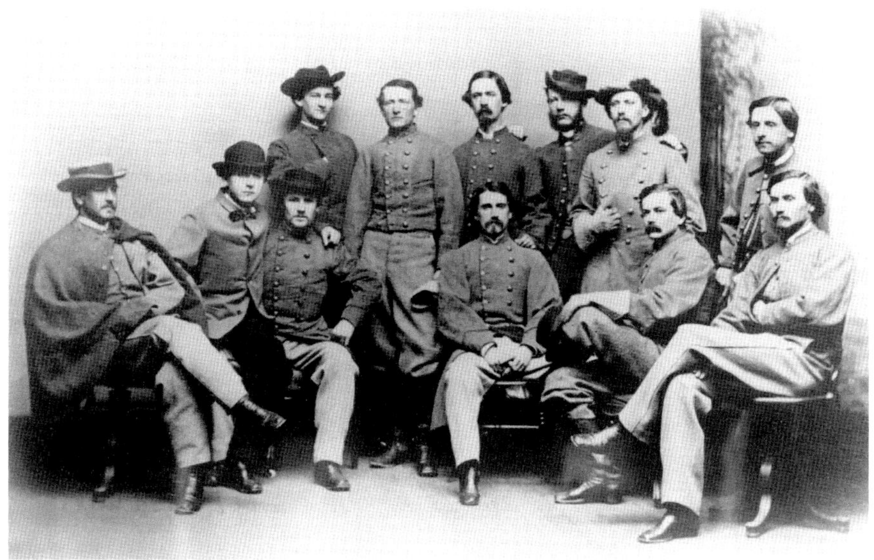

John Singleton Mosby (*fifth from left*) and his officers. *Library of Congress.*

penetrated a Union encampment so boldly that he captured a brigadier general asleep in bed.

Mosby's other great attribute was ferocity in combat. Whenever possible, he and his men fled superior forces, disappearing into the countryside to wait for another day. When Mosby attacked—or decided to hold his ground after being attacked—the fighting quality of his Rangers was superb. Most of them spurned the romantic notion of sabers and rarely had time for carbines. Revolvers at close quarters were their preferred tools, though the Rangers often made lethal use of shotguns, as well.

In choosing his targets, Mosby showed exceptional judgment, always probing his adversaries and striking where risk was least and reward greatest.[73] He devoted much attention to acquiring quality horseflesh from Yankees, thereby guaranteeing his men the means of striking at will and fleeing when necessary. The troopers of the Second Massachusetts Cavalry learned this to their cost on August 24, 1863, when a detail of twenty-five men—mostly Californians—led 102 fresh mounts back to the regiment from the Cavalry Depot at Washington. Each man was in charge of 4 horses, riding one while leading 3 by ropes tied to his saddle. Mosby spotted the detachment, understood their vulnerability and attacked. The ensuing panic among the rider-less horses sent many Yankees to the ground, some of them

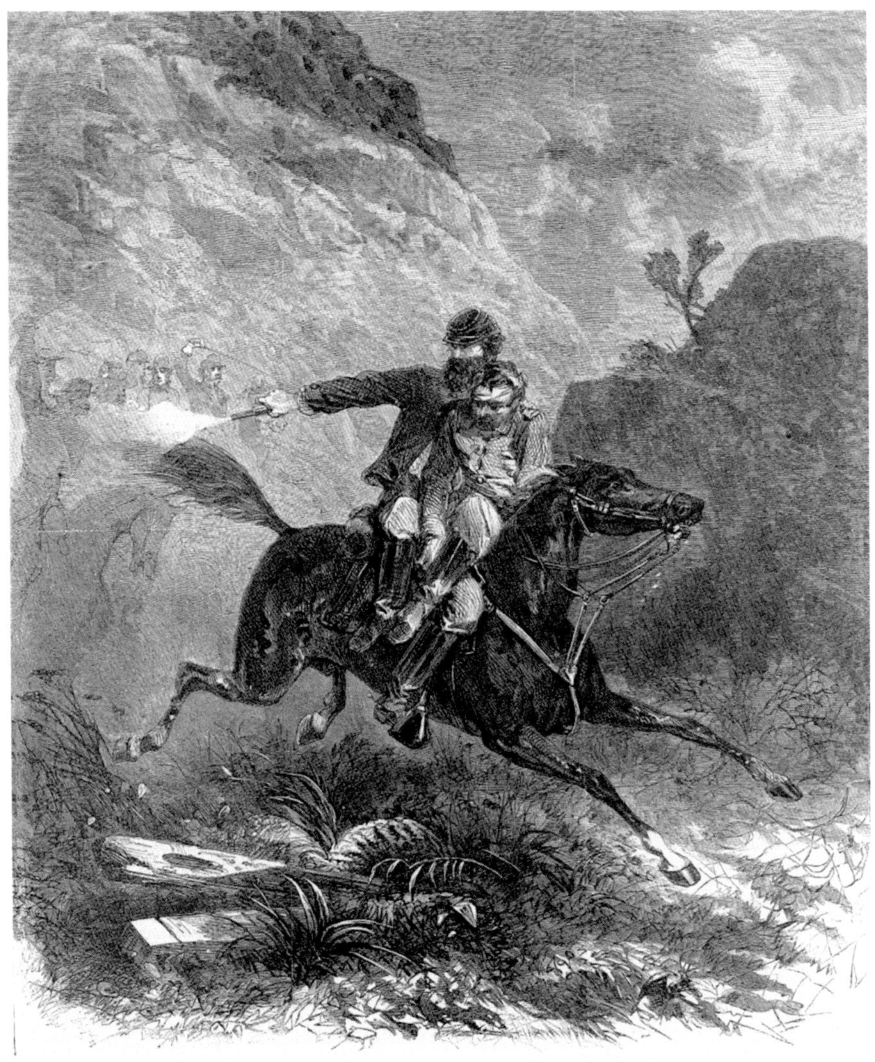

A Cavalry Rescue. Suppressing guerrilla warriors was difficult and dangerous work. *From* Harper's Weekly, *November 29, 1862.*

badly injured by plunging hooves and wild kicks. The Union troops fought back bravely and extracted a price for their horses. Mosby himself took a California bullet in the side and had to withdraw. His men mistook his action as a signal to break off the fight, allowing many of the Yankees to escape. In the final tally, the fracas was an undeniable Confederate victory; they took fewer casualties, captured more prisoners and ended up with most of the

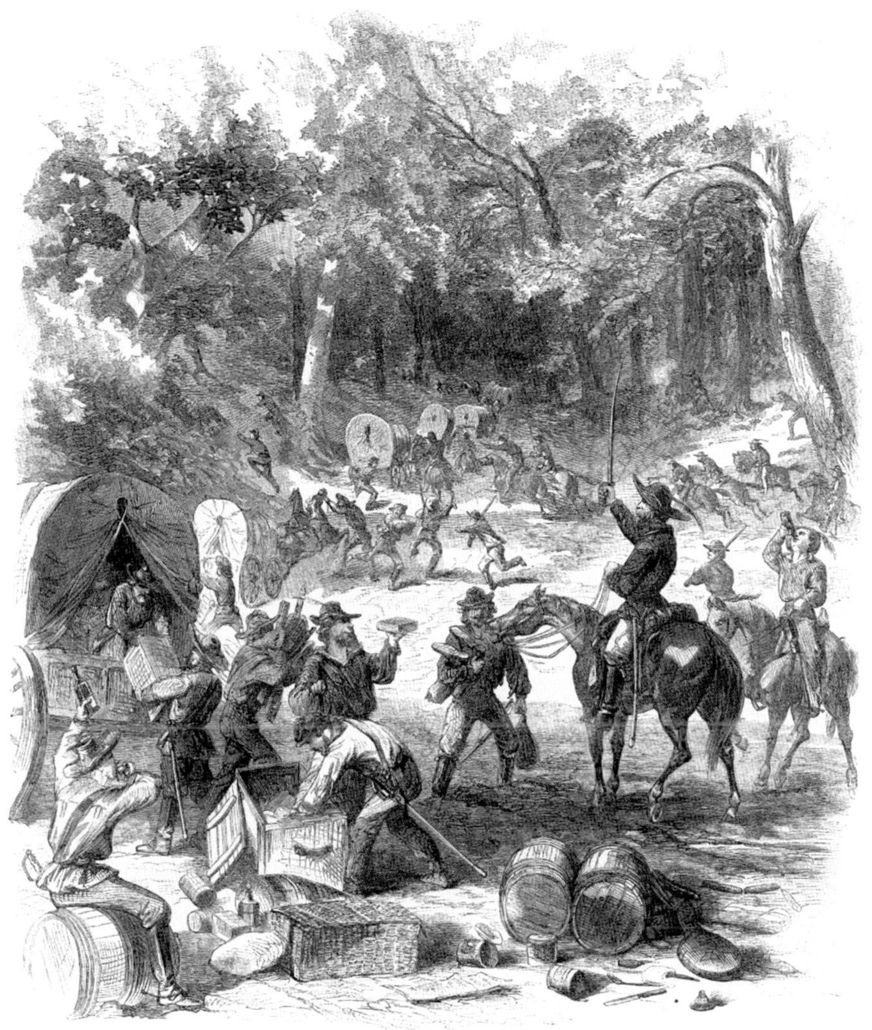

"Mosby's Guerrillas Destroying Sutler's Train." Nothing brought Northern and Southern soldiers together more than the misfortunes of sutlers. *From* Harper's Weekly, *September 5, 1863.*

horses. But Mosby's wound was serious, and during his recovery, the activity of his Rangers dropped off dramatically. From the Union point of view, the losses in men and horses were probably worth the price of putting this most dangerous of Rebel commanders on the sidelines—if only for a little while.

Mosby's Rangers and the Californians battled each other over many months and came to know each other well. Mosby himself recognized the

Californians as a distinct force and paid tribute to them in an anecdote recounted after the war:

> *At one time I captured a lot of loaded wagons in a sutler's train. I thought first of burning them, but finally concluded to carry them off. It was about twelve miles to a place of safety in the mountains, and while on the way we met a part of the Second Massachusetts Cavalry. The California Hundred and Battalion was part of the regiment we came against. They were a fine body of men and the most cheerful fighters I ever met. Well, I was obliged to leave the wagons behind and the sutlers got them back again.*[74]

Capturing and recapturing sutlers' wagons was a favorite activity for both sides, since the soldiers involved extracted a commission on both sides of the transaction. No guilt was experienced during the process. As one soldier observed, "A soldier has no pity at all for the misfortune of a sutler, as they are in the habit of charging soldiers an extortionate price for everything they sell to them, and when a chance offers to make up this extortion, it is gladly taken advantage of."[75]

DRANESVILLE

Colonel Lowell's skill and activity were noted in Washington, and in August 1863, he was given charge of two additional regiments to pursue his campaign against guerrilla bands operating in Northern Virginia. Lowell's elevation to what was, in effect, brigade command brought about a ripple of promotions through the rest of the Second Massachusetts. Sewall Reed, whose leadership of Company A (the California Hundred) was widely respected, advanced to command of the second battalion (though retaining his rank of captain). Other Californian officers and noncoms were advanced inside the regiment at this time or were promoted and transferred to other units. Meanwhile, California troopers remained the fighting backbone of the Second, even as their numbers dwindled in the face of death, wounds and capture. This last was a terrible fate, since Union soldiers captured by Mosby's command generally ended up in Andersonville prison in Georgia, a pestilential hellhole where 30 percent of the inmates died of starvation or disease.

Reed's elevation to battalion command brought increased responsibility, and so it was that he found himself in early February 1864 at the head of a column of 128 men, drawn mostly from the Second Massachusetts, but with 17 troopers provided by the Sixteenth New York. The patrol was routine, the first after a spate of wretched winter weather that had dampened Rebel guerrilla activity and kept the Federals in their camp at Vienna, Virginia.

As it happened, Mosby and his men were also out in force—not on a raid but to attend the funeral of one of their own. When word of Reed's patrol reached Mosby, the guerrilla chieftain reacted swiftly. With around 175 men at his disposal, he had the advantage over Reed in numbers, while his excellent intelligence network allowed him to track the Yankees' direction. Mosby detailed a small force to bird-dog the Federals and then launched the rest of his command on a course to intercept Reed before the latter could reach his base.

Reed's troopers camped for the night at a farmhouse along the Dranesville Pike, where they were joined by 150 men from the Sixteenth New York, who were also out on a scout. Together, the combined Yankee force was too big to attack, and when they set off together the next morning along the pike, there was nothing for Mosby to do but place his men in ambush and hope the Yankee patrols would go their separate ways—which they did. The New Yorkers turned off on a small country lane; Sewall Reed and his men headed straight down the pike for Vienna and home.

Mosby placed fifteen men, dismounted, in a stand of young pines that bordered the road, ready to strike Reed's column on its flank. Mosby knew the Yankees' marching order and placed mounted forces to attack Reed's men in the front and rear once the shooting started. Mosby then placed three men in the road to serve as bait to draw the Union troopers fully into the trap.

Reed's men did not take the bait. After they spotted the Rebel horsemen, they stopped to take stock of their situation, and for a few moments, their fate hung in the balance. Fearing discovery, the Confederates waiting in the pines opened up on the head of Reed's column, emptying saddles and sowing chaos. Two companies of Confederates burst upon the milling mass, and the head and center of Reed's column "broke and fled in every direction."[76] The end of the Federal column held firm, while the rear guard attempted to break down the rail fences by the side of the road so that the remnants of the column could escape and re-form in the fields. But the effort came too late. As one of Mosby's men recorded in his memoirs: "[Reed's] Californians, especially notoriously good fighters, were standing up to the rack like men, dealing out to us the best they had. They rallied at every call on them and went down with banners flying."[77]

After a sharp struggle, the rear of the Yankee column broke and joined the flight. Some headed back down the pike; others tore away northward across country until they escaped by fording the Potomac River. Most were gunned down or captured. Captain Reed took a bullet to the lung while trying to rally his men and died within minutes.

The action was a complete rout. Ten Federals died and seventeen were wounded (one of whom died shortly after). Fifty-seven were captured, of whom thirty-six died in captivity—mostly at Andersonville. Confederate losses included one killed and four wounded.[78] The disaster took a heavy toll of Californians but was taken in stride by the regiment—just another episode in the violent give-and-take that characterized service in that dangerous theater.

Colonel Lowell's cavalry brigade continued its private war with Mosby and his Rangers for the rest of the spring of '64, while greater forces assembled and launched into motion all around them. For it was at this time that General Grant began the vast Overland Campaign that drove Lee back to the gates of Petersburg, setting the stage for the last act of the war.

WITH SHERIDAN FROM WINCHESTER TO APPOMATTOX

As Grant pushed southward toward Richmond and Petersburg, Lee detached General Jubal Early with a sizable force to attack Federal forces in the Shenandoah Valley and then threaten the Federal capital. Lee's hope was that this diversion would cause Lincoln to pull Grant's army back to protect Washington. For a while, the plan worked. General Early swept through the valley and marched to within sight of Washington. All Union forces in the area of the capital were set in motion to resist him—including Colonel Lowell's brigade.

Most of the Californians of the Second Massachusetts Cavalry welcomed this change of duty. Their year spent fighting elusive guerrillas had been a nightmare of bushwhacking and arson. They were thoroughly tired of trying to sort out genuine noncombatants from out-of-uniform Rebel soldiers. Now at last they could get in on the real contest—the one between the great armies—that could end the war and send them all home.

Enter it they did, and in a highly visible way. Their colonel, Charles Russell Lowell, served ably as a brigade commander in the defense of Washington, and he brought his old regiment, the Second Massachusetts, into prominence alongside him. In August, Grant appointed the pugnacious Phil Sheridan to command Union forces in the Shenandoah Valley. After a slow start, the fighting there heated up, and Charles Lowell became one of Sheridan's most trusted commanders. For the Californians in the Second Massachusetts, this meant riding and fighting in large cavalry formations, where they played the role of shock troops. Again and again, they were asked to lead a charge, or stem a rout, or harass a fleeing enemy. By October, their reputation was at its peak, as was their colonel's, who had thirteen horses shot out from under him while fighting for Sheridan.

The crisis of the campaign came on October 19, 1864, at the Battle of Cedar Creek. While Sheridan was at Winchester, ten miles away, Early's Confederates launched a surprise attack on the Federal army and drove it back, capturing many men and guns. Lowell's brigade was called on to help stem the Confederate advance—and did so at enormous cost. Leading a desperate charge against a Confederate force lodged behind a stone wall, Lowell himself was hit in the chest by a spent round.

The wound was serious. Lowell had suffered bouts of tuberculosis before the war, and the smashing impact to his chest collapsed one of his lungs, making it difficult for him to breathe. He was carried to the rear, where his men laid him behind a parapet of earth to protect him. Lowell's commander urged him to quit the field, but Lowell refused, insisting instead on being called when orders came for the climactic charge that everyone knew was coming.

Two hours later, the expected orders came, and Lowell mounted up. He was unable to speak above a whisper, but his strength returned as he assumed his place at the head of his troops. He was able to wave his sword, and his men responded with a cheer.

Confederate grape and canister and musket balls raked the charging Union cavalrymen. One bullet found the brave colonel and tore through his chest from shoulder to shoulder, severing his spinal cord and paralyzing him from the chest down. Remarkably, Lowell's mind remained clear. In the hours remaining to him, he settled the affairs of his command, distributed his possessions among his friends and left loving messages to his wife of less than a year.

General Sheridan expressed the feelings of many in his command when he said of his young subordinate: "I do not think there was a quality which I could have added to Lowell. He was the perfection of a man and a soldier."[79]

The charge that Lowell led was unsuccessful, but the resolute action of the Union cavalry held the Confederates in check for what proved to be the critical period. After a desperate ride, Sheridan arrived on the scene and rallied fleeing Union troops. While the exhausted and hungry Confederates plundered the Union army supply wagons, Sheridan re-formed his men and then led them in a counterattack that destroyed Jubal Early's army and broke Confederate power in the Shenandoah Valley forever. This triumph, along with Sherman's capture of Atlanta, ensured Lincoln's victory in the election three weeks later.

The Shenandoah Valley campaign cost the Californian horsemen many casualties. The onset of winter brought little respite, as the restless Sheridan sent his troopers out on a series of brutal, snow- and ice-covered marches that froze men and killed horses. The approach of spring found the Californians in the countryside outside Petersburg, Virginia, where they fought in the climactic battles that cut off Lee's escape and forced his surrender at Appomattox. They were on their way to join General Sherman in North Carolina when news of General Joseph Johnston's surrender reached them, and they knew that the war in the East was truly over.[80]

The men of the Second Massachusetts took part in the Grand Review of Union forces held in Washington in late May. By August, the regiment was back in Boston, where the Californians learned that neither the Commonwealth of Massachusetts nor the government of the United States felt obliged to pay for their return trip to the Pacific coast.[81]

Of the 502 men who joined the California Hundred and Battalion, 182 were still in service when the Second Massachusetts disbanded.[82] Many had already been discharged due to wounds and illness; others had been promoted and transferred to other units during the war. Of those who survived the campaign, many went to early graves due to the terrible toll their wartime service had taken on their minds and bodies.

The story of the California Volunteers who went east to fight has been well documented, much of it in the men's own voices.[83] The story that emerges is a very human one. At times, some of the men mistrusted their officers' use of company funds. Other men deserted. One Californian major made his colonel's life a misery by pushing incessantly for separate, California-only formations and resigned when his wishes were not granted. The men and officers of the California Hundred and Battalion were not spotless heroes.

They were, however, extraordinarily brave and dedicated men who left the safety of the Pacific shore and sailed back east to fight for their country—risking horrible, disfiguring wounds; captivity; illness; or death. It was their sacrifice, and the sacrifice of other, like-minded men, that ensured that the

United States did not break apart in the 1860s, leaving a Balkanized North America that was a sure invitation to further war. They also prevented the foundation on our continent of a nation dedicated to the right of one race to enslave another.[84] And finally, they proved to a doubting world—almost all of which was ruled by monarchs at the time—that the American experiment in self-government would survive.

Chapter 15

THE SANITARY COMMISSION

California's military contribution to the war effort was remarkable, given the small size of its population and it geographic remoteness.[85] The California Volunteers secured settlements and transportation routes across the West—assuming, in the process, the entire prewar army's job of waging persistent, low-grade warfare across enormous expanses of territory.

The impact of Californian soldiers on the war against rebellion was necessarily limited by the numbers involved, though the presence of California horsemen on the field was much appreciated in the eastern states—especially as their arrival coincided with one of the Union's darkest hours.

There was nothing small-scale or regional about California's contribution to the economic aspect of the war. The steady flow of gold from California proved critical in keeping the nation's credit alive while the Lincoln administration fervently pursued new ways of raising money.

California's financial power also helped the U.S. government in a critical area where it was woefully unable to cope: namely, in the care of wounded soldiers and their families. Common decency demanded that these needs be taken care of, but at the start of the war, the government simply lacked the means. In 1861, the U.S. Army medical establishment (surgeons and assistant surgeons) amounted to eighty-seven men.[86] In early 1862, the Battle of Shiloh showed what the future held in store; at the end of two days of combat, over twenty thousand men lay dead or wounded. Neither the Union nor the Confederacy was remotely prepared to handle casualties

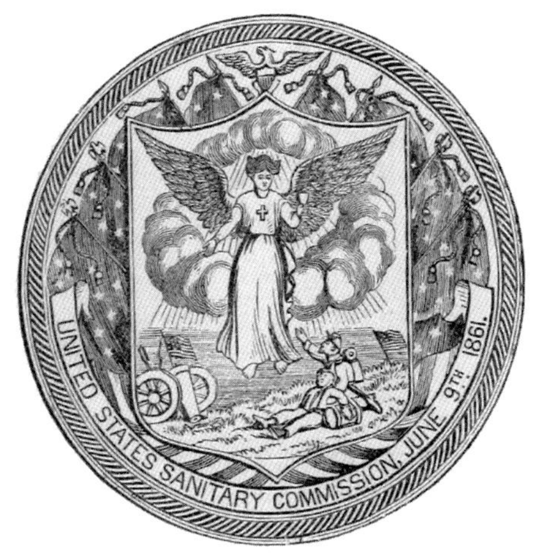

Seal of the United States Sanitary Commission. *From* Roughing It, *by Mark Twain (1872).*

on such a scale. The U.S. Army frantically added medical staff, but in the end, the burden of caring for the wounded—of nursing them and helping their families—fell mostly on volunteer organizations and most especially on the United States Sanitary Commission (USSC).[87]

Founded in June 1861, "the Sanitary" was initially viewed with skepticism by regular army medicos and by the Lincoln administration. But the USSC soon won over its critics. Funds raised by the Sanitary, coupled with massive in-kind donations from across the North, lifted the financial burden for medical supplies off the staggering government, while Sanitary volunteers provided the labor required to care for patients. The source of much of that labor would later prove politically and socially significant: fifteen thousand Northern women worked in hospitals during the war, freeing up men for the battlefield and, along the way, gaining the organizational skills and experience that were later applied to the women's suffrage movement.

Sanitary Commission volunteers and staff also performed as high-level administrators in the hospitals—occasionally by default. A striking example of this is provided by the career of Mary Ann Bickerdyke, affectionately known to the troops as "Mother Bickerdyke" (and to humbled medical officers as the "Calico Colonel"). Bickerdyke had no formal medical training; her rise to responsibility was based entirely on performance in the field. Early in the war, she showed up at a regimental hospital with $500 worth of supplies donated by her village in Illinois. Appalled by the filthy conditions she found, she bribed able-bodied soldiers with food from her stores and set them to cleaning up the mess. She then procured six hogsheads, sawed them in half and began running the lice-infested patients through her twelve new washtubs. From that day to the end of the war, Mary Bickerdyke fought tirelessly and ferociously for the health of wounded men.

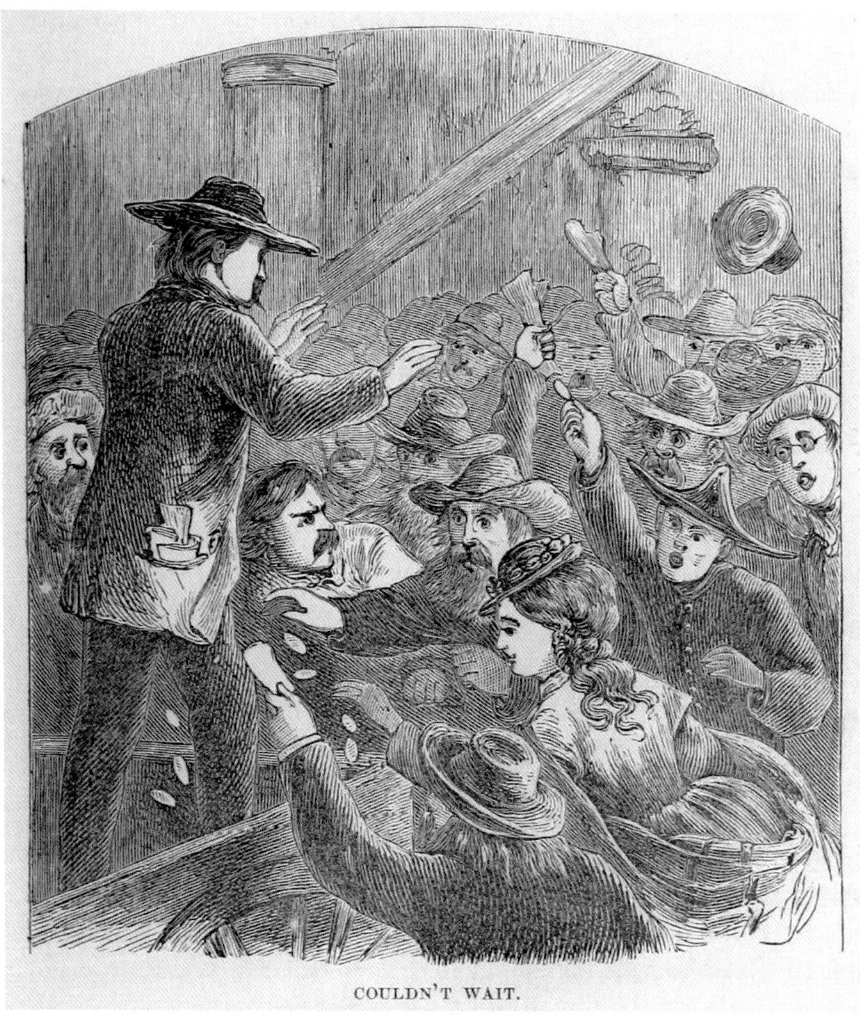

Mark Twain (whose face appears beneath the standing man's elbow) was an eyewitness to the boisterous campaigns to raise money for the USSC.[88] *From* Roughing It, *by Mark Twain (1872).*

Bickerdyke's unusual management style came to the attention of General Grant, who sensed a kindred spirit. Grant kept Bickerdyke near him as he rose in rank and backed her against all comers in the army bureaucracy. The Sanitary Commission appointed Bickerdyke a field agent for her work at Shiloh, giving her a modest salary that provided for her two boys back in Illinois. After Grant captured Vicksburg, he sent a formal request to the Sanitary to have Bickerdyke permanently assigned to his command. When

Grant was summoned back east, he transferred Bickerdyke to General Sherman, whose field hospitals she managed during the Atlanta Campaign and the March to the Sea. Mary Bickerdyke served to the very end, and in May 1865, she rode with Sherman's troops in the Grand Review held in Washington, right alongside Major General John A. Logan.

The make-it-up-as-you-go style of Mary Bickerdyke was typical of service in the Sanitary Commission, which addressed needs so urgent and overwhelming that wild improvisation was called for at every turn. Fundraising, in particular, called for creativity in the highest degree, and nowhere was this challenge met with more flair and success than in California.

MR. GRIDLEY'S WAGER

Ever since the first days of the gold rush, gambling was woven into the fabric of life in the mines. Young men, freed from the constraints of church and society, reveled in placing bets on just about anything that could be bet on.[89] So it was that a pair of rivals for the office of mayor of Austin, Nevada, placed a wager on the outcome of the contest. When the votes were counted, the losing candidate, Reuel Colt Gridley (Democrat), stoically hoisted the prescribed fifty-pound sack of flour to his shoulders and marched the length of the dusty mining camp, accompanied by the din of the town's band and the cheers of its populace. Having thus fulfilled the terms of his wager, Gridley announced that he had no further need for the sack of flour and inquired of his fellow citizens what he should do with it. "Sell it to the highest bidder, for the benefit of the Sanitary fund," came the reply, which was greeted by a round of applause.

Gridley approved the notion and acted as auctioneer. Bids spiraled higher and higher, until the sack was sold to a millworker for the princely sum of $250. When the purchaser was asked where he wanted the sack delivered, he replied, "Nowhere—sell it again." This idea was greeted with cheers, and the auction repeated until the sack had been bought and sold repeatedly for a total of $8,000—without ever leaving Gridley's possession.

When word of the auction reached Virginia City, the heart of the Comstock Lode, a telegram was immediately dispatched to Gridley, ordering him to "Fetch along your flour sack!" There followed an artfully contrived auction that pitted Virginia City against rival communities, with

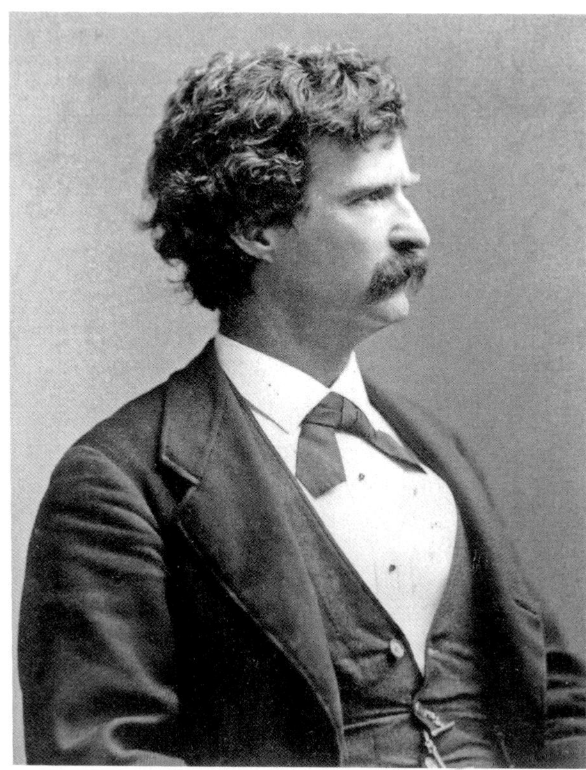

Left: Twain tells the story of Gridley's flour sack in his classic travelogue *Roughing It*, published in 1872. Twain passed through Utah, Nevada and California in the early 1860s; his book paints an indelible portrait of the Civil War–era West. *Library of Congress.*

Below: Communities across California and Nevada bid for the honor of "owning" the flour sack. *From* Roughing It, *by Mark Twain (1872).*

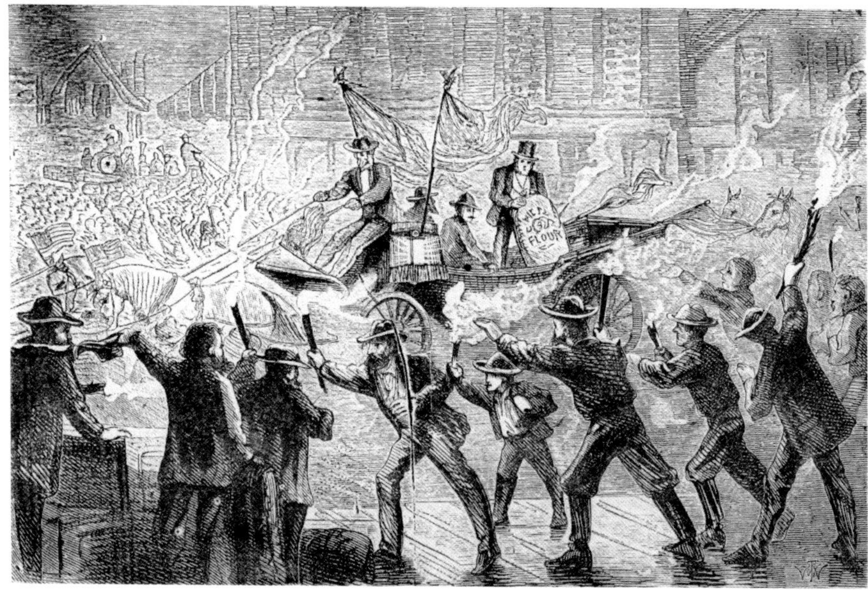

word flying back and forth as the bids mounted up. By the end of a two-day contest, Gridley's flour sack had raised the gold equivalent of $40,000 in greenbacks.[90]

With such successes in hand, there was no stopping the march of the flour sack. It toured California all the way to San Francisco and then traveled back east to be baked into cookies that were sold at a Sanitary Fair (a great fundraising innovation in the East, featuring exhibits of captured Confederate flags, art shows, meals served by society hostesses and anything else that could induce patriotic attendees to part with their money). All told, Gridley's humble sack of flour raised around $275,000 for the Sanitary Commission.

Thomas Starr King and the Sanitary Commission

Gridley's flour sack was a wonderful way to raise money for the Sanitary, but it was by no means the only one. Straight-out appeals, one-on-one or in large public gatherings, turned out to be the most effective tool for raising money—especially when the man delivering the pitch was the most charismatic Unionist on the Pacific coast.

Thomas Starr King, the Unitarian minister who led the movement to keep California bound to the national government, came to USSC fundraising by chance. In November 1861, a band of miners who had journeyed north to seek gold in Canada decided to contribute on a grand scale to the Union cause. They were not sure how to proceed, so they sent a draft for $1,000 to Starr King. A natural-born publicist, King first used the draft (and the patriotic letter that accompanied it) to whip up enthusiasm for U.S. bonds. When Washington was slow to send out the actual certificates, King noticed the public's enthusiasm ebbing, so he switched the destination of the $1,000 draft to the Sanitary Commission and proceeded to drum up business for that cause instead. The ploy succeeded beautifully—and was all the more gratifying because the man heading the Sanitary was Henry Whitney Bellows, a fellow Unitarian minister and an old friend and mentor of King's from his Boston days.[91] The King/Bellows partnership flourished and helped turn the Sanitary into a philanthropic juggernaut.

As a deeply admired public figure, King was ideally positioned to serve as the Sanitary's rainmaker-in-chief. He toured up and down the Pacific coast, adding pleas for the Sanitary to his patriotic exhortations for the Union. The public response to King's oratory was rapturous, but the little minister did his best work in private, in one-on-one discussions with the financial barons of San Francisco (the wealthiest city in the United States at this time). King's foremost asset in the work was his likability. He possessed a sanguine, generous disposition, leavened by a mordant wit. Here, for instance, is King explaining his forbearance after a shipboard encounter with a man in Oregon who would not support the Union unless he found that his own personal interests were at risk: "For one wild moment, I longed to throttle [the] wretch and push him into the Columbia. I looked down, however, and saw that the water was clean!"[92]

King's fundraising efforts carried everyone and everything before him, and by September 1862, he was sending money back to Bellows in $100,000 lots. Over the course of the war, Californians contributed $1,234,000 to the Sanitary Commission's total budget of $4,924,000. The state's population (composing 1.2 percent of the national total) provided more than one-quarter of all the money raised for the Sanitary.

Directing this extraordinary effort was an exhausting labor, and the USSC was far from the only cause King championed. During his tenure at the First Unitarian, he raised funds and supervised the construction of a magnificent new church. He also served on the Board of the College of California at Oakland (afterward the University of California at Berkeley). All these duties lay on top of his ministerial cares for a large congregation. King was never a robust man, and his letters from this time describe the toll taken by his grueling schedule:

> *I have not an abundance of leisure, and now and then have occasion to speak. My lungs being weak, and my nerves rather shattered, I find the occasional strain very severe....I am tolerably well and intolerably at work. Never wrote so much in a year as during last year and am speaking as much as my feeble voice will permit....No constitution delicate as mine can stand it....I am worn out, and yet on the treadmill.*[93]

King's will was always greater than his body, and apart from occasional collapses, he made no concessions to his poor health. Instead, he pushed himself to the limit, touring and speaking across the state. Finally, in March 1864, King's chronic abuse of his health caught up with him. He fell ill with diphtheria and then contracted pneumonia. He remained lucid and composed throughout his illness, solicitously comforting his family and friends to the very end. Thomas Starr King died at the age of thirty-nine, after literally working himself to death in the cause of his country and his faith.

The reaction was an outpouring of grief such as the young state had never known before. The state legislature adjourned for three days so its members could journey to San Francisco to pay their respects. State and municipal courts also went into recess. Encomiums appeared in newspapers around the state, as well as in many papers in the East. On the day of King's funeral, cannons boomed out from Fort Alcatraz at a slow, steady rate and were answered by a battery mounted in Union Square. Governor Low and his staff joined the funeral procession, marching past flags flown at half-staff on public buildings and private. Even foreign consulates and ships anchored in the bay joined in by lowering their flags to half-mast. Though Starr King held no public position (apart from his seat on a college board), his passing was mourned like that of a head of state.[94]

Chapter 16

AFTERMATH

Abraham Lincoln's triumph in the 1864 presidential election signaled the doom of the Confederacy. Southern armies struggled on until the next spring but without any real prospect of success. On April 2, 1865, Grant's army broke through Lee's defenses outside Petersburg, and Petersburg and Richmond fell the next day. Six days later, Lee surrendered the starving, exhausted remnants of the Army of Northern Virginia, effectively ending the war.

The news flashed across the continent by telegraph to California, and the Golden State rejoiced alongside the rest of the Union.[95] That joy turned to horror on April 15, when news of President Lincoln's assassination reached San Francisco in the midst of civic celebration. Shock was the first reaction, followed by grief and rage. Within hours of the news reaching San Francisco, mobs attacked the offices of Secesh newspapers, as well as those of French-language newspapers opposed to the Lincoln administration.[96] General Irwin McDowell, who had taken over the Pacific Department from General Wright, made clear that official patience with treason was at an end. Newspapers, McDowell ordered, that were "so utterly infamous as to exult over the assassination" would be suppressed.[97]

When it became clear that the assassination was an isolated event, civilian and military officials in California began to relax. In June, press censorship was lifted. California Volunteers stationed across the West mustered out of the service as regular army units became available to replace them—a process that took some time.[98]

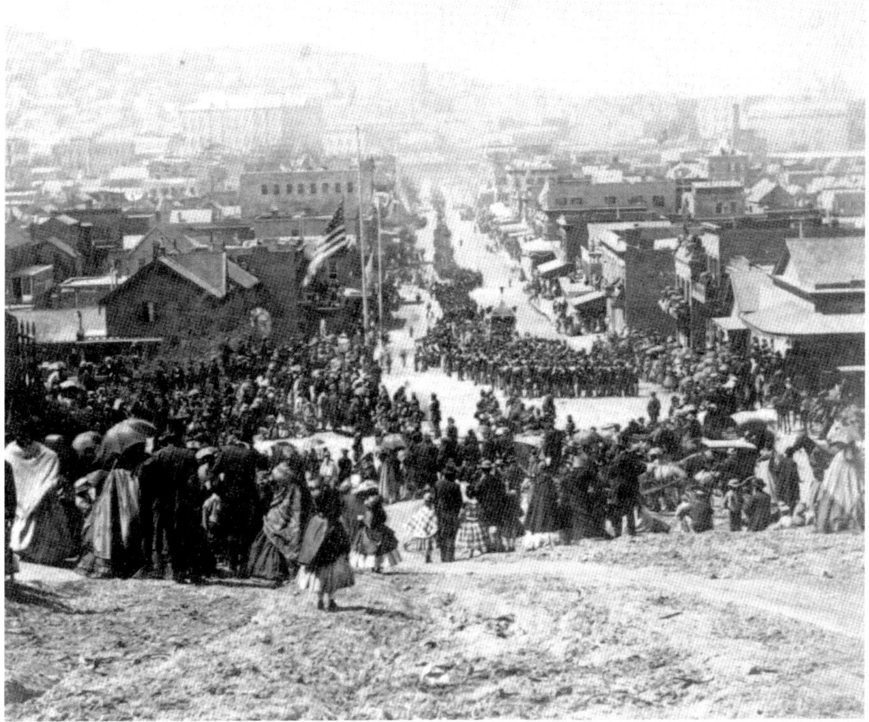

Lincoln obsequies in San Francisco. *Library of Congress.*

As confidence in the new peace grew, the Union Party—the wartime alliance of Northern Democrats and Republicans—begin to weaken, fracture and finally dissolve. In 1867, a resurgent and largely unified Democratic Party captured California's governorship and assembly.

As the demands of war and national politics ebbed, California elections came once again to be dominated by domestic issues. White supremacism, in abeyance during the war, came back with a vengeance, its attention now focused on the Chinese population, whose growing numbers offered serious competition to whites in the labor market.[99] In a key test of racial attitudes, California parted company with the rest of the Union and stood with the South in rejecting the Fourteenth Amendment, the essential Reconstruction measure that guaranteed American citizens equal protection under the law.[100]

Not all the wartime advances in race relations were erased. Black and Indian slavery was abolished forever in California in 1863 (in response to Lincoln's Emancipation Proclamation), and the right of blacks to testify

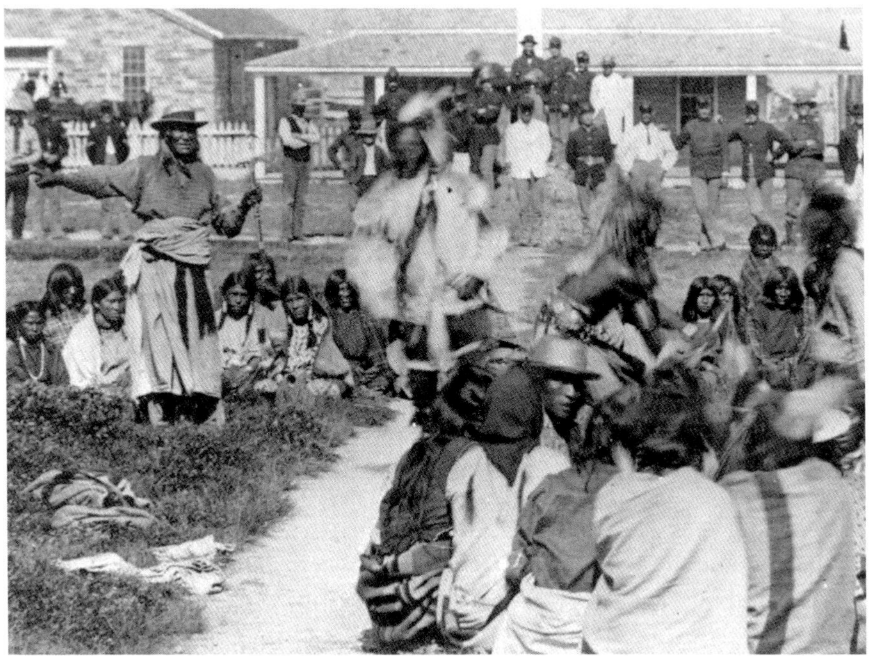

Chief Washakie of the Eastern Shoshone with Dancers at Fort Washakie (1892). *National Archives.*

Colonel Connor's campaign against the Northwestern Shoshone was devastating to the tribe—the worst of a series of calamities that befell them in their interaction with whites. The Eastern Shoshone lived a little more off the beaten emigrant path and had time to brace themselves for the impact of white settlement. They also enjoyed exceptional leadership in the person of Washakie, who befriended Brigham Young and negotiated successfully with other white leaders. The Eastern Shoshone lost vast tracts of land but remained largely in control of their own destiny.

in court was established. The evolution of Indian citizenship was more complicated, since it involved questions of tribal sovereignty that took decades to resolve. It wasn't until 1924 that federal law finally established the right of Native Americans to U.S. citizenship.

During and after the Civil War, the dispossession of native peoples throughout the West continued apace. The subjugation of the Modoc in the early 1870s marked the last armed resistance by Indians in California.[101] The Comanche and Kiowa, who battled California Volunteers at Adobe Walls, were subdued in the 1870s. Remote bands of Apache held out into the 1880s and beyond.

The Impact of the Civil War on California

California's postwar regression in matters of race was cruel but not surprising, given the general tone of the state before the war. But to say that racism survived intact is not to say that the war had little effect on the Golden State. On the contrary, the war transformed California's relationship to the rest of the country, which, in turn, transformed life within the state.

Some modern historians treat California's decision for the Union as a given—an obvious result that could not have fallen out otherwise—but this is to read the past with the 20/20 vision of hindsight. In 1860, no one knew if the remote and neglected Golden State would simply opt out of the troubles that were driving its eastern cousins mad. The idea of standing calmly aloof on the Pacific shore must have been tempting indeed to Californians from both North and South.

In contemporary minds, California was definitely up for grabs. Jefferson Davis was assured repeatedly that the Pacific coast was ready to revolt—that it would at least provide trouble for the national government, if not secede altogether.[102] And Abraham Lincoln would not have dubbed Starr King "the man who saved California for the Union" if he had been sure of the state's loyalty. California at the beginning of the war was a place of widespread fear and uncertainty, with the prospect of political violence very much in the air.

This stands in stark contrast with the California of 1865, which lay firmly in the hands of Unionists, backed by a solid majority of Californians at the polls. Over the course of the crisis, most Californians cast their lot with the national government. At war's end, most Californians felt a bond of shared purpose with the citizens of the other loyal states—and were proud of California's contributions to the Union cause.

The federal government, in turn, was not unmindful of the debt it owed to the Pacific states. In 1862, in the midst of war, Congress voted funds for a transcontinental railroad along a central route—a project that had languished for years as Southerners held out for a more southerly route. Seven years later, a golden spike driven in Provo, Utah, linked California forever to the East Coast—and transformed the state's relationship to the rest of the nation. The distant Pacific shore, which had been little more than myth and romance for most Americans, now became an exotic-but-obtainable destination for tourists and others from the East—many of whom promptly made plans to relocate.

California's politics and economy were transformed by the railroad link to the East. The state's rise to the status of agricultural superpower was a direct result of improved transportation, which allowed California's produce to travel back east, preserved for market by a burgeoning technology of refrigeration.

The net effect of the war on California was to bind the state economically, politically and culturally to the rest of the nation at a speed that would have been unimaginable under the stagnant, gridlocked federal government of the 1850s.

California's Contribution

The mobilization and deployment of California troops throughout the West held Indian resistance in check after the departure of Federal troops in 1861. The hammer blows struck by Californians against the Comanche, Kiowa, Apache, Navajo, Shoshone and Paiute peoples were probably worse than what would have happened if the regular army had stayed in place.

In the end, California's most significant wartime contribution was the same as that made by other Union states. Through massive effort and sacrifice, they delivered the United States from the paralyzing contradiction of being a nation half-slave and half-free. In the process, the nation also determined once and for all that it *was* a nation and not a collection of sovereign states that could recombine themselves in any fashion they chose.

The hard-won victory of the national government guaranteed peace in North America for following generations—a peace that could not possibly have prevailed if the continent had been carved up into competing fragments.[103] Union victory also established—in theory, at least—a more just and humane model for coexistence among Americans of different racial origins. Whatever our failings in realizing that model, the fact that it exists defines our national purpose—and has made possible whatever progress we have actually made toward achieving that great goal.

NOTES

Author's Note

1. Lieutenant Colonel Roger McGrath, "California and the Civil War," California State Military Museum, www.militarymuseum.org.

Chapter 2

2. Details on how the legislature subjugated California's Indian population in the 1850s are available in Johnston-Dodds, *Early California Laws and Policies Related to California Indians*. A broader, more sociologically oriented look at the fate of the native population can be found in Hurtado, *Indian Survival on the California Frontier.*

Chapter 3

3. The duel ended Terry's political career in California. When the war broke out, he went back to Texas and enlisted in the Eighth Texas Cavalry ("Terry's Texas Rangers"), a regiment raised by his brother. Terry's lifelong penchant for violence caught up to him in 1889, when he was gunned down by a U.S. marshal for assaulting a judge who had ruled against Terry's wife in a lawsuit.
4. Andrés Pico was offered command of a battalion of "Native" (i.e., Californio) Cavalry in the Volunteers but had to decline since he was too old to take the field.
5. Quoted in Simonds, *Starr King in California*, 37.
6. Wilkins, *Great Diamond Hoax*, 30.

Chapter 4

7. Taney's name is pronounced *tawny* (rhymes with *brawny*).
8. A color-coded map of the 1860 election by county is available online at the Wikipedia page entitled "U.S. Presidential Election of 1860" (en.wikipedia.org/wiki/United_States_presidential_election,_1860). There is no more useful tool for understanding the regional politics at play in that critical election.

Chapter 5

9. Johnston, *Life of Gen. Albert Sidney Johnston*, ch. 17.
10. Ibid., ch. 18.

Chapter 6

11. Quoted in Simonds, *Starr King in California*, 4.
12. Wendte, *Thomas Starr King*, 18. King added that the two sects would have united long before except for the fact that "they were too near of kin to be married."
13. Wendte, *Thomas Starr King*, 87.
14. Ibid., 195.
15. Unattributed quote in Simonds, *Starr King in California*, 24.

Chapter 7

16. Orton, *Records of California Men in the War of the Rebellion*, 6.
17. Ibid., 16.
18. Figures from Hunt, *Army of the Pacific*, 24.

Chapter 8

19. Baylor's order is contained in *The War of the Rebellion: Official Records of the Civil War.* This quote may be found in "John L. Baylor to Captain Helm," March 20, 1862, Series I, Vol. L, Part 1, 942. Readers wishing to avoid the painful challenges presented by the *Official Records* can find the quote online at the Ohio University site at ehistory.osu.edu/books/official-records/105/0942.
20. Orton, *Records of California Men in the War of the Rebellion*, 43.

Chapter 9

21. Hunter's first name, rank and estimated command size vary from source to source (Sherod/Sherrod, lieutenant/captain, 54 to 120 men).
22. Historians with a more demanding definition of "action" accord this honor to the "Battle of Picacho Pass" (in reality, a brief skirmish), since it resulted in a number of killed (three), wounded (perhaps five) and captured (three). Both Arizonan claims are superseded (in Californian eyes, at least) by some serious gunplay that took place over a gold shipment in the Sierra foothills, a fracas that can be described as "Confederate partisan action" or "garden-variety stagecoach robbery," according to taste. (See chapter 12, "Confederate Partisans," for details.)
23. Hunt, *Army of the Pacific*, 112.
24. Remarkably, the surviving scout succeeded in getting word of the Column's advance to Canby while in Confederate captivity. How the captured courier communicated with Canby is not known.
    General Carleton took a strong interest in spy craft. His couriers carried "decoy" messages while bearing the general's actual communications in their heads.
25. Here, as elsewhere, estimates of the number of Indians involved vary wildly (in this case, from two hundred to five hundred). The Apache did not keep muster rolls, and troops fighting for their lives rarely stop to count their opponents. The fact that Cochise and Mangas Coloradas, leading Apache chieftains, were both present suggests this was an unusually large body of fighters.
26. Civil War–era soldiers were subject to a variety of potentially lethal diseases, including typhoid fever, smallpox, measles, diarrhea, pneumonia, malaria and tuberculosis. Sufferers who did not die during their wartime service were often left seriously weakened.

Chapter 10

27. Both Union and Confederate commanders sought alliances among the political leaders of Sonora and Chihuahua. Of particular interest to the warring *norteamericanos* was the port of Guaymas, strategically located on the Gulf of California. Mexican authorities were distracted by a civil war of their own, however, as pro-Juárez and pro-Maximilian forces battled for supremacy. Establishing a U.S. Army supply line based in Guaymas seemed feasible at one point, but the political situation ultimately proved too unstable to warrant the investment of time and men.
28. The estimated property loss from Indian raids in 1862 was $250,000 (around $7,000,000 in today's dollars), with the Navajo alone accounting for thirty thousand stolen sheep. The death toll of white settlers that year approached three

hundred. (Estimates by contemporary territorial officials, quoted in Sides, *Blood and Thunder*, 380.)

29. Carson bore a special affinity for the Ute people. He represented them in treaty negotiations and got special permission from the War Department to use them as scouts. When on campaign, he often rode with his Ute scouts. Some historians speculate that Carson accepted command of the campaign against the Navajo because he identified with old-time New Mexicans and with the Ute people, both of whom were traditional enemies of the Diné.
30. Hunt, *Army of the Pacific*, 162. Hunt breaks the numbers down as follows: California Volunteers, 215; New Mexico Volunteers, 108; Ute scouts, 75. Twenty-seven wagons were required for food, fodder and ammunition.
31. Edward Beale promoted the idea of using camels in the Southwest, as did Jefferson Davis, when he served as secretary of war in the Pierce administration. The animals were acquired in 1856, but the project was sidelined at the outbreak of war.
32. Sides, *Blood and Thunder*, 463.
33. This and subsequent descriptions of the battle come from Pettis, *Personal Narrative of Events in the War of the Rebellion*, no. 5, *Kit Carson's Fight with the Comanche and Kiowa Indians at the Adobe Walls*, 22–29.
34. The classic cannonball, or "round shot," is a solid iron projectile. Pettis's guns were firing shells, which are designed to explode on arrival at their target, scattering shrapnel and shell casing fragments. This second explosion was outside the Indians' experience, leading to the coinage "gun that shoots twice."
35. Carmony, *Civil War in Apacheland*, 177.

Chapter 11

36. Quote from Hunt, *Army of the Pacific*, 336.

It is safe to assume that the phrase "Equal Rights" in the paper's name does not refer to any notion of racial or gender-based justice. Rather, white Southerners saw themselves as being systematically deprived of their rights by meddlesome Northerners.

"Rail splitter" in this instance is a class-based insult, of a type frequently employed by Southern writers. One prewar Georgia newspaper, for instance, offered up these observations on Northern life: "Free Society! We sicken at the name. What is it but a conglomeration of greasy mechanics, filthy operatives, small-fisted farmers, and moon-struck theorists?…The prevailing class one meets with [in the North] is that of mechanics struggling to be genteel, and small farmers who do their own drudgery, and yet are hardly fit for association with a Southern gentleman's body servant."

One wry Lincoln supporter responded to this diatribe by lofting a banner at a Lincoln-Douglas debate reading: "SMALL-FISTED FARMERS, MUD SILLS OF SOCIETY, GREASY MECHANICS FOR A. LINCOLN." [Above quotes from MacPherson, *Battle Cry of Freedom*, 197–98.]

37. Hunt, *Army of the Pacific*, 337.

38. The purpose of mail banishment was to impose a heavy financial burden on a newspaper's circulation efforts. This kind of soft censorship was not unknown in the nineteenth century, even in peacetime. Southern states employed the technique before the war to suppress abolitionist tracts.

39. Quoted in Chandler, "Fighting Words: Censoring Civil War Journalism in California," *California Territorial Quarterly*, 4.

40. The Confederacy, with much smaller manpower reserves, instituted its first draft in April 1862, almost a year before the North.

The Northern draft of 1863 aimed to restore Union armies bled white by the carnage at Antietam, Fredericksburg and earlier battles. The Battle of Antietam, fought on September 17, 1862, resulted in more than 22,000 Union and Confederate casualties. It remains to this day the bloodiest day in American military history. On December 13, 1862, Union general Ambrose Burnside launched a series of fruitless, brigade-sized attacks on an indestructible Confederate position at the Battle of Fredericksburg. Union casualties exceeded 12,600 men, more than twice the number lost by Confederates.

41. The term "Copperhead" was frequently used in this era to label antiwar Democrats. Republican partisans said the term referred to a venomous snake common in the East. Copperheads claimed the name derived from Liberty head copper pennies they wore as badges. Regardless of origin, the term gained wide acceptance and has been used by historians ever since.

Chapter 12

42. Of Dutch origin, schooners were typically small, two-masted vessels with sails rigged fore-and-aft. Fast and maneuverable, the design was favored by privateers and smugglers throughout the eighteenth and nineteenth centuries.

43. Individual shipments of $1 million to $1.5 million were routine (roughly $20 million to $30 million in today's currency).

44. The Union goal of keeping Southern cotton off the international market was aided by Richmond's initial policy of withholding cotton from nations that did not recognize the Confederacy. This attempt to coerce Britain and France failed, and the imposition of the Yankee blockade removed Richmond's options in the matter.

45. This quote appears endlessly in written sources and on the Internet, but without attribution. Readers are duly cautioned. The author would be obliged if anyone knowing the source of the quote would contact him via the publisher.

46. In a strange twist of fate, Rubery was nephew to John Bright, an eminent British MP and statesman who opposed slavery with a passion. Bright was a firm friend to the Union throughout the war, doing much to prevent Britain from siding with the South. Abraham Lincoln admired Bright and had a photo of him on the desk of his reception room. A clipping from a Bright letter to the press was found in the pocket of the coat Lincoln wore to Ford's Theatre on the night of his assassination.
47. The accuracy—or inaccuracy—of Harpending's memoirs is a source of considerable dispute (and entertainment) among historians. Dr. Robert Chandler leads the skeptics; an article by him highly critical of Harpending is listed in the bibliography.
48. Dr. Chandler asserts that Harpending went no farther than Vera Cruz, where he obtained the letter of marque and naval commission from Confederate agents.
49. Sources differ on how the cannon purchases were explained away. One excuse was that they were necessary to guard mining property in Mexico, another that they were purchased on behalf of the "Liberal Party" for the fighting about to break out in Mexico. It says a lot about prevailing conditions in that unhappy country that neither excuse gave the conspirators away.
50. The Knights of the Golden Circle was a semi-secret organization founded in 1854 to promote Southern expansion into Mexico and Central America, with the long-term goal of founding slave states there. At the start of the Civil War, Knights in California and the Midwest went underground and continued their support for the South. Estimates of the actual numbers of Knights in California vary so wildly as to be useless.
51. Harpending's memoirs are available online, as are the court proceedings against Greathouse. (Both are listed in the bibliography.) A comparison of the documents is instructive. Harpending's narrative is that of a gifted storyteller, recounting youthful adventures at fifty years' remove, bending and shaping the storyline for literary effect. The court proceedings contain a sober tally of evidence and offer many insights into the legal requirements for a prosecution for treason during a time of civil conflict.

Chapter 13

52. A long history of persecution caused the Mormons to flee the United States in 1845 and settle by the Great Salt Lake in what is now Utah. At the time, the area was under nominal Mexican rule, but it was ceded to the United States in January 1848 under the terms of the Treaty of Guadalupe Hidalgo. The Mormon settlers were dismayed to find themselves back under American rule. They essentially ignored the U.S. government until 1857, when President Buchanan sent a small army to Utah to assert the national authority. The troops

were withdrawn in 1860. An American governor stayed behind, but Brigham Young and the senior members of the Mormon Church remained the de facto government of the territory.

53. Three companies of the Third Infantry were detached and sent to deal with persistent problems between Indians and settlers in the Humboldt District, which consisted of the counties of Sonoma, Napa, Mendocino, Trinity, Humboldt, Klamath and Del Norte in Northern California. Connor picked up three companies of troopers from the Second California Volunteer Cavalry on his way to Utah—a useful addition that brought his numbers up to full regimental strength.

54. Quoted in Orton, *Records of California Men in the War of the Rebellion*, 508. The Mormon Church sanctioned polygamy at this time. It was probably this practice that led Connor to his ungallant assessment of Mormon women.

55. Connor's arrival at Salt Lake City made him, as senior officer, head of the District of Utah, an administrative area under the army's Department of the Pacific that included the modern states of Nevada and Utah. The Idaho Territory was added in 1863.

56. Defining Native American polities was difficult for white settlers in the nineteenth century and remains troublesome for historians today. In the first case, white Americans assumed that Indian societies possessed the kind of defined, formal structures white communities favored. White treaty negotiators were forever assuming that the headman of a particular band was the "chief" of an entire "tribe," only to be disappointed when other members of the "tribe" in question went their own ways after diplomatic negotiations. Modern historians are challenged by the fact that written records of interactions between whites and various Indian communities are riddled with errors and false assumptions.

57. This phrase is attributed to Young by many sources, without reference to a particular time and place. It is a customary formulation that he may have repeated. Young did express the essence of the policy in his own words in "Remarks" printed in the *Deseret News* of August 16, 1866: "I wish to impress [all] with the necessity of treating the Indians with kindness, and to refrain from harboring that revengeful, vindictive feeling that many indulge in." [Quoted at history.lds.org, in an article entitled "Brigham Young—An American Moses."]

58. Quote from Madsen, *Glory Hunter*, 57.

59. Connor's actions were not out of line with army policy at the time. In fact, General George Wright of the Pacific command passed along word of Connor's harsh measures to his superiors in Washington with marked approval: "The swift retributive punishment which has been meted out to those Indians will doubtless have the effect of preventing a repetition of their barbarities. It is the only way to deal with those savages." [Quoted in Hunt, *Army of the Pacific*, 508.]

60. Forty miles a day was the rule-of-thumb estimate for daylight cavalry travel under average conditions. The Californians exceeded that rate by 70 percent, riding straight into an Arctic wind by night.

61. The freezing temperature of eighty-proof whiskey is negative ten degrees Fahrenheit. This temperature must be sustained for hours to freeze the contents of a canteen.
62. Mae Parry, "The Northwestern Shoshone," in *History of Utah's American Indians*, edited by Cuch. Ms. Parry was a great-granddaughter of Chief Sagwitch, who survived the massacre. Her essay outlines the subsequent history of the band, who were repeatedly dispossessed by white settlers. Many eventually joined the Mormon Church and gained some degree of protection.
63. Many Mormon settlers were afraid of the Shoshone and were relieved when Connor destroyed Bear Hunter's band. They also resented Brigham Young's policy of providing the Shoshone with food and were glad when the Indians were driven off. This feeling finds full expression in an article on the Bear River fight written for the Logan Chamber of Commerce in 1923 and published online on Mendon Utah Net, www.mendonutah.net/history/cache_county/56.htm.
64. *The War of the Rebellion: Official Records of the Civil War*, serial 102, 1131. (Available online at ehistory.osu.edu/books/official-records/102/1131.)
65. In the mid-nineteenth century, the term "galvanizing" meant to coat iron with tin via an electrical charge. The inference was that the soldiers' new "Yankee-ness" was very thin indeed.
    The Powder River Expedition was undertaken after the collapse of the Confederacy, and many of Connor's volunteer troopers felt it was time for them to go home, rather than go chasing after Indians. Units from Kansas and Nebraska actually mutinied but were suppressed. Connor's Californians and his "galvanized Yankees" served as ordered.

Chapter 14

66. In theory, Civil War–era companies contained one hundred men and were commanded by a captain. A battalion was composed of two or more companies (according to need) and was commanded by a major or a senior captain. Regiments consisted of ten companies (one thousand men) and were commanded by a colonel. A brigade consisted of two or more regiments (according to need) and was commanded by a brigadier general or a senior colonel. In reality, there was a lot of play in all of this. Long-serving regiments could end up with a couple hundred men, due to attrition from death, illness, capture, discharge and desertion. Much depended on a given army's replacement policy, which varied widely according to circumstance.
67. Camp Meigs was also home at this time to the Fifty-Fourth Massachusetts Infantry, the black regiment whose exploits are described in the film *Glory*. Letters show that at least one Californian was resentful of the attention the Fifty-Fourth received (the regiment was a favored project of Governor Andrew).

Subsequent letters show the troopers of the Second Massachusetts revising their opinion of black troops dramatically upward after the Fifty-Fourth's bloody ordeal at Fort Wagner.

68. The four companies that enlisted after the California Hundred are often referred to as the "California Battalion," but they were never a distinct battalion in the organization of the Second Massachusetts Cavalry. California companies were distributed in the regiment's organizational scheme as Colonel Lowell saw fit—a source of considerable dissatisfaction among some Californian troops.
69. An outstanding source of primary material about the Californians is Keith and Larry Rogers's *Their Horses Climbed Trees*, cited in the bibliography.
70. Massachusetts was entering its third year of war when Lowell was commissioned to raise his regiment. The state had suffered horrific casualties in the closing months of 1862. Recruitment was falling, and handsome bounties were required to meet the state's quotas. This, in turn, attracted an unsavory class of men known as "bounty jumpers," who pocketed the cash incentives and deserted at the first opportunity. It was to men like these that Lincoln was referring when he lamented, "Sending armies to McClellan is like shoveling fleas across a barnyard, not half of them get there."
71. Many Californian soldiers resented Lowell's decision to spread them around and said as much in their letters home and to the newspapers. State feeling ran strong in those days, even among Northern troops. The Californians' clannishness was all the more remarkable because many of them hailed from New England in the first place.
72. The term "partisan rangers" was applied in this era to independent forces operating behind enemy lines. (We would call such units guerrillas today.) These forces turned easily to brigandage and often proved more dangerous to friendly civilians than to military adversaries. In 1864, the Confederate government withdrew its sanction of such forces—Mosby's Rangers being one of two exceptions.
73. Mosby was unsentimental about warfare. "In one respect," he wrote in his memoirs, "the charge that I didn't fight fair is true. I fought for success, and not for display. There was no man in the Confederate Army who had less of the Spirit of Knighthood in him or who took a more practical view of war than I did."
74. Backus, *Californians in the Field*, 10. Backus, who served in the Second Massachusetts, cites an article written by Mosby for San Francisco's *Morning Call* as the source of the quote. (After the war, Mosby lived and worked for many years in the San Francisco Bay Area.)
75. From the newspaper *Alta California*, September 8, 1863, cited in Parson, *Bear Flag and the Bay State in the Civil War*, ch. 6.
76. Williamson, *Mosby's Rangers*, 144.
77. Munson, *Reminiscences of a Mosby Guerrilla*, 86.
78. Parson, *Bear Flag and the Bay State in the Civil War*, ch. 7.
79. Ibid., ch. 10.

80. Confederate resistance in the Trans-Mississippi continued into May. The Cherokee general, Stand Watie, didn't surrender to Union forces until June 23.
81. The troops claimed the right to be returned to the point where they had enlisted. A lawyer was retained, and in November, the Federal government agreed to pay passage for the remaining Californians. All who shipped for home before that point did so at their own expense.
82. Figures from the *Oakland Enquirer*, April 23, 1894, quoted in Rogers and Rogers, *Their Horses Climbed Trees*, 389.
83. See especially Rogers and Rogers, *Their Horses Climbed Trees.*
84. In March 1861, Confederate vice president Alexander Stephens summed up the fundamental differences between the U.S. Constitution and that of the Confederacy in an address labeled by historians as the "Cornerstone Speech": "Our new government is founded upon exactly [this] idea; its foundations are laid, its cornerstone rests, upon the great truth that the negro is not equal to the white man; that slavery subordination to the superior race, is his natural and normal condition. This, our new government, is the first, in the history of the world, based upon this great physical, philosophical, and moral truth."

Chapter 15

85. California had a population of 380,000 in 1860. It stood eighth from the bottom in a ranking of states by population, just ahead of Vermont and New Hampshire.
86. From the website "Caring for the Men—The History of Civil War Medicine," citing an article entitled "Fighting For Time" by George W. Adams, published in the National Historical Society's *The Image of War: 1861–1865*, vol. 4 (1983.)
87. Modern usage tends to equate the word "sanitary" with "cleanliness," but the term held broader meaning in the nineteenth century. The term derives from the Latin *sanitas*, meaning "health." The Sanitary Commission was dedicated to the overall mental, physical and spiritual health of its charges.
88. Although the illustration depicts an event that took place in Nevada, the Silver State's population at the time consisted almost entirely of Californians, who poured over the Sierra passes in response to the Comstock strike. The name of the new state was also imported, belonging originally to Nevada County, California.
89. Mark Twain's short story "The Celebrated Jumping Frog of Calaveras County" is a celebration of this aspect of California life. First published in 1865, the story lifted Twain to national prominence.
90. Variations of the Gridley story exist. In Aurora Hunt's version, for instance, Gridley is not the unsuccessful candidate but rather a supporter of one. Other details differ in minor ways. I present Mark Twain's version of the tale because 1) he was a reporter for a nearby newspaper at the time, 2) he knew Gridley personally (they both hailed from Hannibal, Missouri) and 3) Twain makes no

secret of his willingness to lie in the interests of a good story. Such candor is deserving of our respect and support, so long as money is not involved in the transaction.

91. Bellows was the minister of the Church of All Souls (Unitarian) in New York City but was a native of Boston and a graduate of Harvard College and Divinity School. He was a national leader of the Unitarian Church and served as an informal broker for churches seeking new pastors. It was Bellows who brought Thomas Starr King to the attention of the First Unitarian congregation of San Francisco.
92. Simonds, *Starr King in California*, 60.
93. Robert Monzingo, *Thomas Starr King*, 140. (Quotations compiled by Monzingo from three letters by King to friends.)
94. In 1931, California placed statues of two men, Thomas Starr King and Fra Junípero Serra, in the National Statuary Hall in the U.S. Capitol to represent the Golden State there. Both statues remained in the hall until 2009, when King's statue was replaced by one of Ronald Reagan.

    The resolution to replace King's statue was written by State Senator Dennis Hollingsworth, who explained his decision to the *San Francisco Chronicle* thus: "To be honest with you, I wasn't sure who Thomas Starr King was. And I think there's probably a lot of Californians like me." (Quoted by Kimberly Geiger, Chronicle Washington Bureau, in an article published online at www.sfgate.com.) Senator Hollingsworth also objected to Reverend King because he (King) was not a native-born Californian. It is not clear if the senator's concerns about nativity extend to Reagan (born in Illinois) or Serra (born in Majorca, Spain).

    King's statue now stands in the Civil War Memorial Grove in Capitol Park, which surrounds the California State Capitol in Sacramento, where schoolchildren and state legislators can learn more about this crucial figure in California history.

Chapter 16

95. Transcontinental telegraph service reached California in October 1861.
96. Napoleon III took advantage of the fighting in the United States to install a client régime in Mexico, in defiance of the Monroe Doctrine. French-language papers in California that followed Napoleon's line assailed the Lincoln administration, which supported the liberal Juárez government in its resistance to French imperialism.
97. McDowell's order was issued on April 17, 1865. (Quoted by Chandler on page 15 of his article "Fighting Words" in the *California Territorial Quarterly*.)
98. Congress did not authorize payment of the returning Californians' transportation costs until 1867.
99. California's population in 1870, according to the U.S. Census, numbered 499,424. Chinese residents numbered 49,310 (10 percent of the total), blacks

only 4,272 (less than 1 percent). Indians are listed at 7,241 (approximately 1.5 percent), but this figure is certainly low. Many Indians lived in remote locations, and the rest did their best to avoid white officialdom.

100. The Southern states initially rejected the Fourteenth Amendment but were then forced to ratify it as a condition of re-admission to the Union, leaving California alone in its refusal to ratify. The amendment achieved the necessary number of state ratifications in 1868 and has been in effect from that date. In 1959, California saw fit to join the rest of the nation and ratified the amendment.

101. General Edward Canby, who defeated the Confederate invasion of the Southwest in 1862, was murdered at a peace conference with the Modoc in 1873. He was the only U.S. general to die in the Indian Wars.

102. James G. Blaine was a politician who narrowly missed becoming president of the United States in 1884. While not campaigning, Blaine wrote history. His analysis of Southern hopes for California was: "Jefferson Davis had expected, with a confidence amounting to certainty…that the Pacific Coast, if it did not actually join the South, would be disloyal to the Union, and would…require a large contingent of the national forces to hold it in subjection. It was expected by the South that California and Oregon would give at least as much trouble as Kentucky and Missouri, and would thus indirectly but powerfully aid the Southern cause." [Blaine, *Twenty Years of Congress*, 308.]

103. In 1917, Germany's first step in preparing for war against the United States was to offer to restore to Mexico the territory seized by the United States seventy years before, in exchange for Mexico's assistance in attacking the United States. Had the Confederacy succeeded, a long, porous border (over which Southern "property" could escape) and conflicting territorial claims would have provided no end of sparks to rekindle the war. Those sparks would have been assiduously fanned by rival European powers, who would have emulated the German action of 1917 by dangling alliances before the shattered, mutually hostile fragments of the American Union. General conflagrations in Europe along the lines of 1914–18 and 1939–45 would have played out on North American soil, as well.

ANNOTATED BIBLIOGRAPHY

Backus, Samuel W. "Californians in the Field: Historical Sketch of the Organization and Services of the California 'Hundred' and 'Battalion,' 2nd Massachusetts Cavalry. A paper prepared and read before the California Commandery of the Military Order of the Loyal Legion of the United States, 1889." No publication data available.

Backus was an eyewitness to the events he describes, making this account an invaluable resource in the study of the Californians who went east to fight with the Second Massachusetts Cavalry.

Bancroft, Hubert Howe. *History of California.* San Francisco: A.L. Bancroft & Company, 1884.

Bancroft's interpretive work has been superseded in many respects, but he remains the founding father of California history. He collected, sifted and recorded data on a scale that defies imagination. Our debt to him is great.

Blaine, James. G. *Twenty Years of Congress from Lincoln to Garfield.* Vol. 1. Norwich, CT: Henry Bill Publishing Company, 1884.

James Blaine served as speaker of the House of Representatives, U.S. senator from Maine and secretary of state. He narrowly missed becoming president of the United States. In this book, he brings his seasoned political eye to the story of our great national crisis. The title is misleading; most of this book discusses the origins of the war prior to Lincoln's election.

Burns, John F., and Richard J. Orsi, eds. *Taming the Elephant: Politics, Government, and the Law in Pioneer California*. Berkeley: University of California Press, 2003.

The first essay in this collection ("A Violent Birth: Disorder, Crime, and Law Enforcement, 1849–1890," by Roger D. McGrath) offers an interesting new look at the notorious violence of the gold rush era. The argument is that while killings were numerous, they were at some level largely consensual—the result of the code duello that prevailed in California at the time. Robberies in general and crimes against women were few because of the dangers involved. Women could count on community protection; most miners went about armed and were simply too dangerous to rob. Missing from this analysis are crimes against Indians, which were commonplace, rarely recorded and almost never punished.

Carmony, Neil B., ed. *The Civil War in Apacheland—Sergeant George Hand's Diary: California, Arizona, West Texas, New Mexico, 1861–1864*. Silver City, NM: High-Lonesome Books, 1996.

George Hand was a gold miner who enlisted at the beginning of the war. His diary provides a vivid account of his experience with the California Column and his service in the Southwest.

Cremony, John C. *Life Among the Apaches*. San Francisco: A. Roman and Company, 1868.

Cremony was a San Francisco journalist who served as a cavalry officer with the California Column. He may well have exaggerated his military exploits. But he did serve in the Southwest for years as an interpreter and soldier, and his comments on Indian cultures and the details of campaign life make fascinating reading.

Cuch, Forrest S., ed. *A History of Utah's American Indians*. N.p.: Utah Division of Indian Affairs, 2000.

Mae Parry was a granddaughter of Chief Sagwitch. She was born into the northwestern Shoshone tribe in 1919 and served as its historian for many years. Her article in this book, entitled "The Northwestern Shoshone," describes the traditional lifestyle of the tribe and the terrible fate that befell it after white contact. Parry is a good source for the Shoshone view of the events surrounding the Bear River Massacre.

Doyle, Don H. *The Cause of All Nations: An International History of the American Civil War*. New York: Basic Books, 2015.

Foreign recognition and assistance were critical to America's success in winning independence from Britain in the eighteenth century. Both sides in the Civil War knew that the Confederacy's best chance—perhaps its only chance—lay along similar lines. The diplomatic war fought between the North and South in Europe was every bit as important as any battle fought on American soil.

Doyle shows how liberals and conservatives abroad saw the American war as part of a wider struggle between democratic and monarchical forces. Doyle does not trade in airy political theory. He shows, for instance, how this struggle between rival ideologies led to Mexican citizens shooting one another in large numbers in a bitter conflict that directly affected the conduct of the war in the southwestern United States.

Doyle also shows how, in explaining their war aims to foreign powers, U.S. and Confederate leaders explained the war to themselves. These appeals to foreign opinion offer striking insights into the thoughts and motives of the warring parties.

Field, Stephen. *Personal Reminiscences of Early Days in California.* N.p.: privately published and distributed, 1893.

Stephen Field was a California pioneer lawyer who was appointed to the U.S. Supreme Court by Abraham Lincoln in 1863. David Broderick personally saved Field from assassination in 1851. David Terry, who killed Broderick in the famous duel in 1859, was in turn shot and killed by Field's bodyguard while trying to assault Field in 1889.

Field's *Reminiscences* contain a treasure-trove of anecdotes that give the true flavor of American California's first decades.

Goodheart, Adam. *1861: The Civil War Awakening.* New York: Vintage Books, 2011.

In Goodheart's eyes, the South did not secede simply to escape the growing political clout of a booming North's population. He portrays a North caught up in a rapid political and cultural transformation—in some cases, a radicalization—that made peaceful compromise with an increasingly defensive South all but impossible.

California was a step behind the East in this polarization, but it caught up fast. Goodheart's frontispiece is a famous photograph of a vast pro-Union rally in Market Street, San Francisco, in 1861, featuring Thomas Starr King.

Hunt, Aurora. *The Army of the Pacific: Its Operations in California, Texas, Arizona, New Mexico, Utah, Nevada, Oregon, Washington, Plains Region, Mexico, etc., 1860–1866.* Mechanicsburg, PA: Stackpole Press, 2004.

The author deserves much credit for searching out eyewitness accounts of the campaigns of the California Volunteers and bringing this forgotten theater of war to light after decades of neglect. The book was originally published in 1951, and historical sensibilities have changed considerably over the intervening years. In Hunt's eyes, for instance, Major John Chivington is the "fighting parson," bluff hero of the Union victory at Glorieta Pass. Later generations tend to be less enthusiastic about Chivington, remembering him more as the instigator of the 1864 massacre of peaceful Cheyenne at Sand Creek.

Hurtado, Albert L. *Indian Survival on the California Frontier*. New Haven, CT: Yale University Press, 1988.

This book chronicles the harsh fate of the native population of early American California. The approach is sociological, the data horrifying. The massive influx of whites during the gold rush guaranteed that California's Indian communities would be assailed and subjugated at an unprecedented rate. This book provides a close-grained look at the process of dispossession—and the means by which Indian communities survived the onslaught.

Johnston-Dodds, Kimberly. *Early California Laws and Policies Related to California Indians*. Sacramento: California Research Bureau, 2002.

This report, compiled for the state legislature, provides excerpts from key legislative documents pertaining to the treatment of California's Indians in the first decade of statehood, with analysis. It provides a sobering look at how government policy formalized the rapid subjugation of the native peoples who, at the time of the American conquest, outnumbered non-indigenous Californians ten to one.

Johnston, William Preston. *The Life of Gen. Albert Sidney Johnston: Embracing His Services in the Armies of the United States, the Republic of Texas, and the Confederate States, Annotated*. New York: D. Appleton and Company, 1878.

The author was the son of General Albert Sidney Johnston and served in the Confederate army as a colonel and aide-de-camp to Jefferson Davis. W.P. Johnston is an unabashed apologist of the Lost Cause. If you want to hear the authentic voice of the Southern Chivalry on the subjects of honor, white supremacy and states' rights, this is a good place to find it.

Kennedy, Elijah Robinson. *The Contest for California in 1861: How Colonel E.D. Baker Saved the Pacific States to the Union*. New York: Houghton Mifflin Company, 1912.

Edward Baker was a close friend of Abraham Lincoln and a pivotal player in the establishment of Republican political power on the Pacific coast. The author of this biography was an eyewitness to Baker's time in California and writes in the voice of an ardent Unionist. As such, he provides an instructive contrast to Preston Johnston, cited previously.

Lapp, Rudolph M. *Blacks in Gold Rush California*. New Haven, CT: Yale University Press, 1977.

This book brings to light the experience of blacks in prewar California. The state's economic dynamism and diversity offered unusual opportunities for black immigrants, while its murky status as a "semi-free" state created a high-risk environment. Particularly interesting are the stories of black community organizations that battled prevailing prejudices and the legal restrictions that blacks faced.

MacPherson, James M. *The Battle Cry of Freedom.* New York: Oxford University Press, 1988.

MacPherson's 904-page book is widely acknowledged as the best one-volume history of the war. The author is particularly informative on the causes leading up to the war.

Readers who find that nine hundred pages are not enough should turn to Shelby Foote's masterful *The Civil War: A Narrative*, which covers the war in three volumes. Foote was a novelist before he turned to writing history; his storytelling skills are on display throughout the work.

Madsen, Brigham D. *Glory Hunter: A Biography of Patrick Edward Connor.* Salt Lake City: University of Utah Press, 1990.

A well-told, thoroughly researched look into the life of an Irish immigrant who rose to high rank in the frontier army.

———. *The Shoshoni Frontier and the Bear River Massacre.* Salt Lake City: University of Utah Press, 1985.

Madsen lays out the whole tangled and tragic tale of the Shoshone peoples and their interaction with the Mormon settlers of Utah and with the U.S. government.

Masich, Andrew E. *The Civil War in Arizona: The Story of the California Volunteers, 1861–1865.* Norman: University of Oklahoma Press, 2006.

The author has done an extraordinary job researching day-to-day life in the California Column. He also provides a good look at General Carleton's administrative style. As the title indicates, this study is focused on Arizona, which means that the New Mexican side of the Column's duties is only sketched in to provide context.

Matthews, Glenna. *The Golden State in the Civil War: Thomas Starr King, the Republican Party, and the Birth of Modern California.* New York: Cambridge University Press, 2012.

This is a well-researched look into California's experience before and during the Civil War. The author's main interest is the pivotal role played by the Reverend Thomas Starr King in rallying pro-Union sentiment in the early days of the conflict. Considerable attention is given to King's biography and to his intellectual antecedents.

Miller, Rod. *Massacre at Bear River: First, Worst, Forgotten.* Caldwell, ID: Caxton Press, 2008.

Miller provides a rich description of the context behind the January 1863 killings at the Bear River in what is now Idaho. Involved were the Mormons, the California Volunteers, the Shoshone people and remorseless Union commander Patrick Edward Connor.

Writing frontier history inevitably involves *Rashomon*-like episodes, where the historian is confronted by wildly differing, all-but-irreconcilable versions of the same event. Miller is candid about this problem and takes care to present all the data to the reader.

Monzingo, Robert. *Thomas Starr King: Eminent Californian, Civil War Statesman, Unitarian Minister*. Pacific Grove, CA: Boxwood Press, 1991.
The author draws deeply on King's correspondence and other primary sources to paint a full portrait of a remarkable man. An excellent resource for anyone interested in King.

Morrison, John H. *Dying for Our Country: A Sermon on the Death of Capt. J. Sewall Reed and Rev. Thomas Starr King*. Boston: John Wilson and Son, 1864.
J. Sewall Reed, a Massachusetts native and commander of the famed "California Hundred," was killed in battle at the same time Starr King died of illness contracted during his tireless speaking tours for the Union. This sermon was delivered in Milton, Massachusetts, in honor of both men. It illustrates the blend of Christian doctrine and patriotism that sustained the bereaved during that terrible time.

Mosby, John S. *Mosby's War Reminiscences and Stuart's Cavalry Campaigns*. New York: Dodd, Mead Company, 1887.
Mosby's memoirs are a fascinating account of just how dangerous some lawyers can be. With no prior military experience, Mosby defined the meaning of asymmetrical warfare, tying down thousands of Union soldiers with his handful of guerrillas in Northern Virginia. Californians fighting with the Second Massachusetts Cavalry had the unenviable job of trying to chase Mosby down.

Munson, John W. *Reminiscences of a Mosby Guerrilla*. New York: Moffat, Yard and Company, 1906.
A lively recounting of Mosby's exploits by a member of his Rangers who stuck with him to the end. Filled with great anecdotes.

Orton, Richard H. *Records of California Men in the War of the Rebellion, 1861 to 1867*. Sacramento, CA: State Printing Office, 1890.
Orton, a veteran of the California Volunteers, was adjutant general of California when he compiled this text in 1890. It is the best source for wartime correspondence and official data concerning California's military contribution to the war effort.

Parson, Thomas E. *Bear Flag and the Bay State in the Civil War: The Californians of the Second Massachusetts Cavalry*. Jefferson, NC: McFarland & Company, 2011.

Parson tells the story of the California Hundred and the California Battalion fluently and in depth, using traditional historical narration. This book complements the book by Keith and Larry Rogers, which is a compilation of primary sources brought to light by research. Both books have much to offer readers interested in this aspect of California's war.

Pettis, George. *Personal Narrative of Events in the War of the Rebellion*. No. 5: *Kit Carson's Fight with the Comanche and Kiowa Indians at the Adobe Walls, on the Canadian River*. Providence, RI: Sidney S. Rider, 1878.
The author commanded Company K of the First California Volunteer Infantry for most of its service throughout the war. He also commanded the battery of howitzers that saved Kit Carson's command at the First Battle of Adobe Walls. Pettis writes well and paints a vivid picture of the action.

———. *Personal Narrative of Events in the War of the Rebellion*. Third Series, No. 14: *Frontier Service During the Rebellion; or, A History of Company K, First Infantry, California Volunteers*. Providence: Rhode Island Soldiers and Sailors Historical Society, 1885.
Pettis helped recruit Company K of the First California Volunteers at the beginning of the war. This narrative includes a description of the march of the California Column and of Company K's assignments in the Department of New Mexico.

Pittman, Walter Earl. *New Mexico and the Civil War*. Charleston, SC: The History Press, 2011.
Pittman has done a remarkable job assembling primary sources from the New Mexico campaign of 1861–62, in which Union and Confederate forces dueled for control of the Southwest. Pittman's focus is on the military action of this early campaign, which he presents in detail. The California Column arrived in New Mexico only at the end of the period Pittman covers. Readers interested in the California Volunteers' later campaigns should refer to Aurora Hunt's and Hampton Sides's books.

Quinn, Arthur. *The Rivals: William Gwin, David Broderick, and the Birth of California*. New York: Crown Publishers, 1994.
The author has an abundance of good material but presses too hard to present it with literary flourish. On page one, for instance, William Gwin appears on board a ship entering San Francisco Bay. Ten pages later, after an exhaustive visual tour of the bay and examination of what the passengers "must" have felt upon entering it, we are still unsure if Gwin has safely reached shore. Also unfortunate is the author's tendency to build dramatic tension by projecting feelings onto his protagonists that are not suggested by the data or even plausible (e.g., "Broderick would have been at that trial, for it was a perfect chance to size things up. He would have hated Gwin at first sight.").

Richards, Leonard L. *The California Gold Rush and the Coming of the Civil War*. New York: Alfred A. Knopf, 2007.

This book offers a detailed look at the creation of American California and the extraordinary evolution of its politics over the 1850s, illustrated with well-chosen anecdotes. California played an outsized role on the national political stage during this critical period. Richards does a good job of explaining how this came to be.

Rogers, Larry, and Keith Rogers. *Their Horses Climbed Trees: A Chronicle of the California 100 and Battalion in the Civil War, from San Francisco to Appomattox*. Atglen, PA: Schiffer Military History, 2001.

This is a voluminous collection of firsthand sources about the California Volunteers who went east to fight with the Second Massachusetts Volunteer Cavalry. It is a prodigious work of research and an invaluable resource to anyone interested in this aspect of California's wartime experience. The authors' in-depth treatment brings to light many tangential bits and pieces of history that do much to impart the feeling of the time.

Secrest, William B. *Perilous Trails, Dangerous Men: Early California Stagecoach Robbers and Their Desperate Careers, 1856–1900*. Clovis, CA: Quill Driver Books/Word Dancer Press, Inc., 2001, 112–17.

Secrest devotes five pages to the Bullion Bend stagecoach robbery, a daring attempt to finance the transportation of Southern partisans back east to fight.

Sides, Hampton. *Blood and Thunder: The Epic Story of Kit Carson and the Conquest of the American West*. New York: Anchor Books, 2006.

This is a brilliant biography of Kit Carson, the man who was just about everywhere important during American expansion into the Far West, often playing a pivotal role in the story. Carson helped Frémont explore routes to California and Oregon in the 1840s and commanded New Mexico and California Volunteers during the Civil War.

Simonds, William Dan. *Starr King in California*. San Francisco: Paul Elder and Company, 1917.

This is a hagiography of a man who probably deserves a hagiography—a notion that King himself would have been first to ridicule. King's most endearing quality, for this author at least, was his steadfast refusal to allow his intelligence, deeply held beliefs and devotion to his country to get in the way of his appreciation of the ridiculous. There was more than a touch of Sam Clemens in the diminutive preacher from Boston.

Starr, Kevin. *California: A History*. New York: Modern Library, 2007.

Starr's book is a good introduction to the full sweep of California's history up to the present day. Starr, the dean of California historians, is also blessed with a readable prose style. He has a strong interest in intellectual history.

Twain, Mark. *Roughing It*. Hartford, CT: American Publishing Company, 1872.

Twain's famous travelogue takes the reader through many of the scenes discussed in this book. It is also a key primary source on the story of Mr. Gridley's famous flour sack and its happy effect on the fundraising efforts of the U.S. Sanitary Commission.

Twain offers an incomparable view of life in the mines of Nevada and California during the early 1860s.

Wendte, Charles W. *Thomas Starr King: Patriot and Preacher*. Boston: Beacon Press, 1921.

Wendte knew Starr King personally and worked with King's descendants to produce this biography of the great preacher. This is a close-up view of King, replete with primary sources.

Whipple, Edwin P. *Substance and Show, and Other Lectures by Thomas Starr King*. Boston: James R. Osgood, 1877.

A posthumous collection of King's lectures on the Lyceum circuit, showing a master nineteenth-century orator at the height of his powers. The lectures cover a wide range of topics, including King's homage to Daniel Webster, the strongest voice for the Union in the decades preceding the Civil War. The collection is available at archive.org/details/substanceandsho00kinggoog, along with other works by King and discussions of King's work.

Wilkins, James H., ed. *The Great Diamond Hoax and Other Stirring Episodes in the Life of Asbury Harpending*. San Francisco: James H. Barry Co., 1913.

Asbury Harpending was a wealthy young Kentuckian who tried to launch a Confederate privateering cruise from San Francisco Bay—his quarry being the gold bullion traveling by steamship from California to New York. Harpending's prose style is engaging and his gifts as a storyteller are great. His memoirs are available online and make for delightful—if not necessarily factual—reading. (See the article by Robert Chandler for a discussion of Harpending's tendencies toward invention.)

Williamson, James J. *Mosby's Rangers*. New York: Sturgis & Walton, 1909.

This is an eyewitness account of Mosby's amazing career as a partisan leader, told by a man who was with him almost from the beginning.

Periodicals

Chandler, Robert J. "Fighting Words: Censoring Civil War Journalism in California." *California Territorial Quarterly* 51 (Fall 2002): 4–17.

Californians in the early days of statehood loved newspapers—newspapers that were not shy about making their partisan preferences known. Dr. Chandler describes the fate of Democratic and Republican papers as popular sentiment shifted toward the Union cause. Also covered are attempts to suppress Secessionist papers through government action and mob violence.

———. "Liar, Liar! Pants on Fire: Asbury Harpending's Civil War California." *California Territorial Quarterly* 88 (Winter 2011): 37–45.

Dr. Chandler's article pokes holes in Asbury Harpending's account of the latter's activities as a Confederate partisan, including the *J.M. Chapman* affair (an attempt at sailing a Confederate privateer from San Francisco). While Chandler's objections seem valid, it is also the case that privateers, like guerrilla leaders, are under no obligation to always tell the truth. In particular, Harpending's account of having journeyed to Richmond to meet Jefferson Davis could have been a fabrication designed to lift the fighting spirits of men involved in a desperate adventure. In any event, readers of Harpending's memoirs should keep Chandler's warnings in mind, even as they enjoy Harpending's engaging style of storytelling.

———. "The Velvet Glove: The Army During the Secession Crisis in California, 1860–1861." *California Territorial Quarterly* 88 (Winter 2011): 26–36.

Dr. Chandler lays out in detail the rumormongering that led to doubts about Sidney Johnston's loyalty during his tenure as head of the Department of the Pacific (doubts that, incredibly, are still circulated in history published today). Chandler accords high marks to Edwin Sumner, Johnston's successor, for countering the threats posed by pro-Southern activists.

Marion, Doris Wright. "The Making of Cosmopolitan California: An Analysis of Immigration, 1848–1870." *California Historical Quarterly* 19 (December 1940): 323–43.

The article presents a survey of who set off for California, how they reached the gold country and what happened to them after they did.

Posner, Russell M. "Thomas Starr King and the Mercy Million." *California Historical Quarterly* 43, no. 4 (December 1964): 291–307.

California's contribution to the Sanitary Fund was extraordinary—largely due to the efforts of Reverend Thomas Starr King. This article chronicles the development and successful career of this key soldier's aid society in the Golden State.

Robbins, Peggy. "General Grant's 'Calico Colonel.'" *American History Illustrated* 14, no. 1 (April 1979): 4–48.

A look at the remarkable wartime career of Mary Ann "Mother" Bickerdyke, who rose from volunteer nurse to the top level of field hospital management. Her commitment, competence and unflinching defiance of army bureaucracy made her a favorite with both Grant and Sherman.

Robinson, John W. "Los Angeles at Civil War's Outbreak." *California Territorial Quarterly* 88 (Winter 2011): 4–17.

The author provides a detailed look at California's hotbed of pro-Secesh sentiment at the start of the war and at the military measures that secured the Los Angeles area.

Spaulding, Imogene. "The Attitude of California to the Civil War." *Annual Publication of the Historical Society of Southern California* 9 (1912–13): 104–31.

The article is a remarkably comprehensive and generally well-reasoned look at California's experience of the Civil War, especially interesting for being written within living memory of the events described. There is a certain amount of racial stereotyping but comparatively mild for the time. The author offers many quotes from participants and footnotes extensively.

Wagoner, J.A. "The Oratory of Thomas Starr King." *California Historical Quarterly* 33, no. 3 (September 1954): 219–27.

The article describes the technical sources of Starr King's success as an orator, but the impact of King's humor is strangely undervalued. King got his audiences to laugh at him—and at themselves. There is no more powerful device to defuse tensions, and King was a master practitioner of the technique.

Websites

BYU Religious Education, Religious Studies Center. "The Bear River Massacre: New Historical Evidence." rsc.byu.edu/archived/civil-war-saints/bear-river-massacre-new-historical-evidence.

This article describes the controversies surrounding Connor's assault on the Shoshone encampment at Bear River. It is available online courtesy of the BYU Religious Studies Center. The article originally appeared in a book entitled *Civil War Saints*, edited by Kenneth L. Alford. There are useful links after the article, leading to more online information about the massacre.

———. "Civil War Saints." rsc.byu.edu/recent-books/civil-war-saints.

This site offers a wealth of articles describing the Mormon experience of the Civil War, as well as the Mormon War of 1857 (the little-known campaign that was the U.S. Army's largest undertaking between the Mexican-American War and the Civil War).

California Military Museum. www.militarymuseum.org.
This website contains an array of essays on topics relating to prewar militias, the experience of the California Volunteers during the Civil War and biographies of soldiers. Some of the essays have been superseded by more recent research.

Dictionary of Unitarian & Universalist Biography. "Thomas Starr King." uudb.org/articles/thomasstarrking.html.
This site offers a concise biography of Starr King and a useful list of other sources on the great preacher.

Mendon Utah Net, an Early History of Cache County. "Indian Warfare at Battle Creek." www.mendonutah.net/history/cache_county/56.htm.
This site displays an article written in 1923 for the *Logan Journal*, which gives a white settler version of the Bear River Massacre, as told in the days and years following the event. Stress is laid on the fears felt by the white settlers. No mention is made of the fact that the Shoshone might have felt aggrieved by their dispossession.

Reader, Phil. "Copperheads, Secesh Men, and Confederate Guerillas: Pro-Confederate Activities in Santa Cruz County during the Civil War." Santa Cruz Public Libraries. www.santacruzpl.org/history/articles/70.
Hosted by the Santa Cruz Public Library, this three-part article describes Secessionist activity in Santa Cruz County, with particular attention to Tom Poole, Rufus Henry Ingram and the Mason-Henry gang.

"The Second Mass and Its Fighting Californians." www.2mass.reunioncivilwar.com/index.htm.
This remarkable site presents an extensive collection of images and biographies of the men from California who headed back east to fight with the Second Massachusetts Cavalry.

United States v. Greathouse. law.resource.org/pub/us/case/reporter/F.Cas/0026.f.cas/0026.f.cas.0018.2.pdf.
This primary document derives from the treason trial of Ridgley Greathouse and the other *Chapman* conspirators. It provides a good thumbnail sketch of the incident and an interesting glimpse into the legal issues involved in a Civil War–era treason prosecution.

INDEX

D

K

L

M

N

P

R

S

T

U

V

W

Y

ABOUT THE AUTHOR

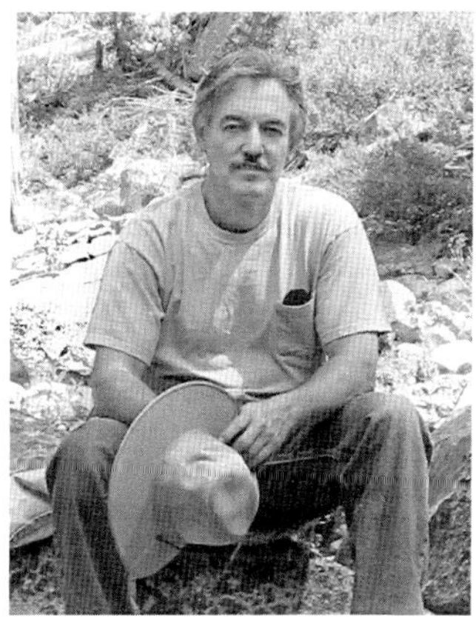

Richard Hurley received his undergraduate degree from Harvard College and wrote for the *Harvard Lampoon*. He worked for three years in the history division of the Oakland Museum of California. He earned a master's degree in architecture from UC–Berkeley, then left the Bay Area for the Sierra foothills and a career in computer-based multimedia. Richard is co-author of the award-winning historical fiction *Queen of the Northern Mines*. He has authored multimedia shows and guest curated a museum exhibit on California and the Civil War.

Visit us at
www.historypress.net

This title is also available as an e-book